929.2 Buc
Buckley, Gail Lumet, 1937-
The black Calhouns : from Civil
War to civil rights with one
African American family

The ⟨

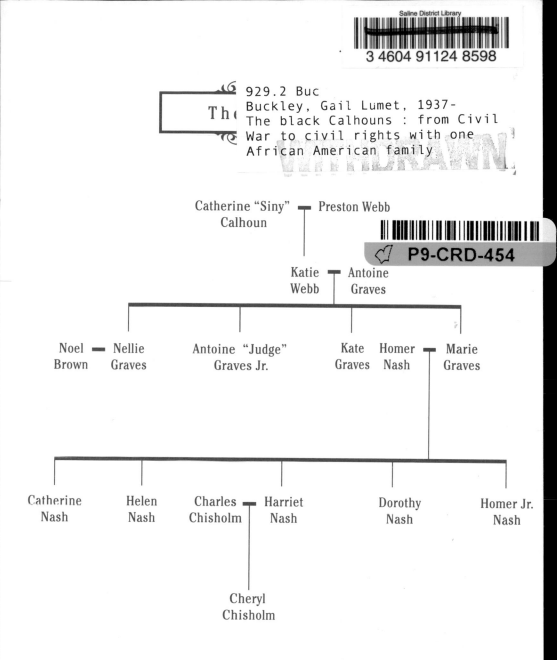

Catherine "Siny" — Preston Webb
Calhoun

Katie — Antoine
Webb   Graves

Noel — Nellie   Antoine "Judge"   Kate   Homer — Marie
Brown Graves   Graves Jr.   Graves Nash   Graves

Catherine   Helen   Charles — Harriet   Dorothy   Homer Jr.
Nash   Nash   Chisholm Nash   Nash   Nash

Cheryl
Chisholm

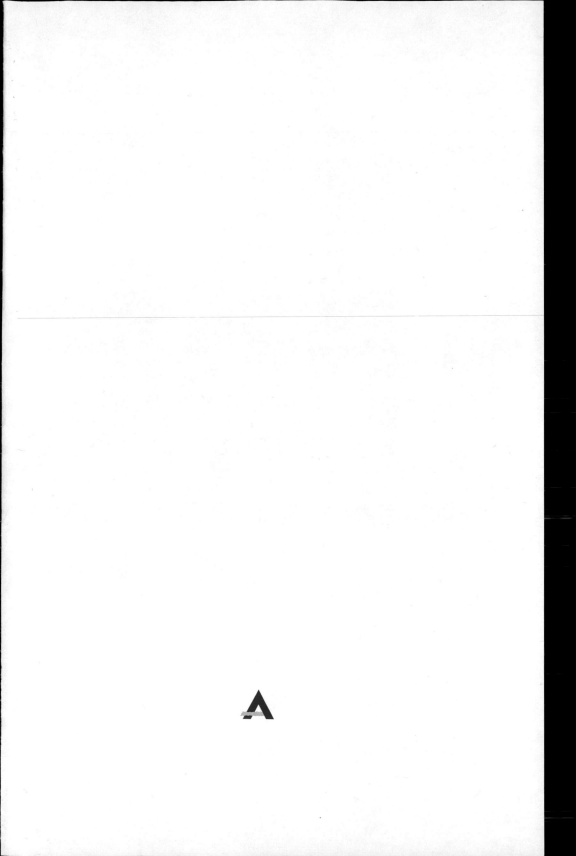

THE BLACK
CALHOUNS

Also by Gail Lumet Buckley

The Hornes: An American Family

American Patriots: The Story of Blacks in the Military
from the Revolution to Desert Storm

THE BLACK CALHOUNS

FROM CIVIL WAR TO CIVIL RIGHTS WITH ONE AFRICAN AMERICAN FAMILY

Gail Lumet Buckley

Atlantic Monthly Press
New York

Published simultaneously in Canada
Printed in the United States of America

FIRST EDITION

ISBN 978-0-8021-2454-8
eISBN 978-0-8021-9069-7

Atlantic Monthly Press
an imprint of Grove Atlantic
154 West 14th Street
New York, NY 10011

Distributed by Publishers Group West

groveatlantic.com

16 17 18 19   10 9 8 7 6 5 4 3 2 1

For Kevin

CONTENTS

CONTENTS

THE BLACK
CALHOUNS

INTRODUCTION

IT WAS 1865. The Civil War was over. Everything my great-great-grandfather Moses Calhoun—the thirty-five-year-old patriarch of the black Calhouns of Atlanta, Georgia—wanted for his future was at hand. It was a brand-new world, at least for a lucky few. The nation that had taken so much away from black Americans would soon give them the three great Reconstruction Amendments to the Constitution: the Thirteenth, which gave them true freedom (the Emancipation Proclamation was only a *proclamation* and could be rescinded); the Fourteenth, which gave them equality under the law; and the Fifteenth, which gave black men the vote. Moses had all the attributes for success in freedom: he was literate; he had been the favored slave of one of Georgia's most powerful men; he had lived in a town, not on a plantation; and his family was intact, which meant that he was not wandering the postwar countryside looking for sold-away loved ones. In this brand-new world, *life* and *liberty* were secure; now he was free to pursue *happiness*.

In 1865 he found a beautiful bride who had always been free. Her name was Atlanta Mary Fernando. Atlanta, whose mother came from New Orleans, was fifteen years younger than Moses and looked white. They produced two beautiful daughters, Cora and Lena Calhoun, and educated them for the free new world. Moses firmly believed in commerce and capitalism—and thanks to Reconstruction, he was agile enough to make the leap from slavery into something like the middle class. Twenty-two years after General Sherman's troops raised the flag of the United States of America over Atlanta's city hall, a newspaper, the *Constitution* of March 12, 1886, called Moses Calhoun "the wealthiest colored man in Atlanta."

One branch of Moses' family would stay in Atlanta and another branch would move north. Moses came from strong women, including his mother, Nellie, and his grandmother Sinai, who bought her own freedom and that of her husband and four youngest children and moved to Chicago three years before the Civil War. Sinai made selling homemade cakes and persimmon beer on a street corner in Newnan, Georgia, a wealthy community outside Atlanta. Sinai's daughter Nellie, a talented cook like her mother, had two children, Moses and his younger sister, Catherine Sinai, called "Siny." Nellie and her children stayed in Georgia when Sinai went north. Moses and his mother and sister were all owned by a relative of John C. Calhoun, Dr. Andrew Bonaparte Calhoun, one of the richest and most important men in the state. His had been the first signature on Georgia's Ordinance of Secession. Because A. B. Calhoun wanted a butler who was literate and relatively sophisticated, Moses had received the rare gift of an education. It was illegal for slaves to learn to read or write, but Moses taught his mother and sister in secret. The year that Sinai left the South, 1857, was the year that Chief Justice Roger B. Taney of the Supreme Court said that Negroes in the United States had "no rights which white men were bound to respect."

After the war the black Calhouns of Atlanta, led by Moses, a flourishing entrepreneur on good terms with his former owner, were fortunate enough to escape the harsh realities of poverty and racism that the vast majority of American blacks faced. They could afford to live in the "best" black neighborhoods, which had less crime—although to travel outside the city limits was incredibly dangerous: beyond Atlanta was, in Mark Twain's words, "the United States of Lyncherdom." Middle-class black women might work outside the home—as teachers, for example—but they did not work as domestics in white households. Middle-class black Southern women seemed to have perfected the survival technique of constructing their *own* South—one in which white people did not exist except perhaps as vague social role models. All black Southerners were exposed to and infected by racism, but normally, middle-class Negroes did not have the usual "black" experiences of racial insults and threats. On the whole, their lives seemed generally quite sunny. They went to college, they went to war, they married their childhood sweethearts, and they raised families. This book is about an extended family with "stars" in every generation, North and South, but Moses' great-granddaughter, my mother, Lena Mary Calhoun Horne, born in 1917, became one of the brightest stars in the family during the second half of the twentieth century.

In the grotesquely lopsided African American story, oversimplification is the truth. Blacks in the North were protected by the U.S. Constitution, but blacks in the South had no constitutional protection at all. The black Calhouns who went north certainly "made it," however "it" is defined. But some urban, educated Southerners like the black Calhouns also had wonderfully successful, happy lives—much happier, in fact, than the lives of cousins who fled to the North. The Southerners who "made it" won respect and honors from both races in every generation, despite living in an oppressive society. Because society at large was closed to them, Southern black families and communities turned inward. There was only family, friends, school, clubs, community, and, highly important, church. Northerners, less frequent churchgoers, seemed to find less happiness and cohesion, and were more prone to divorce, alcoholism, and adultery. Yes, there were Southern alcoholics, but in the church-oriented South families were whole. Southerners had more children and longer and happier marriages. But black Northerners, despite prejudice and restrictions, still had a whole world of outside choices. Northerners had libraries, parks, museums, and schools open to everyone; none of these things was available to Negroes in the South. Yet the black Calhouns prevailed; they were physicians, educators, entrepreneurs, politicians, social workers, journalists, and musicians. Which was more important, political freedom or a happy family life? Living without freedom could be bearable only if one was surrounded by love. Love and personal achievement were the only possible antidotes to the poisons of racism and Jim Crow.

Cora and Lena Calhoun, their cousin, Katie Webb (the daughter of Moses' sister), and the men they married all belonged to the first generation of purposefully educated Southern blacks. As children of free Negroes or favored slaves, they were specifically educated in what were known as "Missionary" schools, founded by Northern philanthropists, to become the first black teachers in the South. The purpose of these schools springing up across the old Confederacy was to train future black teachers to help undo three centuries of enforced illiteracy. Despite the enmity of Southern whites, the Missionary schools were unqualified successes. The Missionary colleges, in particular, represented the dawning of a new day for Southern blacks. Above all, the American Missionary Association recruited dedicated teachers, mostly young Northern whites, who accepted a pittance for the dangerous job of going south to instruct the children of former slaves. They were hated by Southern whites because they treated blacks as social equals, using titles like "Mr.," "Mrs.," and "Miss" and eating meals with them. One of those Missionary teachers was a tough-minded idealist named Edmund Asa Ware, Yale class of 1863, who was head of Atlanta's two Missionary schools—the Storrs School for younger children and Atlanta University. In 1871 he admitted Cora Calhoun to the Storrs School, and in 1881 he signed her Atlanta University diploma. Lena Calhoun chose to go to college at Fisk, in Nashville, another Missionary institution. In 1885 seventeen-year-old W. E. B. Du Bois of Great Barrington, Massachusetts, fell in love at first sight with the beautiful "rosy apricot" vision of his sixteen-year-old classmate, Lena Calhoun of Atlanta.

He not only fell in love but found an iconic label for his fellow black Missionary teachers-to-be. He called them the "Talented Tenth." Theoretically, they were to "uplift" the other 90 percent and take on roles of leadership. The Talented Tenth were very proud people because they were Negroes who *mattered*. Having been programmed for centuries by Southern whites to believe that they were inferior beings, the members of the post–Civil War generation were now being told almost exactly the opposite by their Northern white teachers. Missionary colleges were known to produce extremely confident black men and women. Missionary college elitism sometimes annoyed other blacks almost as much as it annoyed whites, but it would drive the twentieth-century battle for civil rights.

By the time the 1896 Supreme Court decision in *Plessy v. Ferguson* (which upheld racial segregation) basically rescinded the Fourteenth Amendment, Cora and Lena Calhoun had both left the South with their husbands. In October 1887 Cora married teacher-editor-publisher Edwin F. Horn, a.k.a. "the Adonis of the Negro Press," who would add an "e" to the end of his last name when he arrived in New York. On Christmas Day 1888, Lena Calhoun, presumably breaking the heart of "Willie" Du Bois, married Frank G. Smith, a slightly older Fisk graduate who would become a Chicago ophthalmologist. Meanwhile, their cousin, Katie Webb, married Antoine Graves, an early civil rights hero who was the first black licensed real estate broker in Atlanta, and stayed in the South.

It is said that American history is cyclical—but for African Americans it seems more like a vicious circle. The pattern repeats itself over and over: one step forward, three steps back. Is it a coincidence that the three presidents assassinated between 1865 and 1963 were considered "friends of the Negro"? It was amazing, in the first decade of the millennium, that America elected a black president named Barack Hussein Obama. Although some people would never forgive Obama for being black, my ninety-one-year-old mother was thrilled. At first, it appeared that none of Obama's ancestors had been slaves. However, researchers discovered that Obama may have descended from America's first documented African slave, as the eleventh great-grandson of John Punch, an indentured servant who was enslaved in 1640 after an escape attempt. The descent was not, as one might think, from Obama's black father, but through his white mother—a fact that epitomizes the complexities of race in America.

All forms of slavery are cruel, but slavery in the American South was especially cruel in its need to deny blacks their humanity. Blacks, literally, had "no souls," insisted eighteenth-century Southern white Protestants—which may be why the concept of "soulfulness" became so important. Catholics, of course, had a mandate to nurture souls, not deny their existence. The Vatican profited heavily from slavery and the slave trade, but had a civilizing effect on slavery itself. In Catholic areas—Louisiana, for example, as well as Latin America—slave marriages were sanctified, and children could not be sold away from their parents. For the rest of the black South, however, family became as important a concept as soul. After the Civil War, the South had nothing—so poor whites held on to their guns, their dogs, and their battle flag. And poor blacks held on to the concepts of soul and family. Soul was about more than color—country music is poor white soul. For blacks, soul meant faith, fortitude, humor, tenacity, wisdom, and the ability to *overcome*, despite a lifetime of "white supremacy."

I have no memory of childhood talks with my mother about race, but I do remember being told that if anyone asked "what" I was, I was to say, in no uncertain terms and with no embellishments, "I am an American." Many years later, at the 1959 Harvard commencement, I chatted briefly with Senator John F. Kennedy, whose 1958 Senate campaign I had worked on. He asked me what I planned to do, now that I had graduated. I said I planned to go to Paris and never come back. "Oh, yes you will," he said. "You're an American."

Part history and part memoir, *The Black Calhouns* is about six generations of an *atypical* African American family that is also typically American. Broadly, the nineteenth century is history, and the twentieth century, beginning with 1937, the year of my birth, is memoir. North and South, the black Calhouns lived through the civil rights century, 1865 to 1965—surely the most volatile American century of all. The black Calhouns, strengthened by their strong faith as well as their belief in the glowing evolvements of the creed, were lucky—but they were never selfish achievers.

As a child during World War II, it seemed important to stress national unity—however specious the idea. As a hero of that war, John F. Kennedy, a member of a formerly oppressed minority himself, never believed in hyphenated Americanism. Today, however, it is important to let people know "what" I am. I identify myself as African American to let others know that I am one of America's historical stepchildren. The quality of African American life, like that of all stepchildren, depends on the spiritual, philosophical, and political character of the stepparent and stepsiblings. As far as the spiritual is concerned, America boasts of its belief in the Judeo-Christian tradition. Well, we know how the God of the Old Testament felt about racism: when Moses' sister Miriam rebelled against Moses for marrying a Cushite (Ethiopian) woman, God turned Miriam into a "snow-white leper"—so much for "white supremacy." America's philosophical character, as stated in our national documents, our creed, is both impeccable and immutable. The trouble, of course, is politics. The political character of American life is both cynical and changeable—and our political actions have rarely reflected either our avowed faith or our stated creed. African Americans might very well be charged with the task of keeping the country true to its best self.

CHAPTER ONE

South/Reconstruction, 1865–1876
MORNING/1860s

THE STORY of Reconstruction is really the story of what *almost was*, wrote W. E. B. Du Bois—who first *lived* Reconstruction, then studied it. His book *Black Reconstruction in America, 1860–1880*, published in 1935, makes statistics breathe and reads like a novel. Du Bois called Reconstruction the *mythic* time for blacks. It was a window of American opportunity that opened in 1865, the year of the Thirteenth Amendment, and closed in 1876, the election year that saw the final betrayal of blacks by the Republican Party. That single decade, 1865–1876, between the end of slavery and the arrival of Jim Crow, represents the arc in time called "Reconstruction," when for the first time in the South, under the protection of the federal government, blacks were American citizens and all public discrimination was illegal. There were laws to protect black civil rights—and anyone could learn to read and write. This "different world," as Du Bois called it, arrived with the passage of the three great Reconstruction Amendments to the Constitution, the Thirteenth, Fourteenth, and Fifteenth, also known as the Civil War Amendments, which *really* freed the slaves and made them citizens and voters. This was the issue: Alabama, Florida, and Louisiana had almost as many black Republicans as white Democrats, and Mississippi and South Carolina had *more* black Republicans. This was the reality of Reconstruction—the political tables were turned. And this is what the white Democrats of the South were determined to destroy.

Southern cruelty in the form of "Black Codes" brought Reconstruction to the South. Black Codes—laws regulating black life and employment that sprang up all over the South right after Appomattox—were worse than slavery, because black life now had no value at all. During slavery, blacks could be abused or killed with impunity by their owners; under Black Codes they could be abused or killed with impunity by *any* white. Annual work "contracts," with pay at the end of the year, were Black Code staples. In reality, because of deductions for "rent" and "provisions," pay was never seen. The "company store" principle created far more hungry children than the plantation ever did. And ad hoc Black Code enforcers, like the Ku Klux Klan, born in 1865, terrorized the Southern countryside. But from 1865 to 1872, the old Confederacy was occupied by troops of the U.S. Army—sent specifically to protect the rights of former slaves, now citizens and Republican voters, from vengeful whites.

The black Calhouns of Coweta County, Georgia, a small, wealthy community outside Atlanta, were fortunate to have escaped both the Black Codes and the KKK. The black Calhouns came from the small portion of the Southern black population that was both literate and urban. Atlanta was a slave-owning society, but it was also a city whose white business leaders, even in 1865, were almost as interested in Yankee investments as in upholding the "sacred" cause of white supremacy. Run by businessmen, not planters, Atlanta, unlike the rest of Georgia, was concerned with its image outside the South. Georgia was no more and no less viciously racist than Mississippi or Alabama, but Atlanta always wore the smiling face of moderation. Hating confrontations and bad publicity, Atlanta was one of the safest cities in the South for middle-class blacks. And certain middle-class men—doctors, lawyers, businessmen, and entrepreneurs—were as independent of white oversight as any black men in the South could be. Unlike the rest of the South, Atlanta rewarded black ambition—as long as it was not political.

"Calhoun" was an important name in Georgia. There was a town called "Calhoun" in the northwestern part of the state near the Alabama border and a street named "Calhoun" in Atlanta. There was a Governor Calhoun and a Mayor Calhoun of Atlanta. The black Calhouns had been owned by Dr. Andrew Bonaparte Calhoun (A. B. Calhoun), a relative of the former senator and vice president John C. Calhoun, slavery's greatest apologist. A physician and sometime politician, Dr. Calhoun, one of the richest and most powerful men in the state, was a Coweta County delegate to Georgia's Secession Convention—and proudly displayed the pen he had used to sign Georgia's Ordinance of Secession. A. B. Calhoun, born in 1809 in South Carolina, entered medical school in Charleston in 1829. After his 1831 graduation, he moved to Decatur, Georgia, and became a circuit-riding doctor. A year later he settled in Coweta County, in the town of Newnan. Serious about his profession, in 1837 Calhoun spent a year abroad, attending lectures and clinics in the great hospitals of London and Paris. When he returned to Georgia, his friends pushed him to serve a term in the state legislature. Before 1865 Coweta County's population was almost evenly divided between black and white. The blacks were all slaves, of course. Besides homes in Newnan and Atlanta, Dr. Calhoun had a large cotton plantation, the Calhoun Quarter, in the southwest part of Coweta County under the charge of an overseer. But his main family home was the stately mansion, set in a grove of forest oaks on Greenville Street in Newnan, that he built from 1839 to 1840. Newnan, Georgia, was known as the "City of Homes," thanks in great part to A. B. Calhoun's mansion.

Moses Calhoun; his sister, Catherine Sinai, known as "Siny"; and his mother, Nellie, were Coweta County natives. Moses was named for A. B. Calhoun's uncle, Moses Waddel, and Catherine Sinai was partly named for his wife, Catherine Calhoun Waddel. The 1850 Slave

Schedule (slave census) for A. B. Calhoun listed Moses as a twenty-year-old male—and "M" for mulatto. A. B. Calhoun may well have been a father figure to Moses. Like many Southern slave families, the black Calhouns were intertwined with the white Calhouns: Moses was the butler, Nellie was the cook, and Siny was the nursemaid. With her perfect oval face and large, lustrous eyes, Siny Calhoun looked like a beautiful Black Madonna. Her father was generally believed to have been a white man: Judge William Ezzard, a three-time mayor of Atlanta and a good friend of A.B.'s. Moses' father may well have been Ezzard also. Moses was born in 1829 in Creek Indian territory, before "Atlanta" existed. He was considered a "fortunate" slave. While house slaves were under constant scrutiny, they usually led a more comfortable life than other human property. And butlers were the most important house slaves of all. The coachman, blacksmith, and carpenter were important *outdoor* slaves. Moses had grown from a solemn, intelligent boy, surrounded by women, to an imposingly dignified man—the ideal butler. In 1860 only about 5,000 of the 462,000 slaves in Georgia could read and write, and Moses Calhoun was one of them, as the doctor wanted a literate butler. This education was permitted because of his owner's importance. But when Moses secretly taught his mother and sister, it was a criminal act. An ironclad rule throughout the South: no black, slave or free, was permitted to learn to read or write. In the special circumstances in which he found himself—as a favored slave of one of the richest men in Georgia—Moses received more than a boyhood education in letters and numbers; he also learned self-confidence and the ways of the white world.

A forebear of the black Calhouns, Moses' maternal grandmother Sinai, was something of a "liberated" woman. In 1839 Sinai had been discovered by Coweta County authorities living on her own with her husband, Henry, and earning a living by selling baked goods and home-made persimmon beer on a corner of Newnan's Court Square. The authorities mandated that the couple be placed under "the immediate control and management of some white person." Sinai and Henry had been owned by two Newnan residents, Silas Reynolds and William Nimmons. In 1832 Reynolds broke up Sinai's family by, first, selling her youngest child, Felix, to Nimmons and then, in 1834, selling Sinai herself:

> Know all men by these present that I Silas Reynolds of the County Coweta and State aforesaid for and in consideration of the sum of two hundred dollars . . . doth bargain sell and deliver unto William Nimmons of the County and State aforesaid one negro boy slave by the name of Felix about Eight years of age which negro boy slave Felix the said Silas Reynolds warrants to be sound and healthy . . . 5th June 1832.

And two years later:

> Received of William Nimmons three hundred dollars in full payment of a negro woman by the name of Sina about Sixty years of age . . . I have here unto set my hand and seal this 4th day of April 1834.

Sinai somehow convinced Nimmons, her new owner, to let her continue to sell her wares. By 1857 she had saved enough money to buy freedom for herself, her husband, and her four youngest children and move them all to Chicago, where at the time there were fewer than one thousand Negroes. It was extremely rare that North American slave owners allowed slaves to buy their freedom. In fact, it was almost unheard-of, but Sinai was an amazing woman and Nimmons was certainly a "liberal" slave owner—or maybe he just had money troubles. When Sinai relocated to Chicago, she left behind her oldest daughter, Nellie, and Nellie's children, Moses and Siny. She did not feel guilty about leaving these family members. As slavery went, they had a relatively cushy berth as house slaves of a rich man, and because it was the way of "good" slave owners, they would be taken care of in old age. In

1857 Siny married Preston Webb, a free black horse trainer. Although Webb was free, Siny remained a slave and their daughter, Catherine, called Katie, was born in slavery on July 30, 1859. Slavery was for life—and it was matrilineal.

On January 19, 1861, the Georgia Secession Convention was held in the two-story brick courthouse on Newnan's Court Square. A. B. Calhoun, the delegate from Newnan, was the first to sign. During the war, Dr. Calhoun was a member of the surgeon conscript board. When Newnan was chosen as the site for a hospital for the sick and wounded, he had to convince his fellow citizens, who were hostile to the idea of hospitals or refugees in their town. He was so convincing that every public building, including all the churches except the Presbyterian, became a hospital, and sheds were built along Court Square for the wounded. Very soon, soldiers from Tennessee, the Battle of Chicka-mauga, and the Atlanta Campaign were streaming into Newnan station.

Newnan, now a hospital hub, seemed out of immediate danger, but Atlanta could not escape its fate. "I propose to demonstrate the vulnerability of the South, and make its inhabitants feel that war and individual ruin are synonymous terms," wrote Sherman to Grant. In another letter he proclaimed, "I can make this march, and make Geor-gia howl!"

By April 1864 Atlanta was entrenched and under siege, with federal forces moving inexorably toward the most vital supply, manufacturing, and communications center of the Confederacy. Sherman's orders from Grant were "to get into the interior of the enemy's country as far as you can, inflicting all the damage you can against their war resources." Slave prices rose that spring. Slaves were desperately needed to build roads, bridges, and fortifications. By May slaves were being requisitioned at a dollar a day to owners to fortify the city, but on May 4, according to Kate Cumming's *Kate: The Journal of a Confederate Nurse*, Newnan was nonetheless the scene of a celebration—the wedding of Dr. Calhoun's daughter. Cumming, who had a critical eye, described the 11 A.M.

candlelit ceremony in the Presbyterian church by saying that sunlight would have been "in much better taste." She commented on the cost of the nine bridesmaids' dresses ("new Swiss muslin" at fifty dollars a yard) and she noticed one or two "married surgeons" among the nine groomsmen. Nitpicking aside, she confessed that "the whole scene at the wedding was quite pretty and impressive."

Two months later the first Union shells fell on Atlanta. By early August, Sherman's "Big Guns" had reduced much of the city to rubble and collapsed walls. On September 1, after burning or dynamiting everything of military value, Confederate general John Bell Hood ordered Atlanta's evacuation. Andrew Bonaparte Calhoun had already made a lucky escape to the Calhoun Quarter. Dr. Calhoun had the presence of mind, in the fall of 1864, to move his "stock and negroes further south and was absent from home until the close of the war." If Moses ever thought of freedom, it would have been with mixed emotions. Moses was "somebody" in slavery. He was privileged property. It was a clear, hot day on September 2, 1864, when Sherman's triumphant army changed Moses Calhoun's life forever. At the age of thirty-five, Moses became a full person instead of property. Sherman's famous wire to Lincoln read, "Atlanta is ours, and fairly won." Mathew Brady photographed industrial Atlanta in ruins: hulks of brick chimneys among ruined factories, foundries, and railroad yards where, it was said, Sherman's army twisted the ties into the letters "U" and "S." The fall of Atlanta stunned the South; the news ensured both the Confederates' defeat and Lincoln's reelection. "Since Atlanta I have felt as if all were dead within me, forever," wrote the Charleston diarist Mary Boykin Chesnut. "We are going to be wiped off the earth."

After occupying Atlanta for two months, on November 11, just before he began his march to the sea, General Sherman gave orders to burn the city—finally agreeing to spare churches and hospitals after a plea from a Roman Catholic priest. (Sherman had actually been raised in a Roman Catholic family.) Everything the Confederates did not burn themselves, Union soldiers torched. Atlanta was destroyed. In 1864 generals still rode into battle under fire. By the Battle of Atlanta, the thirty-three-year-old Confederate general John Bell Hood had already lost his right leg at Chickamauga and the use of his left arm at Gettysburg. Thirty-four-year-old Union general Oliver Otis Howard, who lost his right arm at Fair Oaks, led Sherman's right flank on his march to the sea. Wherever he went, Sherman liberated slaves. Thousands of former slaves followed his army through Georgia and the Carolinas. They were known as "Contrabands." In 1862 Union general Benjamin Franklin Butler refused to return runaway Louisiana slaves to their owners, calling them "contraband of war." In response to critics who accused him of neglecting the newly freed, Sherman met in Savannah with Secretary of War Edwin M. Stanton and twenty local black leaders. They were reassured by Sherman. A few days after the meeting, Sherman issued Special Field Order No. 15, providing for the settlement of forty thousand freed slaves on land taken from white owners in South Carolina, Georgia, and Florida. Each settler was given a forty-acre parcel and an old army mule, but alas, within a year, the orders were revoked by the new administration of President Andrew Johnson.

Four months after Sherman's army freed the slaves of Georgia, the Thirteenth Amendment to the Constitution, enacted on December 18, 1865, freed all the slaves of the United States and its territories. Lincoln had made another crucial decision affecting black Americans. The emancipation document of January 1863 was only a proclamation—it could be rescinded. Lincoln believed that blacks had suffered "the greatest wrong inflicted on any people." Fearing that the next president might reestablish slavery, he had pushed through the Thirteenth Amendment. Frederick Douglass was ill during the passage of the amendment, but his son Charles Douglass, who had survived the 1863 annihilation of the all-black Fifty-Fourth Massachusetts Regiment in South Carolina, wrote to him from Washington:

I wish you could have been here the day that the constitutional amendment was passed forever abolishing slavery in the United States, such rejoicing never before witnessed, cannons firing, people hugging and shaking hands, white people I mean . . .

At the end of the Civil War, the former Calhoun house slaves from Coweta County all lived together in Atlanta. Here, Moses Calhoun, ex-slave butler, had his eye on property and prosperity. The Emancipation Proclamation of January 1, 1863, freeing the slaves of states in rebellion, had been barely a rumor to the black Calhouns. But 1865 was different. Early in 1865 Moses Calhoun, now free throughout the world, not just Coweta County, chose a beautiful bride who had always been free. Atlanta Mary Fernando was fifteen years younger than Moses and looked white. Ivory-skinned Atlanta, whose mother came from New Orleans, was born in 1845, the year that the city of Terminus was renamed Atlanta, for the Western and Atlantic Railroad. Atlanta and Moses would have two daughters: Cora, born in 1865, when the city was still ash and rubble; and Lena, born in 1869, when Moses first began to climb the ladder of success. Moses always knew that he had to live in Atlanta. And if he was going to become a man of property, he had no time to waste and no time to learn anything new. As a very good butler, he knew about food and drink and how to present them. He had a plan. It involved doing what he knew he did well—and with help from his former owner it could succeed. He opened a combination grocery and catering establishment. He knew these were enterprises in which blacks would be allowed to succeed. Moses had been lucky in slavery—he believed he would be even luckier in freedom.

As far as Moses and Atlanta Calhoun were concerned, probably the most important aspect of Reconstruction was that their children could be excellently, and legally, educated. Frederick Douglass disagreed. He placed education second to the ballot. There was no disputing the Negro's "ignorance and degradation," Douglass wrote. It was "the policy of the system to keep him both ignorant and degraded, the better and more safely to defraud him of his hard earnings." Suffrage was the way out of ignorance. "The only way to guarantee true black freedom is to give blacks the vote," Douglass insisted. He regarded the elective franchise "as the one great power by which all civil rights are obtained." Without the right to vote, to be on a jury, and to serve in the military, there was no citizenship. Douglass believed that the liberties of the American people were "dependent upon the ballot-box, the jury-box, and the cartridge-box, that without these no class of people could live and flourish in this country." Having turned Frederick Augustus Bailey, a slave, into Frederick Douglass, international notable, he did not believe in "special efforts" for blacks. Douglass was a self-made man—he believed others could do the same. Like Lincoln, Douglass had no idea that he was sui generis. Early in 1865 Douglass had two great fears: one, Lincoln would lose the election and the Emancipation Proclamation would be rescinded—and two, Lincoln would win the election and pretend he had never heard of the word "suffrage."

Suffrage aside, the education of former slaves, known as "freedmen" (not *free* men), was now a matter for the combined efforts of the federal government and private philanthropy. The Freedmen's Bureau Bill had been enacted in March 1865 to provide care and relief for the newly liberated. The Freedmen's Bureau, the U.S. Army, and the American Missionary Association (AMA) began to open schools and colleges all over the South. Eager, predominantly white Northern volunteers, mostly from churches and universities, poured into the South to teach former slaves. The Freedmen's Bureau represented everything that white Southerners hated—black soldiers, black voters, black students, black wage earners, and whites extending civil courtesies to blacks. Perhaps the least dishonest and least self-interested bureaucracy in U.S. history, the bureau became a liberal bastion, with leaders who were mostly younger Union officers and Protestant religious activists. Under General Oliver Otis Howard, a hero of Sherman's march through Georgia, the bureau was the model of pragmatic idealism. The death rate of freedmen in 1865 was 38 percent; by 1869 it was 2.03 percent.

One-armed General Howard, the thirty-five-year-old head of the Freedmen's Bureau, known as a "friend of the Negro," made enemies North and South for his support of land redistribution as well as suffrage for blacks. Dark-haired and handsome, with the poignant empty sleeve, Howard was also known as the "Christian general" for making his troops attend prayer and temperance meetings. Born in Maine in 1830, he graduated from Bowdoin College before entering West Point, where he was fourth in his class. After graduation in 1854, he became a West Point math instructor; but in 1857, during the Second Seminole War in Florida, he experienced a religious conversion. He was on the verge of quitting the army and going into the ministry when the Civil War broke out. As colonel of the Third Maine Infantry Regiment, he was at First Bull Run and Fair Oaks, where his right arm was amputated. He returned to battle at Second Bull Run, Fredericksburg, Chancellorsville, and Gettysburg. In 1861 he became a brigadier, and in 1862 a major general. He commanded Sherman's right flank on his march through Georgia. At home, he and his wife worked to desegregate their Washington church. He was well aware of the dangers facing teachers in the South. School buildings and churches used as schools were burned down. Teachers were driven away, beaten, or murdered. Howard led the Freedmen's Bureau its entire life, from 1865 to 1874. In 1867 Howard University, in Washington, D.C., was chartered by act of Congress and named for General Howard, who later became its president.

Although it was a crime in the South to educate Negroes, there had always been a "secret" educated class—usually the illegitimate children of slave owners and house slaves. Many attended Oberlin College, in Ohio, the earliest *officially* integrated college in North America. Oberlin was founded in 1833 in Lorain County in the Western Reserve. Oberlin's first president, Professor Asa Mahan, who had studied under Harriet Beecher Stowe's father at Cincinnati's Lane

Theological Seminary, refused to accept the position unless Negroes and women were admitted. In the 1850s the town of Oberlin, known as "the most-abolitionist place in the most abolitionist county in America," was famous for the integrated rescue of a runaway slave from a bounty hunter.

The institutions of learning established between 1865 and 1870 by the bureau and the AMA were tributes to American liberalism. Former abolitionist Brigadier General Clinton Bowen Fisk, a wealthy St. Louis businessman in banking and insurance before the war, became the Freedmen's Bureau leader in Tennessee, where he established the first free schools in the South for both black and white children. In 1867, with an endowment of $30,000, he made an abandoned Nashville barracks available to the AMA and established Fisk University—home to the magnificent Fisk Jubilee Singers, glorious archivists of spirituals, most notably adored by Mark Twain.

Brigadier Samuel Chapman Armstrong, aged twenty-six in 1865, was the blond son of American missionaries in Hawaii. After attending the Punahou School in Honolulu, he graduated from Williams College in 1862 and a year later found himself at Gettysburg. In late 1863 he led black troops as lieutenant colonel of the Eighth U.S. Colored Troops (USCT) at the notorious Siege of Petersburg, where blacks were cannon fodder. "USCT" was the official designation of black troops who were not organized into state units. Armstrong was given their leadership surely because, in army-think, he was from Hawaii and used to dealing with dark-skinned people. In tribute to his heroic troops, Armstrong joined the Freedmen's Bureau after the war. And with the help of the AMA, in 1868 he established Hampton Institute in Virginia for future teachers. Brigadier Armstrong belonged to the "hand" rather than the "head" school of black education; his students would learn real skills. The theory of educating Southern blacks now fell into two categories (later most notably expressed by W. E. B. Du Bois and Booker T. Washington): to educate the "head" for intellectual learning (Du Bois), or to educate the "hand" for skilled manual labor (Washington).

General Carl Schurz, who had been asked by President Andrew Johnson to study the condition of Southern blacks in the immediate postwar period, had discovered not only the extent of the horrific conditions that led to Reconstruction, but another aspect of the Southern attitude toward blacks: "Aside from a small number of honorable exceptions, the popular prejudice is almost as bitterly set against the Negro's having the advantage of education as it was when the Negro was a slave."

In 1865, twenty-eight-year-old Edmund Asa Ware (known as Asa), two years out of Yale, never in war, and hiding his youthful features behind a very imposing blond beard, was an American Missionary Association agent assigned to a white public school in Tennessee. His ability to bring order out of chaos so impressed General Clinton Fisk that Fisk recommended Ware for the big job in Atlanta—as superintendent of two new Missionary schools: the Storrs School and Atlanta University. The Storrs School, for younger children, was named for the Reverend Henry Martin Storrs, a white Congregational minister from Cincinnati, who contributed $1,000 toward new buildings. While professing to be nonsectarian, the AMA was heavily Congregational.

Asa Ware belonged to the "head" school of black education. Seemingly diffident, Ware combined soaring idealism with a steely sense of command and a talent for organization and administration. Ware confessed without embarrassment that Harriet Beecher Stowe made him an abolitionist. Born on a Massachusetts farm in 1837, he moved to Connecticut with his family in 1852. He was a fifteen-year-old student at Norwich Free Academy when he first read *Uncle Tom's Cabin* and attended antislavery lectures by Wendell Phillips and the Reverend Henry Ward Beecher, Stowe's brother. (Following the abolitionist pattern, he also listened to temperance speakers.) He graduated as "first-boy of the school" in 1859. Asa Ware was the kind of young man whom older men noticed and approved of. It happened at Yale, and it happened again when he went to work for the AMA. At Yale, class of 1863, he held a scholarship provided by a group of four older male benefactors. Known for "modesty, simplicity, a keen sense of humor, a repugnance for pretense and sham, and a dedicated and deeply religious concern for his fellow man," Ware was popular with eminent university professors. After Yale, he taught for two years at Norwich Free Academy and repaid his benefactors.

Atlanta University and the Storrs School, two of the jewels in the AMA crown, had both been founded in November 1865. That autumn, many of Atlanta's people, black and white, were still living in makeshift tents on the edges of the city, and thousands of former slaves were still being fed by the army. By the end of 1865, luckier than most ex-slaves, Moses and Siny shared a house on Atlanta's Fraser Street with their mother, Nellie; their respective spouses; their two small babies; and Moses' mother-in-law. Moses had a grocery store, Nellie was a laundress, Siny was a hairdresser, and Siny's husband, Preston Webb, was a horse trainer. Much of Atlanta's population, black and white, had to start over with nothing. Although the city had been consumed by fire and mostly destroyed, its people were resilient. Moses stood in the ash and rubble of Atlanta like a character out of *Gone with the Wind*, determined to succeed. Aged thirty-five when he was emancipated, Moses was too old to tolerate a boss. He knew that he was going to be a man of business and property, not a wage earner. And he knew how to do it without raising white ire. He opened a grocery store on the lot next to his house and later bought a lot nearby and opened a restaurant. He began to make money to support his family. He may well have received financial assistance from Dr. Calhoun, with whom he presumably remained on affable and respectful terms. In 1867, as a new citizen of the United States of America, Moses registered to vote.

When Asa Ware arrived in Atlanta in September 1866, he had not been surprised to find that his classrooms were an old boxcar and a former Confederate commissary. This was his second posting in the war-ravaged South, so he was well aware of the conditions. Ware's role was to make the Atlanta Missionary schools the models for the education of future teachers and members of what would become the new Negro middle class. Storrs very quickly became more than a school; it became a center for social services, education, and worship for ex-slaves, who had petitioned for a church of their own. On May 22, 1867, a school committee voted to organize a Congregational church. The first church service was held a week later in the Storrs School chapel, conducted by Reverend Erastus M. Cravath, who was the white secretary of the AMA, a founder of Atlanta University, and the first president of Fisk University. The new church was a block away from the Storrs School, and the parsonage was built by students in the Atlanta University trade department. Atlanta's First Congregational Church was actually the second black Congregational church in the United States. For seventeen years, the church's interracial congregation was served by white pastors recommended by the AMA.

In private, the slender Ware had a laconic Connecticut Yankee manner of speaking, but in speeches and lectures, he was brisk and no-nonsense. He was not robust, but he had charisma. His *eyes* and his *voice*, people said, had power. "I could not but feel that I had met a man of strong personality, a man with force of character enough to impress himself upon others," wrote William H. Crogman, the future president of Clark University, as a student in the early 1870s.

Devoted to academic excellence, Ware rejected the Southern concept of educating the "hand," not the "head." He dreamed of establishing a centrally located university to train talented black youth and educate teachers. He also rejected all notions of racial inferiority. As principal of the Storrs School, Ware made an enormous impression on the students. It was a new and strange thing to see a *white* man carrying wood and making fires for *them*. When a white Atlantan asked Ware how he was able to live among Negroes, he replied: "Oh, I can easily explain that; I'm simply color blind."

The beginning was shaky. It had been necessary to find a substantial house, a "Teachers' Home," where all the teachers could live together for safety—because no one in Atlanta would rent a room to Yankee teachers, who were known locally as "NT," for "nigger teachers." A large house had been purchased at the corner of Houston and Calhoun streets, where the principal and his wife would live, and where Asa Ware lived as a bachelor. More teachers were needed, and places to house them. The school was seriously overcrowded. Children attended in the mornings and afternoons. And those aged fifteen to sixty who were unable to read listened to teachers from seven to nine in the evenings. There was also a Sunday school. The AMA believed that black advancement lay in "the religious element in their character." Piety and utter sincerity were the hallmarks of the Missionary teachers. Most of the teachers were New England or Midwestern Congregationalists, and they clung together in the Teachers' Home–Storrs School–Atlanta University–First Congregational Church neighborhood with other Northerners, AMA workers, and occupying Union officers in the face of hostile natives—*white* this time.

Among the dedicated young volunteers arriving in Atlanta in the fall of 1868 to teach at Storrs was twenty-four-year-old Sarah Jane Twichell, known as Jane. Like Ware, she was a New Englander, descending from a prominent family in Connecticut. A graduate of the Hartford Female Seminary, Jane joined the AMA in 1865 and was said to have a "strong, attractive and commanding personality." In other words, she was an opinionated New England woman and no shrinking Southern belle. Atlanta was actually her third Southern post, after Norfolk and Charleston. Asa Ware's courtship of Jane Twichell was practically instantaneous. They were married in Connecticut in the summer of 1869.

Moses began to buy more property in 1869, when his second daughter, Lena, was born. In August 1869 Nellie went to Chicago to the deathbed of her mother, Sinai, and wrote a beautiful letter to Moses. "She diede [*sic*] happy in the Lord," wrote Nellie. In the autumn of

1870, at the start of the school year, Moses drove his daughter Cora and his niece, Katie Webb, to the Storrs School in his grocery delivery wagon. The 1870 census listed Moses as a "Retail Grocer," with "Real Estate" valued at $830 and a "Personal Estate" of $700. Under "Color," Moses is listed as "B" for black; all other family members are "M" for mulatto. Meanwhile, Moses, Atlanta, Cora, Lena, Nellie, Siny, and Katie all lived together in the house on Fraser Street—although Siny, whose husband had died, would soon remarry, and she and Katie would move away. Thanks to Reconstruction, and his own well-educated intelligence, Moses would give his daughters the education and sense of family that slavery had denied him.

Chapter Two

South/Reconstruction
NOON 1870s

In 1870 Moses owned a café, a boardinghouse, and a grocery store and was becoming a pillar of Atlanta's black community. He was able to make it into the American middle class precisely because, as usual, his timing was excellent. He was at the right time and place to take advantage of everything the earliest days of Reconstruction had to offer himself and his children. Later, it would become more difficult. In 1870 blacks voted for the first time in new elections in which all adult males, regardless of color, could vote. Moses Calhoun had registered and presumably voted Republican—like the vast majority of black men throughout the South. That year was both the high-water mark and the beginning of the end for black Republicans, whose downfall began being plotted the moment the ballots were counted. Blacks were not just voting—they were winning elections. Between 1870 and 1901, twenty-two Negroes from Southern states served in the U.S. Congress: two senators and twenty representatives. Unlike Mississippi and Alabama, though, Georgia always had a white majority. But while no black from Georgia went to the Reconstruction Congress, in 1870 Coweta County elected a black man named Sam Smith to the Georgia legislature. The black Calhouns were lucky because Atlanta, whose business community courted Yankee investment, demonstrated less overt violence against black Republicans.

Georgia was in the "vanguard" of the New South—commercial rather than agricultural. The state had gone through a leadership transition, from the planter class (not as old as Virginia's or South Carolina's) to a new business class. By 1870 its cotton crop surpassed the largest crop under slavery, and business and industrial prosperity was equally impressive. Georgia had safely returned to the status quo, with a small difference: now some Negroes were allowed to prosper.

In January 1870, Dr. Calhoun, whose relations with Moses's sister Siny were somewhat ambiguous (daughter or mistress?), deeded a house and lot to her in Newnan. There was no information beyond the deed to "a woman of color, Catherine Sinai":

> . . . for and in consideration of good will . . . and an interest in her welfare which he has by reason of her fidelity as a servant . . . does grant and convey unto the said Siny Webb for and during her natural life and after her death . . . to the daughter of the said Siny Webb namely Catherine Webb . . . one lot in the city of Newnan . . . on the land of said Andrew B. Calhoun.

By 1874 Georgia Negroes owned more than 350,000 acres of land. Moses had found a niche and would become a wealthy man. Besides equal American citizenship, Reconstruction for blacks also meant equal opportunity to succeed or fail. This is exactly what Southern whites wanted to take away. They did not want blacks to have *choices*. As Southern blacks claimed more and more to be American citizens with "certain unalienable rights," the old Southern power structure flexed its considerable muscle and its new terrorist arm, the KKK, to refute those claims. The KKK was founded in Tennessee in 1865 as a response to the Thirteenth Amendment by ex-Confederate officers, among them Nathan Bedford Forrest, perpetrator of a massacre at Fort

Pillow, Tennessee, against surrendering black soldiers and black civilians, including women and children. The KKK was a secret organization whose masked, night-riding members' basic activity was committing acts of terror against rural blacks and intimidating or murdering white Republicans. When it was not committing murder and arson and other evils, it was working to stifle the education, economic achievement, voting rights, and right to keep and bear arms of blacks. In April 1868 in Columbia County, Georgia, there were 1,222 votes for the Republican candidate. By the November presidential election, Columbia County reported *one* vote for Ulysses S. Grant. Republican voters had been either driven out or wiped out. In 1870 a federal grand jury declared the Ku Klux Klan to be a terrorist organization.

October 25, 1870, was a day of mixed blessings for Atlanta University. The good news was that the Georgia legislature had made an appropriation to the university of $8,000. The bad news: Atlanta University was now under the same regulations and restrictions as the University of Georgia, whose rules required a governor-appointed board of visitors and examinations on behalf of the state. Asa Ware knew that the examinations were about not just Atlanta University, but the whole question of higher education for Negroes. Because he had a point to prove, he asked the governor to appoint most of the board from the old slaveholding class. "I know these Negroes," said Joseph E. Brown, who had been governor during the war. "Some of these pupils were probably my slaves. I know that they can acquire the rudiments of an education, but they cannot go beyond. They are an inferior race, and for that reason, we had a right to hold them as slaves, and I mean to attend these examinations to prove we are right."

The examination lasted three days, June 26 to June 28, 1871. The youngest children, surely including Cora Calhoun and Katie Webb, performed only satisfactorily. "This is just as I expected," said ex-governor Brown, "and confirms my belief." The next day, however, the examiners were stunned when the teachers of Latin and Greek asked the examiners themselves to select the passages and choose the pupils to be tested. To the amazement of the examiners, the students performed brilliantly. In the rhetorical exercises the examiners were especially impressed by the students' ability to answer questions in their own words, not just parroting the text. The examination in geometry was equally stunning. Ware asked a young girl why she had seemed nervous during the geometry exam. "Oh, Mr. Ware," she said, "I was not on examination, nor our class, nor our school; my race was on examination before these Visitors . . . to God be the praise for my examination that day."

"The exercises of the two preceding days has dispelled the opinion, heretofore entertained, that the members of the African race were incapable of a high degree of mental culture," said Brown. "I was all wrong. I am converted." The board even praised the "missionary spirit with which the teachers entered upon their self-assigned task, and have performed their duties while receiving salaries barely sufficient to sustain the necessaries of life." The performance of the Atlanta students was reported in the press, North and South. "We are not prepared to believe what we witnessed," wrote the *Atlanta Constitution*:

> To see colored boys and girls fourteen and eighteen years of age, reading in Greek and Latin, and demonstrating correctly problems in Algebra and Geometry, and seemingly understanding what they demonstrated appears almost wonderful.

Now prominent businessmen stopped to shake the hands of Atlanta University teachers; there was white community support for building projects; the legislature was inclined to grant more appropriations; and the morale of students and faculty soared. People believed that Asa Ware could convince anyone to do whatever he wanted, especially recalcitrant white Southerners. But for Asa Ware trouble lay ahead.

Georgia was now entirely in the hands of white Democrats. In 1871 the Klan murdered seventy-four men in Georgia.

From 1865 to 1871, Moses Calhoun, aspiring capitalist, had an account in the Atlanta branch of the Negro-owned Freedman's Savings and Trust Company. In 1871 Freedman's Bank (as it was also called) had thirty-four branches and deposits of $20 million. When the bank failed in 1874, how much Moses lost is unknown. But Frederick Douglass, who became president of the bank in early 1874, very much tarnished his own reputation. In the mid-nineteenth century, Douglass was a new kind of black leader. Before the Civil War, the evil of slavery gave rise to half-mad leaders of doomed rebellions, men like Denmark Vesey and Nat Turner. But Douglass was not only sane; he was canny. He went from being a moral leader before the war to being a political leader after the war, having the ear of presidents Lincoln, Grant, Hayes, and Garfield.

Oddly enough, Reconstruction was not a happy period in the life of Douglass, for so long the voice of black aspirations. In 1870 the fifty-one-year-old Douglass was on the wrong side of two important issues: he had supported President Grant's Santo Domingo annexation fiasco (hoping to build an American "empire," Grant sought unsuccessfully to annex Santo Domingo), and he had opposed Negro migration to Kansas. Now, as president of Freedman's Bank at its collapse, he was distanced all the more from the ordinary black people of the South. Douglass seemed to have totally succumbed to a power structure that fed his ego with titles and sinecures. To be fair, Douglass felt old, tired, and useless. His lifework, his religion, had been abolition—once it was achieved, he was having a kind of post-emancipation *tristesse*. Douglass had a right to his ego; he was a self-made star, a brilliant and generous man, and a sincere proponent of all progressive values—William Lloyd Garrison made him a pacifist (they disagreed on the Civil War) and Lucretia Mott made him a feminist.

In 1874 Frederick Douglass made a mistake. He agreed to become president of the Freedman's Bank. The list of the bank's incorporators and trustees—which included the industrialist Peter Cooper, editor William Cullen Bryant, Treasury comptroller John Jay Knox, Dr. Samuel Gridley Howe (husband of Julia Ward Howe), and Chief Justice Salmon Chase—was stellar; but its board of directors was made up basically of crooks. "No more extraordinary and disreputable venture ever disgraced American business disguised as philanthropy than the Freedmen's Bank," wrote Du Bois. Douglass had the grace to admit that one of the reasons he said yes was the thought of the vast gulf between little Fred, the nearly naked slave boy, and being president of a bank.

"It is not altogether without a feeling of humiliation that I must narrate my connection with 'The Freedmen's Savings and Trust Company,'" wrote Douglass, describing it as an institution designed to furnish a place of "security and profit" for the hard-won earnings of black people, especially of the South. There were bank branches throughout the old Confederacy, and "money to the amount of millions flowed into its vaults." In typical nouveaux riche style, the bank decided to build itself a showplace in order to display its prosperity. "They accordingly erected on one of the most desirable and expensive sites in the national capital one of the most costly and splendid buildings of the time," wrote Douglass, going on (with not a little irony) about "marble counters" and "elegantly dressed colored clerks with their pens behind their ears and buttonhole bouquets in their coat-fronts."

Douglass became a trustee of the bank when he moved to Washington in 1872 to work on his new paper, the *New National Era*. He deposited $12,000 and loaned the bank $10,000 of his own money, but when it was too late, he learned that the other trustees had *nothing* deposited in the bank. Some, while assuring Douglass of the bank's soundness, had withdrawn their deposits. Douglass also discovered a matter of $40,000 that could not be traced. "Not to make too long a story, I was, in six weeks after my election as president of this bank, convinced that it was no longer a safe custodian of the hard earnings of my confiding people." Douglass contacted the Senate Committee on Finance—while a group of trustees tried to make him the villain. But Douglass insisted that the bank should close, and the Finance Committee soon agreed.

It was a hollow victory. "[It] brought upon my head an amount of abuse and detraction greater than any encountered in any other part of my life," wrote Douglass. He was accused of "bringing the Freedman's Bank into ruin, and squandering in senseless loans on bad security the hardly-earned moneys of my race," despite the fact that all the loans were made prior to his presidency. "Not a dollar, not a dime of its millions were loaned by me, or with my approval," he wrote. "The fact is . . . I was married to a corpse . . . the life, which was the money, was gone." Douglass believed that he had been placed in the position with the hope that by "'some drugs, some charms, some conjuration, or some mighty magic,' I could bring it back."

Despite the demise of Freedman's Bank, by 1875 black Americans, especially those in the North, had reason to feel optimistic— Massachusetts senator Charles Sumner's great civil rights bill was law. The Civil Rights Act of 1875 had originally been proposed by Sumner in 1870. It was an equal rights bill for transportation, hotels, theaters, churches, cemeteries, juries, and schools, but when it passed in 1875, equality in schools was deleted. Sumner had died in 1874 in his rooms at Washington's Wormley House, an exclusive private hotel, with James Wormley, the Negro hotel owner, at his bedside. In the art of the time depicting Sumner's death, Wormley stands out as the only Negro in the picture. Samuel Cutler Ward, the anti-abolitionist brother of Julia Ward Howe and the most important lobbyist in D.C., famous for saving Andrew Johnson from impeachment, was both a political foe and a beloved friend of Sumner's. He communicated the details of Sumner's death to their best friend, Henry Wadsworth Longfellow. The three had been friends since their Boston boyhood. Ward, a rotund, Pickwickian figure, wrote to "Longo" that he had been "in the bath," when word came that Sumner was dangerously ill. Dressing hurriedly, he had rushed to Sumner's bedside to find him in extremis. "A vast crowd of freed men with the gloomiest faces darkened the street before his door," wrote Ward. "The last audible words he uttered, with the old ring in his voice, were 'Don't let the bill die!' Shortly after, again in a loud voice, 'I mean the civil rights bill!'"

Charles Sumner's bill did not die. It passed in his honor. The passing of the first civil rights bill in America was a momentous event for American blacks—and an event of concern for many whites. In always free Indiana, the white *Evansville Journal* asked sixteen-year-old Edwin Horn, a young Negro schoolmaster-journalist, to write about the bill from the black point of view. Horn, who called himself "colored" but looked white, warned that the bill gave only *equal rights*. Hoping to forestall any excuses for racism, Horn spoke directly to young black people, warning them against "impertinence and insolence." The primary object of the bill, he said, "is to *protect* you in the enjoyment of your rights as American citizens." He warned that any indiscretion committed by a black man in asserting his rights under the civil rights bill would "not only bring injury upon its author, but also do a great harm to the colored race as a whole." Edwin was conveying what whites wanted to hear—but he was also warning young Negro men to watch their step.

Edwin Horn, an exceptionally handsome young man, worked for two Evansville papers—one white, one black. On his way up in black journalism, Horn was the editor of a colored weekly, *Our Age*, and he was also the official "colored correspondent" for the *Evansville Journal*, a white daily. His real job was teaching in Evansville's colored school. Edwin first came to the *Journal*'s attention in January 1875, when he gave the dedication speech at the opening of the new colored school. The *Journal* quoted the major theme of Edwin's speech:

> To be the full equal of the white man, there are two particular things we need—education and wealth . . . See that your children are educated . . . If they be educated and virtuous, the greatness of our people is assured.

In March, the *Journal* noted:

At the close of the written examination of the Second Intermediate Schools, it was discovered that the pupils of the colored school of that grade, taught by Edwin F. Horn, had the highest general average in the city.

Edwin was born in 1859 in racially unfriendly Tennessee to a mixed-race couple, a white British-born father and an Indian-black (or entirely Indian) mother. But he grew up in Quaker-influenced Indiana, which came into the Union in 1816 as a free state. Edwin's hero, Indiana's Civil War governor, Oliver Morton, had been an ardent abolitionist. In Indiana, the Horn children were classified as "colored," a slightly more acceptable category than "Indian." Thanks to the Quakers, Indiana had a relatively peaceful Civil War, except when Morgan's Raiders used it as a shortcut to Ohio. Edwin grew up in Evansville, a placidly pretty Ohio River town, half Midwestern, half Southern. His father, the captain of a river trading boat, instilled a love of poetry in his four children, three boys and a girl. Edwin had a relatively comfortable time growing up "colored" in Evansville. A true child of Reconstruction, he showed the importance of education in both his speech and his comments. He started a night school for black adults. Whatever his talent, Edwin loved poetry. "Give children the best of poetry," he wrote in a note to himself as a young teacher. "There is born in every man a poet who dies young." Later, in 1887, the journalist-editor-teacher would marry Cora Calhoun.

In 1876 the country was one hundred years old. Edwin Horn played the flute in the Evansville Centennial Concert. It was a great year to be an American—except for Southern Republicans. Although the state of Mississippi did not recognize the Thirteenth Amendment until 1995 and did not ratify it until 2013, the rest of the Confederate states were ratifying the Fourteenth Amendment and pledging allegiance to the

United States. But in 1876 the South was once again solidly Democratic. The country was clearly divided, but sectional differences were less important than economic unity. Post–Civil War America was in the business of advancing the machine age; machines made money. What better way to advance America's vision of machine age leadership than to have a birthday party and invite the world? The Philadelphia Exposition, in the city where it all began, was the site of the great centennial party: a heady mix of patriotism and commerce, a passing recognition of the arts, and the glorification of the machine. It probably reflected the American character. Tycoons and titans of industry clearly revered machinery in all its forms. After Lincoln, who was sui generis, the greatest American men of the age were mechanics, engineers, inventors, and industrialists—not presidents.

By 1876, however, Reconstruction in the South was politically dead—although its spirit certainly survived everywhere, the letter of Reconstruction had died. It was a terrible turning point. There would be no more Union soldiers in the South to protect former slaves; there would be no more effective Republicans in the South, black or white; and there would be no more black freedom. Moses Calhoun thrived, however, amassing property because his interests were economic, not political. By 1876 Moses was as successful as any black man in Atlanta could hope to be. The postwar migration of Georgia blacks to Kansas and points west and north had caused some alarm among whites. Moses might have felt it was "good riddance." Like many upper servants, he probably had conservative views. The *best* people, he might have believed, stayed to rebuild Atlanta, which soon became as brash and money-grasping as it was before the war, with Democrats back in charge. Moses was no political activist. He was a Republican, but he knew how to get along with Democrats. Moses' particular pursuit of happiness throughout the 1870s meant expanding his business, becoming a pillar of the black community, and organizing parties for his daughters and their friends. There were other black churches in Atlanta, but Moses naturally joined First Congregational—not only a house of God, but a doorway to the future. Asa Ware, a founder of First Congregational, was elected the first clerk and treasurer of the church, which was a block away from Storrs School. By the fall of 1875 Jane and Asa Ware had moved out of their dorm quarters and into an old cabin that they decorated like a New England cottage—and which became a "source of sweetness and light" to hundreds of student guests. The two Ware children illegally attended Storrs School. Georgia law prohibited black and white children from attending the same school.

Ironically, in 1876 Mississippi became the first state to elect a Negro, forty-one-year-old Blanche Kelso Bruce, to a full term in the U.S. Senate. Educated with his master's son (possibly his half brother) in Virginia, Bruce was intelligent and articulate, with polished manners. A self-described carpetbagger, he settled in Mississippi in 1870. When Bruce took his seat in the Senate, the white senior senator from Mississippi, James Alcorn, refused to escort the newly elected junior senator down the aisle, contrary to established custom. As Bruce, embarrassed, started to walk down the aisle alone, Senator Roscoe Conkling, the powerful Republican "boss" of New York, instantly stepped in to escort him. Bruce was the only Negro senator—and, for two years, the only Negro in Congress. Befriending Bruce, Conkling saw that he also received appointments to important committees.

The Republicans had won the war and saved the Union, and they spent sixteen consecutive years in the White House. The party was in disarray—it had been in power too long. There were no strong candidates and too many factions: radicals, moderates, conservatives, and reformers. The Republican Party itself was now commonly perceived to be a sinkhole of graft, corruption, and patronage. It looked like an easy win for the Democrats. Their candidate was the very popular former New York governor Samuel Tilden, aged sixty-two, a barn-burning (antislavery) Democrat known as the "giant killer" because he sent Boss Tweed to jail in 1873. Tilden, a bachelor who later gave $3 million to the people of New York City to establish a free public library, won both the popular and the electoral vote; but disputed returns, and accusations of fraud and violence in several Southern states, caused the election to be decided by Congress. Hayes won by one vote. The election was utterly corrupt, as was the resulting "compromise." "The Republican Party is the ship," Frederick Douglass famously often said, and "all else is the sea." Unfortunately, the ship was dashed on the rocks of the stolen election of 1876. The election was actually decided in a smoke-filled room in the Negro-owned Wormley House hotel. Southern Democrats did not really care about the White House—they cared about "home rule" over Negroes. The secret "compromise" stated that Southern Democrats would acknowledge Republican Rutherford B. Hayes as president only if all federal troops were removed from the former Confederate states. The Wormley Compromise was a double betrayal. The Republican Party betrayed Southern blacks—as well as the Thirteenth, Fourteenth, and Fifteenth Amendments. And the Democratic Party betrayed its own candidate. It was another terrible turning point.

The Republican candidate Rutherford Birchard Hayes, aged fifty-four, was not just another bearded Union general from Ohio—he was a genuine war hero. Leading a regiment of Ohio volunteers, he was wounded five times and had four horses shot out from beneath him. His wife, the former Lucy Ware Webb, was sometimes known as "Lemonade Lucy" because she was a member of the Temperance League and had banned alcohol in the White House. Hayes took the oath of office in March 1877 in a quasi-secret ceremony in the White House, because outgoing President Grant feared mob violence by Tilden's supporters. The only happy people were Southern Democrats, who got exactly what they wanted—total control over *their* Negroes, without constitutional restraints. It was not a "stolen" election. It was a *trade.* The South gave the North the White House in exchange for a free hand in erasing all traces of both Reconstruction and the black Republican vote. The end of black freedom in the South officially came in April 1877, when President Hayes withdrew all federal troops.

The end was in the beginning, of course. The minute blacks began to vote, the white South began to plot their downfall. No longer at war with Yankees, the South was openly at war with blacks. The former Confederacy was determined to reinstate slavery by any means necessary and to organize society as if the Confederacy had won the war. Poor Southern blacks, some having glimpsed a different world, were on their way back to the *new* bondage of Jim Crow, sharecropping, and lynching—all virtually nonexistent during slavery. By 1876 black life in the South was back to Justice Taney's comments of 1857; if you were black and lived below the Mason-Dixon Line, you *still* had no rights "which the white man was bound to respect." Blacks had discovered that life in freedom, as twentieth-century poet Langston Hughes wrote, was "no crystal stair."

Georgia was somewhat different. As soon as the army was withdrawn in 1877, the Georgia legislature ejected its Negro members—three in the senate and twenty-nine in the house—on the grounds that they had not been citizens for the requisite nine years. However, shortly after the ejection, one of Georgia's congressmen came down to tell the state's political bosses that some very important people in Washington wanted the Negro members of the legislature reseated—and the Fourteenth and Fifteenth Amendments ratified. It seemed that Georgia was wooing Northern business investors. Georgia liked to look good to Yankees—in Atlanta at least. That left plenty of room in the countryside for the KKK to foment terror. The year 1876 was the last when blacks in the South voted for nearly another century.

In the state report on Atlanta University in 1877, the year that Cora Calhoun was a freshman at the school, the committee noticed a "remarkable docility" on the part of the students, who were like "clay in the hands of the potter." Atlanta University was in a position to "shape the public opinions of the colored race, and make them true and loyal citizens of Georgia . . . or it can turn all their prejudices and feelings against their native state." The board urged Asa Ware to remove certain books that presented a "sectional bias" and suggested that he instruct his teachers to promote friendly relations between students and native whites. Ware, who was courageous but not rash, removed the objectionable books and urged his teachers to make serious efforts to avoid alienating the students from Atlanta's white citizens.

Perhaps Ware was conscious of the growing relations between the students at Fisk and the friendly citizens of Nashville, due in particular to the Fisk Jubilee Singers. In the 1870s America discovered and fell in love with Negro spirituals: Bible stories, both light and serious, retold in Negro dialect and set to vocal harmonies of an almost transcendent beauty and power. Audiences, black and white, flocked to hear the Fisk Jubilee Singers, fresh on the concert scene and currently touring America, Europe, and the British Isles to raise money for their university. One of their earliest and most eloquent fans was Mark Twain (Samuel Clemens), a longtime friend of the Negro. (Huck Finn, of course, is the perfect "closet" abolitionist.) Twain first heard the Jubilee Singers in a German beer hall on their first tour of Europe in the summer of 1871:

> To my mind—their music made all other vocal music cheap . . . It is utterly beautiful, to me; and it moves me infinitely more than any other music can. I think that in the Jubilees and their songs America has produced the perfectest flower of the ages; and I wish it were a foreign product, so that she would worship it and lavish money on it and go properly crazy over it.

Suddenly, black American spirituals were being sung around the world in every language, and the Jubilee Singers became internationally known. These very polite and well-groomed young people, ranging in all the shades of black, from ebony to ivory, raised enough money from the 1876 tour to construct the first important building at Fisk.

Beyond the schools and churches of both races, vox populi was not exactly clamoring for spirituals—but it was clamoring for black music and dance. And it was clamoring for an ersatz version of black life in minstrel shows. Before the war, minstrelsy was about whites performing in blackface (burnt cork makeup). After the war, the most successful minstrel troupe was Charles Callender's Original Georgia Minstrels, formerly the Georgia Minstrels, who were blacks in blackface. Black minstrels accepted and copied the image created by racist white minstrels. Callender's Original Georgia Minstrels entered every new town with a parade, a brass band, and, if possible, an elephant.

Also popular were "Tom" shows—performances of *Uncle Tom's Cabin*—a theatrical perennial for at least eighty years. At one point, four companies performed the play simultaneously in New York City. And touring companies continued to play to packed houses all over America—generally with all white actors. The more successful companies, however, had Negro extras, often advertised as "a passel of darkies and a brace of hounds." Or—if really high end—"200 genuine colored people." In February 1881, ninety-two-year-old Reverend Josiah Henson, "the real Uncle Tom," who lived in Dresden, Canada, near Detroit, gave one of his last lectures on slavery in an American church. White-haired Henson was indeed the "original." His lecture was free. This is what Reverend Josiah Henson said about slavery: "It turned the slave into the cringing, treacherous, false, and thieving victim of tyranny."

By the 1880s, twenty years past slavery, Moses and Atlanta Calhoun were leaders in Atlanta's black middle-class community, and Cora and Lena Calhoun and their cousin, Katie Webb, were definitely top girls. The Calhoun girls, with their youthful good looks, were photographed— Cora, small and pretty, and Lena, tall and beautiful. In the 1880 census,

Moses Calhoun, aged fifty-one, of Fulton County, Georgia, was listed as "Merchant & Restaurant," "married," and "mu" for mulatto—the census could never make up its mind about Moses; sometimes he was "bla" and sometimes he was "mu." His household now consisted of Atlanta, Cora, Lena, and Atlanta's mother, Charlotte Fernando. The family names are followed by six unknown men, presumably the cook and waiters from Moses' restaurant, living in his boardinghouse next door. Moses had become a pillar of the First Congregational Church, which remained unapologetically integrated—with a white pastor and a substantial group of whites in the congregation, mostly teachers and staff at Storrs and Atlanta University—sitting *among* rather than separate from the black members, contrary to Georgia law. The black Calhouns were now leaders of their community. As the hopes of Reconstruction began to fade, they continued to embody its promise.

CHAPTER THREE

South/Reconstruction
NIGHT/1880s

By 1880 the country was clearly speeding backward on the subject of race—and the extent of the racist oppression would go far beyond anything seen in antebellum days. Jim Crow, the KKK, and the "separate but equal" lie all held sway over black Americans from the late nineteenth century through most of the twentieth century. The 1880s could be called the Dark Ages—everything won in the war and Reconstruction was basically lost. Southern blacks had absolutely no constitutional safeguards. Jim Crow would soon spread its shadow over the region and the country. Outside the larger Southern cities, black life was less than cheap. It was a tyranny that was worse than slavery. The only thing that made it marginally better than slavery was the ability to escape, which was available to only very few.

Above the Mason-Dixon Line, it was the Gilded Age—with tycoons, trusts, and the iron tentacles of the railroads relentlessly pushing westward. It was a new age of steam, steel, speed, and communication. There were new inventions, some by black Americans, to make life easier and faster. For example, Canadian-born Elijah McCoy, the son of runaway slaves, was trained and certified as a mechanical engineer in Scotland, but in America he could get only a job as a railroad fireman. In the 1870s he invented a steam engine lubrication device that was so superior that purchasers began asking for the "real McCoy." And Massachusetts-born Lewis Latimer, also the son of runaway slaves, drafted the patent drawings for his friend Alexander Graham Bell's telephone; he also invented the railway water closet and, most important, the carbon filament for electric lightbulbs. Working for Hiram Maxim (inventor of the machine gun) in 1881, Latimer supervised the installation of electric lights in New York City, Philadelphia, Montreal, and London. In 1884 he became Thomas Edison's chief draftsman and the only black "Edison pioneer"—and in 1890 he cowrote the book on the Edison electricity system. (In the 1890s he would become a good friend of the New York–based black Calhouns.) Special black achievement might be recognized—but the explosion of southern European and Chinese immigration was making an impact on black employment. There was racial and labor violence. There was also a robber baron mentality among the powerful. "The public be damned!" said the richest man in the world, William H. Vanderbilt of the New York Central Railroad. It summed up the attitude of almost every politician in Washington in the last quarter of the nineteenth century. The Negro electorate and the Negro leadership continued to follow the Republicans without protest. How could they support the Democrats?

In the summer of 1880 Edwin Horn, the young man who would marry Cora Calhoun, was an alternate delegate from the First District in Indiana to the Republican National Convention in Chicago, pledged to Senator James G. Blaine of Maine. Edwin was now a spectacularly handsome twenty-one-year-old middle school principal and editor-publisher of a black weekly newspaper. Senator Blaine was leader of the "half-breeds," the liberal Republican faction that wanted continued federal protection for black Southern voters. But conservative Republicans, known as "stalwarts," believed in sacrificing the black vote for an alliance with disaffected Southern Democrats. The 1880 Republican convention was deadlocked between "half-breed" Blaine and "stalwart" Ulysses S. Grant, seeking an unpopular third term. The convention desperately needed a dark horse. Senator Blanche Kelso Bruce was presiding when Representative James A. Garfield of Ohio asked for recognition. Bruce recognized Garfield, who made such an impression on the exhausted delegates that, on the thirty-sixth ballot, he became the "dark horse" nominee. Garfield's victory was slim and achieved without a single Southern state. He campaigned on the "bloody shirt" platform—of helping Southern Negroes. The Senate itself was evenly divided between the two parties.

Despite being a Blaine man, Edwin Horn was happy to support Garfield, a former abolitionist and the youngest brigadier in the Union army, and to see Blaine chosen as secretary of state. They were both "half-breeds." They would save the beleaguered black Republican South from the depredations of the Democrats. Garfield, who was the last president to be born in a log cabin, and whose campaign biography, *From Canal Boy to President*, was written by Horatio Alger, attended Western Reserve Eclectic Institute (later Hiram College), then transferred to Williams College, where he graduated in 1856. After college, he taught classical languages at Western Reserve Eclectic during the week and preached for the Disciples of Christ on Sundays. He became principal of the Eclectic Institute in 1857. The ambidextrous Garfield's classicist parlor trick possibly explains the meaning of "Eclectic": he could simultaneously write an answer to a question in Latin with one hand and ancient Greek with the other—surely uniquely in American politics.

There was a notable black presence at the Garfield inauguration. Black troops, heroes of the Indian Wars, marched in the inaugural parade. (After the Civil War, the army established four all-black units—two infantry and two cavalry—to fight hostile Indians.) It was said that more Negroes than whites bought tickets for the inaugural ball. And in a historical first, on March 4, 1881, as marshal of the District of Columbia, sixty-three-year-old Frederick Douglass had the duty of escorting both president-elect Garfield and outgoing president Hayes to the inauguration ceremonies. Appointed by Hayes in 1877 to be the first black marshal, and still handsome and imposing with his lion's mane of white hair, Douglass led the parade of officials from the Senate chamber to the Capitol rotunda, where Garfield took the oath of office.

In his inaugural address, President Garfield stated that all the powers of the government, the states, and volunteer services should be directed at solving the problem of educating the Southern Negro. "There can be no permanent disfranchised peasantry in the United States," he said, essentially speaking of all the people the Missionary schools were unable to reach. The South disagreed, of course.

On March 5, the day after the inauguration, President Garfield named Frederick Douglass the first black recorder of deeds of the District of Columbia. Douglass had not been entirely for Garfield. He preferred men of sterner stuff, like General Grant. Most blacks loved Grant—graft, "stalwarts," and all. But recorder of deeds was a more lucrative patronage job ($1.50 per deed) than marshal. It would also mean less time on the lecture circuit and more time to write. His third book, *The Life and Times of Frederick Douglass*, would be published that year. As recorder of deeds, he had a new secretary: a forty-two-year-old Mount Holyoke graduate, Helen Pitts, a white feminist from a Rochester, New York, abolitionist family.

By now, Senator Bruce of Mississippi, the first black senator to serve a full term in Congress, was one of the wealthiest Negroes in America and the most famous black elected official. His senatorial term ended on Garfield's inauguration day. His political future now depended entirely on Republican Party patronage. He requested the position of register of the Treasury and it was granted. It was the highest appointed position ever held by a Negro—his signature would be on U.S. currency. As long as there was a Republican in the White House, black Republicans like Bruce and Douglass would have good federal jobs. Black Republicans no longer won elections in Mississippi, of course, but they still controlled delegates to the Republican National Convention and could make a difference in tight races.

Bruce's 1878 marriage to the beautiful Josephine Wilson, daughter of an important Cleveland Negro, had been highly publicized, and the honeymoon abroad was a success—with all courtesies from the Department of State. The newlyweds were a political and social success in London. The London *Times* called Bruce as "accomplished as any man in the Senate." Back in Washington, the Bruces attended a white church, had many white friends, and entertained lavishly in their imposing Washington house. The senator now owned three thousand acres of Mississippi Delta land, plus several successful Washington businesses, and commanded high fees for speeches. "His complexion is café-au-lait, and his slightly curly hair is well-brushed," wrote a contemporary. "He dresses well and is as intelligent and polite a gentleman as you will find in Washington." Mrs. Bruce, it was noted, had "Caucasian features, large, beautiful eyes, a somewhat brunette complexion, and long, slightly waved hair. She is well-educated and said to be an intellectual." A photograph of the young Mrs. Bruce reveals a delicate-featured, seemingly white beauty who is really a Negro—at least according to the "one-drop" rule of Southern law. Bruce and his wife had one son, Roscoe Conkling Bruce, born in 1879 and named for Bruce's senatorial mentor, the Republican boss of New York.

By the late winter of 1880, up-and-coming young Indiana Republican Edwin Horn was about to marry his second wife and move to Indianapolis, where he would become principal of a colored school and found a weekly newspaper, the *Colored World*, later the successful *Indianapolis World*. Extremely high-minded, and steeped in Romantic poetry and literature, he had joined a colored literary society in neighboring Nashville, where he had met his first love, Callie Hatcher. Two 1878 Nashville newspaper clips tell the story:

Married . . . Saturday, November 30th . . . Mr. Edwin F. Horn of Evansville, Indiana to Miss Callie Hatcher of this city . . .

Died . . . On Saturday, December 14, Mrs. Callie L. Hatcher, the wife
of Edwin Horn . . .

They had been married only two weeks. The cause of Callie Hatcher
Horn's death is unknown. Maybe she was ill when they married. Maybe
she had a sudden accident. Edwin married again two years later. His
second wife's father, H. Ford Douglass, had been a noted Illinois abolitionist and "agent" on the extraordinary Ohio Underground Railroad.
The great Frederick permitted Ford to add an extra "s" to his name
and spoke well of him in print. In the bloody 1850s Ford Douglass
had advocated black emigration to Central America or Haiti. Despite
his faith in emigration, however, he was the first black man in Illinois
to try to enlist in the Union army. Eventually, he became captain of
the army's only black regiment of light artillery and died of typhus at
the Battle of Vicksburg. Edwin understood his father-in-law's sense of
exile, as it became less and less possible for black Republicans to survive
or have freedom in the South. Edwin's second wife, Ford Douglass'
daughter, Nellie, died in childbirth.

After presenting herself for examination concerning her Christian faith,
on February 9, 1881, sixteen-year-old Cora Calhoun was chosen for
admission into the Congregational Church. And on March 13 she was
baptized by immersion, as was the practice, with a group of thirteen
others. Cora was now a member of the senior class of the higher normal
course at Storrs. (A senior in high school, more or less.) She was studying
algebra, art history, Milton, and Shakespeare; her classes included "Mental
Philosophy and Moral Philosophy" and "Evidences of Christianity."
High school may be where Cora discovered that she was a religious seeker.

On April 7, 1881, Tennessee, the birthplace of the Ku Klux Klan, created the first Jim Crow law, mandating separate railway carriages for
Negroes and whites. It was the first law of its kind in the South—but its

title came from an old song. According to historian C. Vann Woodward, by 1838 the term "Jim Crow" had become an adjective that applied to all aspects of Southern Negro life. Over time, "Jim Crow" became synonymous with the South's entire legal system. The name came from a minstrel song, "Jump Jim Crow." The original Jim Crow(e) may have been a crippled black man who entertained workers at Thomas Crowe's livery stable in Louisville, Kentucky, circa 1830:

> He was very much deformed, the right shoulder was drawn up high, and the left leg was stiff and crooked at the knee, which gave him a painful, but at the same time ludicrous limp . . . He was in the habit of crooning a queer old tune, to which he had applied words of his own . . . and these were the words of his refrain: "Wheel about, turnabout, do js so, an ebery time I wheel about I jump Jim Crow."

This deformed man apparently so convulsed white minstrel star Thomas "Daddy" Rice when he was a young man that he put it into the blackface act that made him famous.

It is important to understand that Jim Crow laws were the model for Hitler's Nuremberg race laws and South African apartheid. Nazis sent Jews to death camps. Apartheid kept black people penned into "homelands." And Jim Crow kept blacks isolated, oppressed, impoverished, uneducated, liable to lynching, and still working without fair recompense. Tennessee's Jim Crow law became the Southern model in the long twilight of Reconstruction. Tennessee laws were copied by Florida in 1887; Mississippi in 1888; Texas in 1889; Louisiana in 1890; Arkansas, Georgia, Alabama, and Kentucky in 1891; South Carolina in 1898; North Carolina in 1899; Virginia in 1900; Maryland in 1904; and Oklahoma in 1907. These ironclad laws were the bane of black Southern life for most of the twentieth century.

In June 1881 Cora Calhoun completed Atlanta University's higher normal course of study and become a member of its fourth graduating class. Her diploma was signed by Asa Ware. Besides her religion and philosophy courses, she had studied geometry, geology, geography, botany, chemistry, physics, astronomy, literature, composition, history, government, and Latin. She also learned household science: plain sewing, cookery, and nursing. The pretty sixteen-year-old Southern girl from a reasonably well-off family, bluestocking and feminist though she might claim to be, was always ready to go to a party. Cora kept party invitations as souvenirs: There was the New Year's Eve 1880 "Entertainment" at Odd Fellows Hall given by "a committee of 12 bachelors." The bachelors were slightly older young men whom she had known all her life. The "Gate City Girls" ("G.C.G.") and "The Married Ladies Social Club" had a masquerade party "At Mr. Calhoun's" (Moses' restaurant) at No. 34 Decatur Street, on March 24, 1882; the committee included "the Misses Webb and Calhoun." In 1883 Cora was cordially invited to attend "a Reception given by the Young Men, at Golden Rod Hall, Whitehall St. Dec. 28, 8 o'clock." Christmas and the New Year, a social time for Cora and other middle-class blacks of Atlanta, had traditionally been festive times on plantations—the holidays were even more festive in freedom.

But education was the eternal issue—and "Head or hand?" was the question. On May 31, 1881, Booker T. Washington, a twenty-five-year-old Negro graduate of Hampton Institute, received $2,000 from the Alabama state legislature to open a new school for Negroes in Tuskegee, Alabama. At the age of sixteen, Washington, a former child coal miner, had walked barefoot to Hampton Normal and Agricultural Institute and asked to be admitted. Students received a postsecondary education, learned job skills, and paid for their education through manual labor. They were advised to ignore politics and concentrate on character development and economic self-help. When the Alabama legislature asked Samuel Armstrong, Hampton's founder, to recommend a white teacher as principal, he instead recommended Washington. Tuskegee Institute officially opened on July 4, 1881, with one teacher, Washington, using space rented from a local church. Tuskegee stressed the "hand" above all—thus it received more Northern industrial largesse than any other Missionary college.

Two days earlier, on the morning of July 2, 1881, a failed civil servant crackpot named Charles Guiteau shot President Garfield in the busy waiting room of Washington's railroad station. As Garfield entered the station, Guiteau stepped directly behind him and shot him twice in the back, then was seized by angry witnesses who held him until a policeman arrived. It was at the police station that Guiteau made the statement that caused so much trouble to Garfield's successor: "I am a Stalwart of the Stalwarts! I did it and I want to be arrested! Arthur is President now!" Vice President Chester A. Arthur, a stalwart (essentially a Republican willing to accommodate the anti-Negro South), would enter the presidency under a large cloud of suspicion.

Frederick Douglass, for one, had always been suspicious of the "self-indulgent" vice president. Douglass distinctly remembered when he first heard the name "Chester A. Arthur" at the 1880 Chicago Convention. He had felt a shudder "such as one might feel in coming upon an armed murderer or a poisonous reptile":

> For some occult and mysterious cause, I know not what, I felt the hand of death upon me. I do not say or intimate that Mr. Arthur had anything to do with the taking off of the President . . . I state the simple fact precisely as it was.

Party reformers had no love for Arthur, either. There was no place in which Arthur's "powers of mischief will be so small as in the Vice-Presidency," said the *Nation* magazine. The *New York Times* said that Arthur's previous career had been a "mess of filth." He was a well-dressed fat man, collector of the Port of New York, and chief lieutenant to Senator Roscoe Conkling. During the 1880 campaign, political rivals insisted that he was ineligible to be president because he was not born in America. Some insisted that he was Canadian because his parents had briefly lived there. Another group said he had been born in Ireland and came to the United States at the age of fourteen. Even his so-called friends were aghast. "Chet Arthur, president of the United States? Good God!" said one unnamed acquaintance.

Once again, America was plunged into mourning over the assassination of a president. This was different, however. Although gravely wounded, Garfield still lived. Public prayer vigils were held throughout the country. At first Garfield's condition fluctuated; then it was mostly bad. In the Washington summer, navy engineers lowered the temperature of the president's sickroom by blowing fans over a large block of ice. Sam Ward, who personally carried some hundred-year-old rum to the White House, wrote to his sister Julia, saying he was "backing divine Providence to win the race." The problem was the bullet—doctors couldn't find it. One bullet had grazed the president's arm; the second was possibly in his spine. Looking for the bullet, a team of doctors stuck unwashed fingers into the wound and infected his liver in the process. Alexander Graham Bell announced the invention of a special metal detector to find the bullet—a "telephone probe," he called it, for the detection of bullets in the human body. But the metal frame on Garfield's bed threw the instrument off. Bell had asked the doctors to move Garfield from the bed, but they rejected his request. What did Bell know about medical science? When Garfield finally succumbed, his medical treatment had been such that his assassin could fairly say that the doctors, not he, had killed the president.

Douglass had some final thoughts on Garfield and Arthur:

The death of Mr. Garfield placed in the presidential chair Chester A. Arthur, who did nothing to correct the errors of President Hayes, or to arrest the decline and fall of the Republican party, but, on the contrary, by his self-indulgence, indifference, and neglect of opportunity, allowed the country to drift (like an oarless boat in the rapids) towards the howling chasm of the slaveholding Democracy.

In December, Atlanta University established the Garfield Scholarship Fund, as a memorial to the late president who had been considered a friend of the Negro.

If there was anyone who understood political disappointment, it was Edwin Horn. Senator Charles Sumner's great Civil Rights Act of 1875, which he reported on for two Indiana papers, was declared unconstitutional in October 1883. Black despair followed. It was the end of all Reconstruction benefits. The Republican-dominated Supreme Court ruled that the bill's guarantees of equal rights went beyond the powers granted to Congress in the Reconstruction Amendments.

Republicans and Democrats were now united in seeking to make life hell for blacks in America—52 blacks were lynched in 1883. Between 1883 and 1896, 1,280 Negroes, including women and children, were lynched. And Alabama, Florida, Mississippi, Texas, and Georgia enacted Jim Crow laws on everything from railroad cars to burial plots to checkers games. Ida Wells-Barnett, the militant antilynching crusader, would begin keeping statistics in 1892.

On July 4, 1885, an item appeared in the *Washington Bee*, one of the most popular black newspapers, that "Miss Cora C. Calhoun, of Atlanta, Ga., and Miss Carrie Walton of Augusta, Ga.," were "expected in this city daily." They had been in Raleigh, North Carolina, for the wedding of a friend. "Both are accomplished young ladies, besides embracing all other charms demanded by the critical eye." Belles of the Eastern circuit black bourgeoisie of Boston, New York City, Philadelphia, Washington, and Atlanta, they were great travelers, despite Jim Crow. Cora was now twenty. She hoped to see new (male) faces—Atlanta's faces were far too familiar.

"He Fell Going Uphill" was the *Atlanta Constitution* headline. In the late summer of 1885 Asa Ware returned to Atlanta ahead of his family to prepare for the opening of school in the fall. After dinner on the evening of September 5, he felt ill and went for some air. As he was walking uphill from his home to the university, he had a seizure, or stroke, and died. His burial posed a problem for the local cemetery. Ware had stated his wish to be buried where he had done his lifework and "not with those . . . who had not been friends to the colored people." Because Ware was held in such esteem by whites as well as blacks, the cemetery made a concession. President Ware was buried in the middle of the road that divided the Negro and white sections of the cemetery. Thus, one-half of his body lay in the burial ground of each. Nine years later, on December 22, 1894, Ware's remains were moved to Atlanta University and placed beneath a granite boulder from Ware's Massachusetts birthplace.

In the fall of 1885, sixteen-year-old Lena Calhoun went away to college at Fisk, where among the new faces in her class was a seventeen-year-old youth from Massachusetts with a decidedly Yankee accent named William Edward Burghardt Du Bois—known as "Willie." Du Bois, who was at Fisk to prepare for Harvard, entered Fisk already a sophomore and was suddenly running the paper and the student government. He had only one academic rival, the daughter of Fisk's white German teacher. Du Bois, the star student-athlete of Great Barrington High School, had been one of three blacks in his high school—the others were his cousins. Of African, French Huguenot, and Dutch ancestry, they were all descendants of the colonial "Black Burghardts," who had lived free in the Berkshires for generations. An admirer of beautiful Lena Calhoun, Du Bois wrote of her in retrospect:

> Never before had I seen young men so self-assured and who gave them-selves such airs and colored men at that; and above all for the first time I saw beautiful girls . . . Of one of these girls I have often said, no human being could possibly have been as beautiful as she seemed to my young eyes in that far-off September night of 1885. She was the great-aunt of Lena Horne and fair as Lena Horne is, Lena Calhoun was far more beautiful.

Du Bois did not learn about being black until he attended Fisk. And he was happy that he went to the school before he went to Harvard:

Had I gone from Great Barrington High School directly to Harvard, I would have sought companionship with my white fellows and been disappointed and embittered by a discovery of social limitations to which I had not been used.

At age eighteen, Du Bois began teaching summer school, leaving Nashville for the Tennessee countryside—where, living and teaching in log cabins built before the Civil War, he learned about slavery after the fact:

No one but a Negro going into the South without previous experience of color caste can have any conception of its barbarism . . . Murder, killing and maiming Negroes, raping Negro women—in the 80's and in the southern South, this was not even news; it got no publicity; it caused no arrests; and punishment for such transgression was so unusual that the fact was telegraphed North.

The process of "learning" to be black was a kind of rite of passage for certain black men—usually middle-class Northerners. In the process of learning, Du Bois found hope instead of futility. At Fisk he discovered a "civilization in potentiality," into which he leaped with enthusiasm. "A new loyalty and allegiance replaced my Americanism," wrote the Massachusetts Yankee: "henceforward I was a Negro."

After college, it was time for Katie Webb and the Calhoun girls to marry. Katie was actually the first. She found a hero—a romantically handsome fellow with ambition. In October 1885 Katie married Antoine Graves, of Rome, Georgia, who graduated from Atlanta University two years after Cora. In June 1883, twenty-one-year-old Antoine was appointed principal pro tem of the Gate City Colored

Public School (also known as the Houston Street School), and he was reelected as principal by the Atlanta Board of Education for the school years 1884–1885 and 1885–1886. He was the second principal of the school. In 1886 the body of Jefferson Davis passed through Atlanta on the way to reburial in Richmond, and the white citizens planned a celebration. All schoolchildren, teachers, and principals were ordered to march in the parade. Antoine Graves told his teachers and students that he did not believe they should honor a man who fought to keep them in slavery; therefore he would not march—but the teachers and students were free to do as they wanted. He was fired. After job-hunting as far afield as Texas and California, he eventually returned to Atlanta and opened a real estate business, which he would operate for fifty-five years. He was the first black broker in Atlanta and would handle some of the largest transactions in the city: selling the governor's mansion to the state, and appraising and selling land to and for the city. During the late 1880s and early 1900s, he was active in the Republican Party South, now virtually an all-black party. He was also a past grandmaster of the Odd Fellows Lodge, an organization established after the Civil War to aid former slaves in adapting to a new way of life. Katie and Antoine had four children, all born in Atlanta: Nellie, July 1886; Antoine Jr., called "Judge," June 1888; Catherine, April 1890; and Marie Antoinette, March 1892.

On March 12, 1886, the pleasant world of Moses Calhoun fell apart on the front page of the *Atlanta Constitution*. The white population may have read the article with amusement:

An Irate Mother

She Gives a Young Darky a Good Thrashing

Ras Badger, the son of the colored dentist, makes slanderous remarks about Cora Calhoun, the daughter of Mose Calhoun—the mother gives Badger a thrashing.

The upper crust of the colored society is now enjoying a smothered
sensation in which the Badgers and the Calhouns are the star characters.
Cowhides and injured characters are the features of the sensation . . .

The article went on to describe Moses and Dr. Badger, the dentist, as
two of the most prominent Negroes in Atlanta—both being "sober"
and "industrious," with "considerable property" and "the confidence
of a long list of white friends." Both were described as having families
and as occupying the "highest social position in colored society." It
seemed, however, that Dr. Badger's son, Ras, had been overheard making "unkind and slanderous remarks" about Cora Calhoun, whom the
paper described as "quite pretty and a decided belle with her race."
The paper does not reveal the content of the slander, but Atlanta
Calhoun, Cora's mother, took it seriously enough to confront young
Badger, who strongly denied having made any remarks about Cora.
When he refused Atlanta's demand that he put a denial in the papers,
the *Constitution* reported that "the mother knocked him down and
gave him a good genteel thrashing." She then purchased "an old-time
cowhide which she says she will use upon Badger the first time she
meets him." The affair was hushed up immediately after it happened,
the paper said, "but leaked out yesterday and is now the talk of the
town among the colored people." Moses is singled out in the story as
having "amassed enough money to make him the wealthiest colored
man in Atlanta," with "a handsome home on Wheat Street." Like his
wife, the paper said, Moses Calhoun "is devoted to his children and
out of what he makes sets aside a liberal amount for their wardrobes
and education."

Records are scarce, but it appears that sometime shortly after this
article appeared Moses Calhoun suddenly sold his businesses and moved
his family lock, stock, and barrel to Birmingham, where, once again,
he opened a restaurant-catering establishment. Why did he move to

Birmingham? It seems he was so humiliated that he felt he literally could no longer show his face in Atlanta. Dignity and pride were huge elements of his personality. In any case, the dream was shattered just when Moses could actually hold it in his hand. He moved to Birmingham for two reasons: it was in another state, and it was a city without a past. He was starting over where no one knew his name. No sleepy Old South town, Birmingham was born in the 1870s from rich iron and coal works, and borne on the backs of black convict labor slaves who were bought and sold to work in the mines, living in unspeakable horror and filth, beaten four or five times a day, and often working naked on very little of what passed for food. "Convicts," by the way, were usually convicted of "crimes" like vagrancy and were sold by sheriffs to work off the bonds they were forever unable to post for their bail. Convict labor was the post-slavery way for individuals as well as communities to make revenue from free human labor.

How did the Calhoun family feel about being "the talk of the town"? Cora and Lena were doubtless mortified, Atlanta was chagrined, and Moses was both furious and afraid. What was he without his good name? He was a laughingstock and felt utterly humiliated. I think Moses had what is called a narcissistic mortification—a death of the ego. He could not hold his head up in Atlanta. How interesting that he would seek to re-create himself in Birmingham, a new city that had no identity beyond its mineral resources. And no one in Birmingham appeared to have read the Atlanta papers.

Moses found the prosperous center of Negro Birmingham and opened a grocery-catering service. This was very lucky since his two daughters would marry, one a year after the other. Cora was first. This item appeared on October 29, 1887, in the *Cleveland Gazette*:

An invitation to attend the marriage of Miss Cora C. Calhoun, of Birmingham, Ala., and Edwin F. Horn, editor of the Chattanooga, Tenn., *Justice*, and formerly a resident of Indianapolis, Ind., and Chicago, Ill., has been received. The wedding occurred the 26th at the residence of the bride's parents, in Birmingham, Ala. That theirs may be a long and pleasant marriage life is the earnest desire of the *Gazette*.

In 1887 Edwin might have still been optimistic about the black future in the South—Chattanooga, like Birmingham, was still a Republican town. Edwin had been successful in Chattanooga, publishing the paper and teaching. The *Chattanooga Justice*, the paper Edwin started, became the leading colored paper in the state. He was also a budding capitalist— perhaps inspired by his new father-in-law—as part owner of a "modern" drugstore, the People's Drug Store, where "electric cars pass the door."

After the death of his second wife, Edwin had moved to Chattanooga, which was one of the rare Republican-dominated Southern cities. It was known to be a place where blacks could get ahead. But Cora and Edwin probably met in 1886, when he was briefly coeditor of the weekly *Atlanta Defiance*, and still visibly grieving after the deaths of two wives. They were both in a state of upheaval. Cora, with her sister and parents, was about to start life over in Birmingham. Not only was Edwin a new face, but he was the handsomest man she had ever seen. That could be worrisome. But he seemed so melancholy. At some point she learned the story of his two tragically brief marriages. What woman could resist? In 1887, twenty-two-year-old Cora was slender and petite, with large nearsighted hazel eyes, a generous mouth, curly brown hair, and a tiny waist. The colored press delighted in the marriage of one of its own to a belle of Atlanta and Birmingham:

> The marriage of Mr. E. F. Horn of this city [Chattanooga] and Miss Cora Calhoun of Birmingham, Ala. was a brilliant event in the history of the magic city . . . The groom came to this city about one year ago, since then he has made a great success in editing and publishing a weekly paper called JUSTICE . . . Mr. Horn is also a teacher in the Gilmer Street school . . .

Everyone agreed that while Cora was a pretty little thing, dark-eyed Lena—at sixteen already tall, majestically poised, and gravely smoldering—was a beauty. Lena broke Willie Du Bois' heart when she married an "older man," as Du Bois described Frank Gatewood Smith, Lena's husband, who had been a senior during her and Du Bois' first year at Fisk:

> Frank Smith of the class ahead of me was a yellow dandy, faultlessly dressed and a squire of dames. He later married Lena Calhoun with whom I was hopelessly in love; but Smith was over 25 years of age and ready for a wife.

Lena married Frank on Christmas Day 1888 in her father's Birmingham house. They followed Cora and Edwin to Chattanooga, but later returned to Nashville, where they had both gone to college. At some point before they married, Frank had passed as "Cuban" to attend an Illinois ophthalmology school. So he was Dr. Frank G. Smith, optometrist—but he was also, in typical black middle-class fashion, the first principal of Pearl High School, attached to Fisk, the only black high school in Nashville. Frank and Lena had two children, both born in Nashville: Edwina, 1891; and Frank Jr., 1893.

Moses was known to have owned a grocery store in Birmingham in 1887. And he was listed in the Birmingham directory for 1890. The house address given is the same as the one on Cora Calhoun's wedding invitation. First Congregational Church records list Moses and Atlanta Calhoun as having left the church by death in 1890. More likely, they both died between 1888 and 1890.

After Cora and Edwin Horn married, they followed the dying Republican Party across the South—from Atlanta to Birmingham to Chattanooga. Edwin finally met his idol, Frederick Douglass, in Washington in 1888, at the National Negro Editorial Association convention. Douglass had returned to Washington to work for the

Republican Party in the 1888 election. The new president, Benjamin Harrison, made Douglass minister and consul general to the Republic of Haiti and chargé d'affaires for the Dominican Republic. There was even a small flurry that year for Indiana native Edwin Horn to be recorder of deeds when Harrison, a friendly acquaintance of Edwin's from Indiana, became president. This was great excitement for Edwin, but in the end the job went to veteran former senator B. K. Bruce. The Republicans had two important black tokens in Douglass and Bruce, who interchanged a round of jobs. Edwin and Cora had their first son, Errol, in 1889, in Chattanooga.

Poor health and arguments over the U.S. occupation of Haiti caused Frederick Douglass to resign his consular posts. Douglass died on February 20, 1895, after speaking to a meeting of the National Council of Women. Douglass' controversial second marriage to his white secretary in 1884 seemed to have no effect on his party standing. In theory, he spoke *for* and *to* the black people of America. And he was, after all, the most recognized and important *token* of all.

On the other hand, Booker T. Washington would soon become far and away the most important black man in America—so important that he stood alone between all that money from Carnegie and Frick and the entirety of Southern black education. In modern terms as well as in the context of their own times, Washington was pretty far right and Du Bois was pretty far left. Douglass was the most centrist. Washington basically distrusted middle-class blacks, especially the NAACP. He did not believe that voting rights or civil rights were essential to black success. As far as whites were concerned, Washington believed in strict accommodation—and educating the "hand" instead of the "head." Washington never shared his good fortune, which he reaped because he mostly said only what whites wanted to hear—as in his famous "Atlanta Compromise" speech of 1895: "in all things that are purely social we can be as separate as the fingers, yet one as the hand in all things essential to mutual progress."

There were few friends of the Negro in the years between 1890 and 1900, when the Supreme Court entrenched segregation and disenfranchisement. The final assault on blacks came thirteen years after the Supreme Court declared Charles Sumner's Civil Rights Act to be unconstitutional. In 1896 *Plessy v. Ferguson* upheld both Jim Crow and white supremacy, ruling that it was "powerless to eradicate racial instincts or to abolish distinctions based on physical differences." Against this blatant support for white supremacy, the great Justice John Marshall Harlan's lone dissent was a powerful rebuke to the racist court: "Our Constitution is color-blind, and neither knows nor tolerates classes among citizens." Although some Northern states enacted state civil rights acts, *Plessy v. Ferguson* remained the national law of the land for more than fifty years. White supremacy was the American way of life.

It would be a very long and dark night for black Americans in the South. Between January 1896 and December 1897, two hundred Negroes were lynched. In Atlanta the black Calhouns survived by creating their own insular world, by staying out of controversial politics, and by always supporting the church, the community, education at all levels, and, most important, the concept of family life. They loved Atlanta. There were rednecks everywhere, and race riots were not unknown, but there were no night riders in the streets of Atlanta. Atlanta was the *New South* ideal.

Reconstruction became part of Southern folklore: *once upon a time, a decade or so after the Civil War, there were laws in the South by which Negroes were not reduced to third-class citizenship and were permitted to vote freely, and state universities, supported by black taxes, were open to black students.* This was the Reconstruction message to blacks: You are free American citizens, equal under the law with every other free American citizen. You have the duty as well as the right to vote—your life may depend on it. Reconstruction died because the white South did not want the ex-slave to be either a citizen or a voter or even, necessarily, an American. The white

South wanted blacks to be returned to some form of slavery. And the form of slavery that the mass of ex-slaves and their descendants had returned to by the end of the nineteenth century was in many ways far worse and far more terror-filled than the antebellum variety. But the spirit of Reconstruction went north, where it found a home in Harlem and created the Harlem Renaissance, whose talent pool came from Missionary colleges. It would also find a home in Washington, D.C., at Howard University Law School, a perfect place to plot the legal downfall of Jim Crow.

Reconstruction produced an entirely different sort of black leadership. Instead of revolutionaries, or token "great men," by the late 1880s there would be a growing army of highly educated young Negro men and women, dedicated to teaching and uplifting the race—and also to *standing up* for the race. They had been educated for leadership by their Missionary teachers; and their duty, in turn, was to educate future leaders. This was leadership en masse. The message of a Missionary education was clarity of purpose, strength of dedication, and a crucial sense of amour propre: "If you know who you are, and what you are doing, then nothing and no one can put you down." These new educator-ambassadors, or envoys between the races and generations, had all come of age during Reconstruction. They all grew up with white teachers. They would always strive for respect and friendship between the races because they knew it was possible. They were building the bridge to real freedom.

Reconstruction taught blacks that they had human and civil rights, and if they had little else, they had a friend in the Constitution. The new century began with everything won by blacks in the Civil War and Reconstruction lost. Freedom, equality under the law, citizenship, and constitutional protection no longer existed. For more or less the next hundred years, Negroes in the South were reduced to de facto slavery, and Negroes in the North to second-class citizenship. The North won the Civil War—but as far as blacks were concerned the South won the peace. A 1912 editorial in the *Raleigh News and Observer* described the true meaning of Jim Crow and the Southern mind-set: "The subjection of the negro politically, and the separation of the negro socially, are paramount to all other considerations in the South short of the preservation of the Republic itself."

CHAPTER FOUR
North/1900–1919
THE NEW NEGRO

T HE NORTHERN migration of the Talented Tenth, Du Bois' name for the 10 percent of highly educated American blacks, began about fifteen years before the Great Migration of World War I. The Great Migration was about jobs— about leaving the South to find work. The Talented Tenth migration was about personal fulfillment— leaving the South to *do* work. Members of the Talented Tenth were also known as "New Negroes." There was a common denominator between those who left the South and those who remained. The daughters of Moses could afford to leave—just as the daughter of Siny could afford to stay. Negroes with money had some choices.

Plessy v. Ferguson, which made white supremacy the law of the land, gave Cora and her Republican activist husband, now known as the "Adonis of the Negro Press," the impetus to leave the South. And Moses Calhoun's death gave them the wherewithal. Pregnant with her third son, and wearing the heavy black-veiled mourning clothes of the period, Cora set out for New York City with her handsome editor husband. Facing an ever more powerless Republican Party, Edwin and Cora decided that they did not want their two sons, Errol and Teddy, to grow up as prisoners of their race. The North might not be free of racism, but at least the boys (whose two younger brothers would be born in New York) could go to public schools, museums, libraries, theaters, parks, and zoos without facing "whites only" signs.

Cora and Edwin were *successful* Northerners because they were *meant* to be Northerners. It was not about money. It was about a certain kind of self-fulfillment for each that would not have been possible had they remained in the South. The self-fulfillment involved a change of political party for him—and a slight change in name. He added an "e" to the end of Horn—possibly because he had formerly been well known as a black Republican and hoped to forestall confusion. The Northern move also meant a change in lifestyle for her. Cora and Edwin arrived in Manhattan's West Fifties sometime in 1896, just at the birth of a new center of black life, which had moved uptown from Greenwich Village. Known as "Black Bohemia," the West Fifties were the best section of black New York. Cora and Edwin's new neighborhood (around what is now Columbus Circle) would soon be known as San Juan Hill, for the turning point in the 1898 Spanish-American War in Cuba, where black U.S. cavalry troops fought side by side with Teddy Roosevelt's Rough Riders in the first (and last until Vietnam) integrated U.S. fighting force since the War of 1812. There were two black-owned hotels on West Fifty-Third Street: the Maceo, which was very sedate; and the Marshall, which was glamorous and fun and had the best jazz orchestra in New York. San Juan Hill became the center of black culture and nightlife. The West Fifties were a precursor of Harlem—vibrant, creative, musical, and home to black New York's most talented citizens: Charles Chesnutt, Paul Laurence Dunbar, James Weldon Johnson, and Edwin's new theatrical friend, Bert Williams of the *Ziegfeld Follies*.

Cora and Edwin fled the South in 1896; four years later they received a belated New York greeting in the form of a race riot that could easily have come from Dixie. The riot occurred in the neighborhood known as the "Tenderloin"—home to Manhattan's poorest blacks, living almost cheek to jowl with some of its poorest whites, the Irish of Hell's Kitchen. From the *New York Times*, August 16, 1900:

RACE RIOT . . . SET UPON AND BEAT NEGROES . . . For four hours last night Eighth Avenue, from Thirtieth to Forty-second Street, was a scene of the wildest disorder that this city has witnessed in years. The hard feelings between the white people and the Negroes in that district, which had been smoldering for many years . . . burst forth last night into a race riot . . .

The black-Irish issue was discussed in *Harper's Weekly* of December 22, 1900:

In 1890 the city's population was 1,515,301 and that of the negroes 25,674 . . . It will be seen from the figures given above that the negroes in New York do not constitute a very considerable proportion of the population . . . Why there should be any race feeling against such an insignificant element of the population seems superficially strange. It is quite true that the Irish seem to have a natural antipathy to the negroes . . .

"Natural antipathy" is putting it mildly. The Irish *hated* American Negroes. The New York City Draft Riots—when in 1863, Irish mobs lynched blacks from lampposts and set fire to the Colored Orphan Asylum with the orphans still in it—seemed like yesterday. George Templeton Strong, the patrician Republican diarist, called blacks "the most peaceable, sober and inoffensive of our poor." He was sorry to say that "England is right about the lower class of Irish. They are brutal, base, cruel, cowards, and as insolent as base." Irish-black hatred was based on the deep psychology that in America, the Irish were thrilled to finally find people who were lower on the social scale than themselves. They bitterly resented the fact that in some American locations—Boston, for example—the Irish were treated worse than Negroes. But in New York, the Irish ruled absolutely—not in the corridors of real money and power, but in Little Old New York, which was all that mattered.

The *Harper's* article stated that black employment had been much higher earlier in the century. It mentioned all the "good" waiter, bootblack, and barbering jobs that first belonged to Negroes, and then to the Irish, but were now taken over by newer immigrants like Greeks and Italians. Tammany captured immigrants as soon as they stepped off the boat. Negroes, Republican for so long, were the newest "immigrants" to be ensnared by promises, some of which were actually kept. Tammany was extremely eager to capture the black vote—which is why Edwin Horne (now with an "e") spent his days surrounded by Irishmen. And it is probably why Cora became a Roman Catholic.

Edwin began his New York life in 1896 as a teacher, but after unsuccessfully suing the city for promoting a white teacher with less seniority over him, in 1898 he gave up teaching and became secretary of the newly organized United Colored Democracy, a.k.a. the Afro-American Tammany Hall Organization, otherwise known as "Black Tammany," a lobbying group that sought to lure black voters away from the Republicans. The United Colored Democracy was the brainchild of T. (Timothy) Thomas Fortune, publisher in 1896 of the *New York Age*, a hugely successful black newspaper. Three years older than Edwin, and born a slave in Jackson County, Florida, Fortune learned the printer's trade in Jacksonville. After attending Howard University, he moved to New York and began his newspaper career in 1881 with two papers, the *New York Globe* and the *New York Freeman*—both of which soon failed because of Fortune's radicalism. Because Negro papers were barred from membership in the Associated Press, Fortune was among the group that founded the Colored Press Association. Fortune attacked the Republican Party and urged blacks to resort to self-defense if the government refused to help them. His disgust with the Republicans extended to encouraging blacks to support Democratic hopeful Grover Cleveland. By 1889 he was disgusted with the Democrats, too, and called for a National Afro-American League, but it failed for lack of political and financial support.

He advocated using the term "Afro-American" instead of the Spanish word *Negro*, because blacks were "African in origin and American in birth."

Meanwhile, Fortune encouraged Edwin's political switch. Nothing if not ambitious, Edwin saw which way the political wind was blowing. Influenced by his mentor, Edwin changed his party affiliation and the spelling of his name. Edwin Horne was definitely a new man, a *political* New Negro—a *Democrat*. Enlisting in the Democratic Party was a revolutionary concept for black Americans. Edwin did so well for Black Tammany that in 1899 he was given the patronage job of assistant inspector in the combustible division (bomb squad) of the New York fire department in Brooklyn. It was an extraordinary job for a black man (indeed for anyone who was not Irish), so he may have passed for white—not with Tammany, but with the fire department. In 1898 New York City consolidated all five boroughs, joining Brooklyn, Queens, and Staten Island with Manhattan and the Bronx. Cora and Edwin now decided to leave the West Fifties and move to tranquil, bucolic Brooklyn, buying a new brownstone row house at 189 Chauncey Street, an integrated street around the corner from Bushwick Avenue in a section of Brooklyn then called Stuyvesant Heights. While mostly white, it was also known as a black middle-class enclave. The four new brownstones on Chauncey Street clearly represented gentrification or urbanization or both. The new row houses symbolized bustling modern Brooklyn, part of a great city, but they were bordered on one side by a Swedish livery stable and on the other by an Irish farmhouse. Across the street were wooden tenements inhabited almost entirely by Irish families. The new Horne home was a microcosm of New York's history and of its ethnic mosaic. Anyway, it was a better place to raise sons than West Fifty-Third Street. There was no nightlife.

Black Tammany, meanwhile, was thriving. From the *New York Times*, January 16, 1904:

The United Colored Democracy of Greater New York, which is better known as the Afro-American Tammany Hall Organization, had
a ball last night at Tammany Hall, and every colored Democrat of
prominence in the city attended the affair. Not only were the colored
Democratic leaders at the ball, but also many leaders in Afro-American
social circles. The costumes of the women folks were not only beautiful
but expensive . . .

The reporter noted that "half a dozen women who are well-known
in colored social circles in Brooklyn" were seated in "one of the hand-
somely decorated boxes."

T. Thomas Fortune was also a feminist, speaking of the "New Afro-
American Woman" and supporting the new organization to which Cora
belonged, the National Association of Colored Women, organized in
1896 by firebrand Brooklyn suffragist Victoria Matthews, who assured
black men that women wanted the vote only so they could elect more
black men. Cora considered herself a feminist and a suffragist. She was
also a New Afro-American Woman with three small sons and spiritual
and political yearnings.

On May 1, 1904, Cora, ever a religious seeker, was confirmed as a
Roman Catholic and took the name "Elizabeth," for the mother of
John the Baptist, who was miraculously pregnant in old age. She received
the sacrament of confirmation from Archbishop John Murphy Farley,
but the priest who instructed her was the charismatic Monsignor John
Burke, the white pastor of St. Benedict the Moor, New York's first
black Catholic church. Named in honor of a sixteenth-century black
Sicilian saint, the Church of St. Benedict the Moor moved up from
Bleecker and Downing streets in Greenwich Village to the Tenderloin
in 1898, soon after Cora and Edwin arrived in New York. Cora was
surely influenced by Tammany when she gave up Congregationalism to
become a Roman Catholic, but she remained a Republican without a
vote. Privately, she scorned Black Tammany. Why would she leave the

party of Lincoln for the party of the Draft Riots? In 1905 Cora, age forty, had her fourth son and named him John Burke Horne for the priest who instructed her in her new faith, but called him "Burke." Cora and Edwin's three older boys—Errol (b. 1889); Edwin Jr., called "Teddy" (b. 1893); and Frank, named for Aunt Lena's husband (b. 1899)—all left Public School 54 and entered St. Vincent Ferrer School. It was about this time that Teddy Horne got an after-school job as a page boy at the old Plaza hotel and, unbeknownst to his parents, having learned to gamble, vowed to spend the rest of his life in very bad company. He would be rescued, briefly, by sports.

In 1904 the Brooklyn bourgeoisie was caught up in the St. Louis Olympics because George C. Poage of Milwaukee, the first American Negro to enter the games, won two bronze medals in track and field. With the Olympic ideal in mind, in 1905 several families, including the Hornes, founded the Smart Set Athletic Club of Brooklyn, a middle-class family organization that stressed sports. It was ideal for the Horne boys. Teddy Horne had a growth spurt and outgrew his hotel job. His morals were probably already beyond repair, but he became a member of America's first independent, all-black basketball team. The Black Fives Organization, which researches and preserves the history of pioneering all-black basketball teams from 1904 to 1950, described the Smart Set:

> The Smart Set Athletic Club of Brooklyn was founded in 1904 and is created with assembling the first formally organized fully independent African American basketball team, which debuted in 1907 . . . [Its] members came from a tight knit clique of well-educated, affluent "old money" African Americans who resided in what was then predominantly white Stuyvesant Heights of Brooklyn . . . [T]heir complete dominance of other black basketball teams earned them the nickname the "Grave Diggers." [The team] won the first two Colored Basketball World Championships, for 1907–08 and 1908–09.

In 1908 the "Grave Diggers" defeated the Washington, D.C., Crescent Athletic Club at home and away. Both Teddy Horne and Charlie Scottron, cousin of Teddy's future wife, Edna Scottron, were on the team. (The "Grave Diggers," including Teddy and Charlie, would be prominently featured in publicity surrounding the opening of the new Barclays Center sports complex in Brooklyn in 2012.)

The Smart Set and George Poage were one side of the 1910 black sporting picture—the other side was Jack Johnson, the heavyweight champion so hated by white America that the mere mention of his name could start a race riot. In 1908 Johnson knocked out Tommy Burns to become the first black heavyweight champion, and millions of young black boys thought about boxing gloves. Johnson, with *two* white wives, charged the racial climate simply by existing. Riots at screenings of the film of the Jack Johnson–Jim Jeffries heavyweight bout caused an interstate edict against fight films and may have helped convince producers to keep blacks out of movies. Jack Johnson, heavyweight champion of the world and racial provocateur, defeated Jim Jeffries, known as the "Great White Hope," in Reno, Nevada, on July 4, 1910.

Despite factional disputes, no money to speak of, and Booker T. Washington's refusal to support it, the formal organization of the NAACP had been completed in May 1910. The officers of the organization, at 20 Vesey Street in downtown New York, included Oswald Garrison Villard (a descendant of William Lloyd Garrison) and W. E. B. Du Bois; Moorfield Storey of Boston served as the first president. The only "colored" officer, Du Bois was the director of research and publicity and editor of *The Crisis.* A very professional, sophisticated, and intelligent magazine, *Crisis* did not talk down to its readers—nor pander to them. There was literature, art, criticism, human interest, and, certainly, politics. In November 1910 *Crisis* sold one thousand copies; by 1918 circulation would be one hundred thousand. In some people's minds, the presence of Du Bois on the staff branded the organization as radical from the beginning. Many feared it would fall apart, like his Niagara Movement. Instead it grew. The New York branch of the NAACP was organized in January 1911. Cora and Edwin Horne were early members. There would be nine branches by 1912. That number would double between 1913 and 1914. Meanwhile, starting in 1910, the NAACP publicized lynching stories—sixty-seven blacks were known to have been lynched that year. In 1911 a story about a Negro being lynched appeared in the papers on an average of every six days. That year, in another political move sure to confound his rival Booker T. Washington, Du Bois left both the Republicans and the Democrats to join the Socialist Party.

Black Tammany had actually been doing well since 1906 and the Brownsville, Texas, riot, where white townspeople attacked black soldiers, and President Theodore Roosevelt indicted the soldiers. Blacks took this as an unforgivable betrayal on the part of a man who in 1898 said he owed his life, and the lives of his Rough Riders, to the black Ninth and Tenth cavalries. It was becoming less difficult to convince Negroes, if not to support Democrats, at least to reject Republicans.

Edwin Horne also took a big political step in 1910, running for city council on the Tammany ticket. His nickname back in Indiana was "Windy," which might be the reason for his loss. Edwin lost his run for city council, but won the thanks of Tammany for the gift of the black vote. Thanks to Edwin's attacks on Theodore Roosevelt in his *What Do We Want?* pamphlets, sponsored by the United Colored Democracy, nearly fifty thousand black men voted Democratic for the first time in New York history and a Democrat, John A. Dix, was elected governor of New York. "Some Negros would vote for the Republican party even if the party put them back in slavery," Edwin's pamphlet asserted. Tammany had a nice way of thanking new voters. Nearly everything Edwin asked for in *What Do We Want?* was given to the Harlem community by Tammany:

> [We want] colored policemen, colored firemen, garbage removed from our streets before noon, crooks driven out of the tenements, work for

our boys, protection for our girls . . . civil rights as citizens in theatres and restaurants . . . a colored regiment in the National Guard.

Edwin's pride and joy, the new Fifteenth New York National Guard Regiment, organized in 1912, the first black National Guard unit in the state, was known as "Harlem's Own." In war, the Fifteenth New York became the 369th Regiment, the "Harlem Hellfighters," one of the most storied military units of World War I. Thanks to broken Republican promises, Roosevelt's blunder at Brownsville, and the new Republican policy of dismissing black officeholders, the congressional election of 1910 had seen a revolutionary shift in black voting away from the Republican Party. New York Negroes, thanks to Edwin, became permanent Democrats—but even Tammany could not save New York Negroes from the "Black Peril" hysteria.

The year 1910 saw the so-called Black Peril edict against blacks in Manhattan—as if less than 2 percent of the population could actually invade and overwhelm the city. The Black Peril hysteria kept black talent out of the theater and black audiences out of the theater district. Blacks could perform only in Harlem—and black theatergoers could not attend Broadway houses. The Lafayette, at 132nd Street and Seventh Avenue, was the leading Harlem theater, producing all-black musicals, Broadway hits, and classic European theater. But the Black Peril was actually something of a "green" invention. In 1903 the black musical comedy team of Walker and Williams (the great Bert Williams) had a smash hit Broadway show called *In Dahomey*. It was the same year that George M. Cohan, the king of Broadway, put forth a so-so effort called *Running for Office*. Cohan, a well-known racist and union-buster who refused to join Actors' Equity, did not want any black competition. From Cohan to Eddie Foy to Chauncey Olcott, the Irish owned Broadway for at least the first quarter of the new century. They not only wanted no black performers; they wanted to prevent perfectly respectable Negroes from going to the theater or dining in the theater district. But Edwin's friend, the great black *Ziegfeld Follies* star Bert Williams, was immune. In 1910 Williams was listed above the title, along with Fanny Brice, Eddie Foy, and Lillian Lorraine. He was such an enormous star, and his blackness was so extremely comic, that he was forgiven. No one who saw Williams' pantomime poker game ever forgot it. Onstage, Williams was a black caricature. Offstage, he was a tall, light-skinned Negro from the Danish West Indies who "blacked up" to become an audience favorite. His *Follies* act, as a Pullman porter dealing with small, inebriated white passenger Leon Errol, was so hilarious that diehard fans came two or three times a week just to see what Williams and Errol were up to in the ad-libbed act. (Errol's solo drunken act later became a staple of early movies.) Meanwhile, Edwin constantly listened to Williams' deep, lugubrious voice singing "Ace in the Hole" and "I Ain't Got Nobody" on his big wind-up Victrola.

Blacks may have been barred from Broadway, but they still had the Marshall Hotel. On any Sunday night, circa 1910, great black talent met white talent as stars from Broadway came up to the Marshall to dance to Jim Europe's Clef Club Orchestra—booking a table in advance was recommended.

James Weldon Johnson wrote in *Black Manhattan*:

In the brightest days of the Marshall the temporary blight had not yet fallen on the Negro in the theatre. Williams and Walker and Cole and Johnson were at their height; there were several good Negro road companies touring the country, and a considerable number of colored performers were on the big time in vaudeville . . . the first modern jazz band ever heard on a New York stage . . . It was a playing-singing-dancing orchestra, making dominant use of banjos, mandolins, guitars, saxophones, and drums in combination, and was called the Memphis Students—a very good name, overlooking the fact that the performers were not students and were not from Memphis.

The Memphis Students were such a hit that they played in Paris, London, and Berlin later that year and stayed abroad a further year. The Marshall, which advertised in the first issue of *The Crisis*, was apparently under secret police surveillance because of "race mixing." It was *the* meeting place of black and white celebrities and politicians. James Reese Europe, a.k.a. Jim Europe, was a "Memphis Student." Born in Mobile, Alabama, in 1881, he grew up in Washington, D.C., where he studied violin with the assistant director of the U.S. Marine Corps Band. He came to New York in 1904 and became a musical director for the team of Bob Cole and Billy Johnson and for Bert Williams. In 1910 Jim Europe organized the Clef Club. James Weldon Johnson describes it:

> He gathered all the colored professional instrumental musicians into a chartered organization and systematized the whole business of "entertaining." The organization purchased a house in West Fifty-third Street and fitted it up as a club, and also as booking-offices. Bands of from three to thirty men could be furnished at any time, day or night. The Clef Club for quite a while held a monopoly of the business of "entertaining" private parties and furnishing music for the dance craze, which was then beginning to sweep the country. One year the amount of business done amounted to $120,000.

The crowning artistic achievement of Jim Europe and the Clef Club was the famous Carnegie Hall concert in May 1912. It was the first jazz concert ever in Carnegie Hall—with a 125-member orchestra and ten upright pianos. James Weldon Johnson described the audience reaction:

> New York had not yet become accustomed to jazz; so when the Clef Club opened its concert with a syncopated march, playing it with a biting attack and an infectious rhythm, and on the finale bursting into singing, the effect can be imagined. The applause became a tumult.

In 1913 Europe and his Society Orchestra, including young violinist-vocalist Noble Sissle, played at Delmonico's and the Hotel Astor—proof positive that the Black Peril had been successfully put to rest by an NAACP suit the year before. Europe was approached by white dancing stars Mr. and Mrs. Vernon Castle (as they were billed, lest anyone think they were brother and sister) to become their musical director. Irene and Vernon Castle were America's greatest dancing stars, and rich tourists flocked to the Marshall to fox-trot and turkey-trot to the Castles' favorite orchestra. Besides composing, arranging, conducting, and recording Castle dance steps, in 1913 Europe made the first jazz recordings by a black band for the Victor Talking Machine Company. Some modern critics say that the Clef Club orchestra did not really play "jazz." What it played was "pre-jazz hot ragtime"—a popular style in the Northeast in the 1910s. "Hot ragtime" is perfect. The band was hard-edged, driving, and red-hot, like Bessie Smith singing "Alexander's Ragtime Band."

While the racial atmosphere for black musicians was good, it was very bad for black politicians. In 1912 a surprising number of Negroes voted for Democrat Woodrow Wilson, who actually appeared to be leading a campaign against black Americans. Blacks could only blame themselves when the first Southern Democrat elected president since the Civil War resegregated every aspect of federal Washington, including the lunchrooms and cafeterias—all desegregated since the Civil War. They could have chosen the flawed but bighearted Teddy Roosevelt; even better, Eugene Debs. But Wilson was a racist who told Thomas Dixon, author of *The Clansman*, that as president he would put blacks back "in their place." Practicing what historian James Chace called "draconian segregation," Wilson made the District of Columbia as racist as Dixie. He dismissed black diplomatic appointees to traditionally "black" countries like Haiti and the Dominican Republic and replaced them with white men. Even his famous aide, "Colonel" Edward House, wrote in his diary that Wilson's "prejudices are many and often unjust." How could blacks vote for Wilson? Edwin may well have voted for Wilson since he could not vote for Roosevelt. Poor Roosevelt. His instincts on race were those of a decent man—but every time he said a kind word to a Negro, the South went berserk. Teddy Roosevelt's last public speech, which he was invited to give by Du Bois, would be in November 1918 at Carnegie Hall for the Circle for Negro War Relief. It is possible, of course, that Edwin voted neither Democratic nor Republican, but for the Socialist Debs.

Eugene Debs, of course, was some sort of saint. "What is socialism?" he was asked. Debs replied, "Merely Christianity in action. It recognizes the equality in men." He was more of a charismatic preacher than a politician, attracting large crowds but not so many votes. In William Howard Taft's hometown, both had speeches the same night. According to James Chace, Taft spoke free and Debs charged 10 cents for admission, but Taft's meeting hall was barely filled, and Debs' audience was overflowing, with people turned away. Debs actually did better than expected in 1912, winning the largest share of the popular vote ever won by a Socialist candidate (6 percent). A man remarked to Debs that the audiences all seemed to love him. "They love me because they know I love them," he said. In September 1918 Debs was sentenced to ten years in prison for violating the Espionage and Sedition Acts by making speeches against the war. After attesting to his "kinship with all living beings," Debs uttered his famous credo: "While there is a lower class, I am in it; while there is a criminal element, I am of it; and while there is a soul in prison, I am not free."

World figures appealed for clemency for Debs, who was sixty-two years old and in very poor health—but Woodrow Wilson refused. In 1921 President Warren Harding, a Republican, pardoned Debs and he was released from prison. James Chace described the scene:

> When Debs was released from prison, the warden suspended all rules so that 2,300 convicts could crowd along the front wall of the prison to shout their farewells. Debs turned to them, with tears streaming down

his face, and held his hat in tribute to them high above his head. Finally, a drawn and terribly thin Debs offered a last good-bye and drove away.

A photo of Cora and Edwin, taken in 1912, shows Cora looking lovely in an age-appropriate black evening dress and Edwin, as usual, looking impossibly handsome and melancholy. Despite four sons, and good looks, Cora and Edwin's marriage was not happy. By 1913 they were leading separate lives under the same roof. There were New Women as well as New Negroes—and Cora had become a New Woman. The mother of four was a teacher, social worker, do-gooder, "uplifter," and suffragist. After twenty-six years of "the business of raising a family," as she would say in a 1920s newspaper interview, she came into her own in 1913 by becoming active in the YWCA. This was only the beginning—she was shedding the role of dutiful wife. Cora must have had many a lonely day and night at home in Brooklyn with the boys while Edwin was doing Tammany business. His fire department job took up very little time, but Edwin spent most evenings across the bridge. He loved the theater, the opera, and the city's nightlife. He liked going to the Marshall. This was the political and social free participation he had left the South to find. Meanwhile, life at home was toxic. Edwin was rumored to have a white lady friend. She was Edna Woolman Chase—a suffragist and, of all things, an editor at *Vogue* (whose first issue had appeared in 1892). In photographs, Chase resembled the young Cora—small and pretty with a direct gaze. No one knows if the rumors were true, but it seemed that Cora believed them. She also may have believed that Edwin spent a great deal of his time away from the family living as a white man.

In 1915 *Birth of a Nation* was released, a film that Woodrow Wilson adored, but that was one long pro-KKK, antiblack diatribe played by white actors in blackface. The NAACP made sure that pickets appeared wherever the film was shown, but its suit to stop screenings was unsuccessful—although several states later agreed with the NAACP that the film fostered racial hatred and violence in a time of national crisis. Blacks seemed to have no friends in America. In the first three months of 1915, Congress introduced six Jim Crow bills affecting only Washington, D.C., including an anti-intermarriage bill. Happily, the NAACP defeated a House bill forbidding even literate Negroes from entering the country. But Wilson ordered the U.S. Marine Corps to invade and occupy Haiti.

That year, caught up in war fever with the sinking of the *Lusitania*, and also looking for a career, twenty-five-year-old Errol Horne, eldest son of Cora and Edwin, joined the army. Known in Brooklyn as an athlete, with the famous Horne charm (which probably came from Edwin), Errol was handsome in his uniform in the studio portrait he sent home from Texas. Taught to ride and shoot by old black Indian fighters at Fort Huachuca, Arizona, by 1916 Sergeant Horne had very quickly reached the highest rank blacks could expect to attain. He was twenty-six. In March 1916 he was part of Brigadier John J. Pershing's punitive expedition in pursuit of Mexican bandit-revolutionary Pancho Villa, who had invaded an American border town. Pershing was known as "Black Jack" for the color of the troops he led in both the Spanish-American War and the Mexican campaign. In the pursuit of Villa, who was never captured, Major Charles Young (the last black graduate of West Point in the nineteenth century) and members of the black Tenth Cavalry rescued the white Thirteenth Cavalry from an ambush and both Major Young and the Tenth Cavalry became national heroes. Young was promoted to lieutenant colonel, but army doctors declared him physically unfit for combat and removed him from active duty. If he went to war a full colonel, he could come home a brigadier—which would not do. The U.S. Army was not going have any black brigadiers. Young fought back, proving his physical fitness by making a nonstop Pony Express ride from Ohio to Washington, D.C. Young was finally made a full colonel but was not called to active duty until the last week of the war.

Errol Horne, however, was promoted to second lieutenant after the Villa campaign. He also won a bride, marrying a young woman from Texas called Lottie. He sent home a picture of a pretty, smiling girl who might be Mexican in a white middy dress with a big ribbon on her long braid of hair. Popular opinion had made Errol the "best" Horne brother: best looking, best athlete, and nicest. Errol was the golden boy. In the picture, taken by Errol, whose shadow holding the box camera is clearly seen, Lottie poses with an older man, possibly her father, who wears a big Mexican sombrero. Errol was sent to France to officer black labor troops, but within a year was dead from the 1918 influenza pandemic. Cora wrote a black-bordered note to her cousin, Katie Webb Graves:

> Everything possible was done for him, and he was buried with every military honor, but O, it is a deep, deep sorrow . . . Am here in the country trying to rest mind and body . . . I have Lottie with me and she is a wreck.

Errol may have been buried with every military honor, but on August 17, 1918, General Pershing sent an official directive to the French military:

> Although a citizen of the United States, the black man is regarded by the white American as an inferior being with whom relations of business or service only are possible . . . The vices of the Negro are a constant menace to the American who has to repress them sternly . . . We must prevent the rise of any pronounced degree of intimacy between French officers and black officers . . . We must not eat with them, must not shake hands or seek to talk or meet with them outside the requirements of military service. We must not commend too highly the black American troops, particularly in the presence of Americans.

Negroes might be "citizens," but they were not really "American." And Pershing was directing the French to give U.S. black officers the West Point silent treatment. The NAACP's *Crisis* magazine would report in 1920 that the French gave orders to burn copies of Pershing's directive. The French already had black generals, colonels, captains, and lieutenants, as well as Senegalese and Moroccan troops who helped save Paris in 1914. When Americans continued to harass the French about their colonial troops, the French replied succinctly:

It is because these soldiers are just as brave and just as devoted as white soldiers that they receive exactly the same treatment, every man being equal before the death which all soldiers face.

It was a brilliant reply. Neither the Wilson administration nor the U.S. military, puffed up with the hubris of their own racism, which saw black deaths as unimportant, could have any idea of the contempt that was behind every carefully chosen word: "brave," "devoted," "same treatment," and "equal." Among America's many crimes against black people, their treatment in the world wars by their own government was among the most sickening. Black American soldiers in World War I were treated in ways that can only be described as war crimes. On some American ships, black troops were not issued life jackets but expected to use floating debris. A young lieutenant and future general, George C. Marshall, was on such a ship and was appalled. In the terrible winter of 1918, at Camp Lee, Virginia, Wilson's home state, white troops slept in barracks and black troops slept in tents without floors or bedding. "Men died like sheep in their tents," read a report to the secretary of war, "it being a common occurrence to go around in the morning and drag men out frozen to death."

News of the armistice came to a brokenhearted Horne family. But there had been a bright spot in 1916. On the home front there was a civilian wedding in Brooklyn. Ted Horne and Edna Scottron were both twenty-two years old and had known each other all their lives. They were popular, attractive members of the Brooklyn "crowd." The Scottrons, a big family from Springfield, Massachusetts, had always been free. They were among the first fifty black families to settle in Brooklyn. There were two Native American grandmothers on Edna's side—from Eastern tribes like those that met the *Mayflower* or inspired James Fenimore Cooper. Edna's father, Springfield-born Cyrus Scottron, was the first black railway postal clerk in New York. Her mother, Louise Logan, was a Brooklyn-born teacher, whose grandmother had been a French-speaking free African immigrant to the United States in the 1850s. Edna's uncle Samuel Scottron, Cyrus' much older brother, was an important black Brooklyn figure. He owned a large furniture store and was the third black member of the Brooklyn Board of Education. Edna, green-eyed and freckled, with a pocket-Venus figure, was considered one of the best-looking girls in the "crowd." Ted and Edna seemed a perfect couple. What better reason to marry? Moreover, Ted had a job—a Tammany patronage job. He was the first black member of the claims division of the industrial commission of the New York State Department of Labor. His boss was Frances Perkins, later the first female U.S. cabinet member in history, under FDR. Ted actually had a white staff under him. They posed with him for a photo outside their office, all looking very young and happy. Written on the back of the snapshot was "Horne and staff." With Errol gone, Ted and Edna lived rent-free on the top floor at Chauncey Street (above Cora). Edna was spoiled and basically uneducated. Her only reading material was movie magazines. Her intellectual habits and coterie of chattering girlfriends must have driven her mother-in-law mad—fortunately, Cora was rarely at home in the daytime.

Edna and Ted's only child, Lena Mary Calhoun Horne, was born in Brooklyn on June 30, 1917, in a Jewish lying-in hospital, where the nurses marveled over her "coppery" color. Edna was passing as white—specifically Jewish, I suppose. Cora, but not Ted, came to the hospital.

The baby was called "Lena" for Cora's sister—and "Mary" because Cora was a Roman Catholic at the time. Edna, for whom Cora had little respect, seemed to have no say on the subject. Cora herself would soon move on spiritually to Ethical Culture—but Lena was baptized at Holy Rosary Catholic Church on Chauncey Street.

When Lena was growing up, Cora refused to address her husband by name. "Please tell Mr. Horne . . ." she would say to one of her sons. Cora herself was never at home. She had decided to get busy, and a 1925 article in the black newspaper *Chicago Defender* reported after the fact on this era in her life as an activist New Negro Woman. With the outbreak of World War I, she became a Red Cross organizer and headed a unit of seventy-five women. At the same time she was secretary of the Brooklyn Urban League, an officer of the Sojourner Truth House for delinquents, a director of the Big Brothers and Big Sisters Federation, a member of the International Council of Women of the Darker Races, and the mayor's appointee to the Brooklyn victory committee.

On the board of Big Brothers and Big Sisters, Cora became a mentor to young Paul Robeson, who was the youngest son of a minister from Princeton, New Jersey, and had lost his mother. She helped him get a scholarship to Rutgers after Woodrow Wilson refused to consider the idea of a black at Princeton—even if the young man was brilliant at everything, including football, and even if Princeton was his hometown. (In 1917 "Robey" Robeson, playing for Rutgers, became the second Negro named by celebrated sportswriter Walter Camp to his "all-American" list.) Harvard and Yale had both desegregated their undergraduate schools in the mid-1870s. But Princeton was still all-white in 1917. There was never any doubt that Paul Robeson was black. But the big black Robeson of the glorious smile and blinding charisma was always an icon and never a stereotype. (At later political events, people literally stood on chairs to see him.) Like Frederick Douglass, Robeson was a natural leader since boyhood. His biographer Martin Bauml Duberman wrote of the "astonishing range of his gifts in sports, studies, singing and debating," saying that "Robeson's natural talents were so exceptional that he had to make a proportionally large effort in order to forestall resentment in others." Admired by whites for "his unfailingly courteous, Christian demeanor," he was an "amazingly popular boy," said one teacher, because "he had the faculty for always knowing what is so commonly referred to as his 'place.'" Duberman quotes another: "He is the most remarkable boy I have ever taught, a perfect prince. Still, I can't forget that he is a Negro."

On July 2, 1917, the worst and most horror-filled race riot in U.S. history took place in East St. Louis, Illinois, a blue-collar town with a conflux of black and white Southerners fleeing the boll weevil and seeking war industry jobs. East St. Louis had a special issue with blacks: it was a Democratic town that feared elections would be stolen by newly arriving black Republicans. The weeks before the riot saw the white press stirring up trouble with bogus stories of black crimes, especially rape. There was also an underlying labor issue. The riot began over the hiring of black scabs at the striking Aluminum Ore Company. The union did not admit blacks, of course. The riot exploded on a rumor that an armed black man had killed a white man. White mobs now surged through the town to kill or maim any black man, woman, or child they came across. This riot may have been as bad as the 1863 New York Draft Riots. In New York at least there were white people willing to help Negroes evade the mobs. Both white Irish police and white Irish priests, for example, helped save most of the inhabitants of the Colored Orphan Asylum. East St. Louis seemed to have no civic-minded upper class and very few good-hearted cops or priests. It was a classic, old-fashioned, Southern-minded, American small town— violent and prejudiced. Blacks and whites, mostly Southern, did not live that far apart from each other. Mobs set fire to black homes, then shot victims as they ran out. Sometimes they nailed boards over doors and windows before setting fire to the houses. A white army reserve officer reported seeing a white man snatch a baby from a fleeing black woman's arms and toss it back in the flames. The police and National Guard did nothing except encourage the mobs and shoot at fleeing blacks. There were reports of blacks being burned alive as well as lynched. There are few records of what actually happened in East St. Louis, because the mayor's secretary ordered police and guardsmen to arrest anyone with a camera and to smash the cameras, but eyewitnesses told their tales—and at least one picture was smuggled out. It is a photo of a mob swarming a streetcar to drag off blacks. Six thousand blacks soon left East St. Louis. Too late, the local chamber of commerce demanded that the police chief resign. German propaganda had a field day. But Woodrow Wilson said nothing.

Du Bois compiled a report, "Massacre at East St. Louis," published in *The Crisis*. And the NAACP brilliantly organized the first Silent Protest march any American had ever seen. On July 28, eight thousand to ten thousand blacks marched down New York's Fifth Avenue behind men carrying banners reading, "Mr. President, why not make America safe for democracy?" Leading the parade were little children dressed in white who held hands across the avenue. Women in white marched behind the children. At the very front were NAACP officials and the drummers. Besides the tread of the marchers, the only sound coming from the parade was muffled drums. It must have been a stunning sight to New Yorkers, for whom the word "demonstration" naturally meant "noise." Although baby Lena was less than a month old, it is impossible to imagine that Cora was not there. It was the first large-scale, organized public demonstration for civil rights in the twentieth century.

When America entered World War I in 1917, at first no one wanted black soldiers—then labor troops were clearly needed and draft boards could not sign blacks up fast enough. Labor troops did manual work and heavy lifting: loading and unloading ships, building roads, and so forth—anything, except carrying a gun or firing a weapon. Ironically, the only black troops who were treated with anything like respect were in Wilson's Washington, D.C. Washington's black National Guard troops were stationed at all government buildings on the theory that blacks could not be infiltrated by German spies or saboteurs. Buffalo Soldiers—trained black professional combat troops—stayed in the Philippines or on the Mexican border during the war. Black troops could fight Filipinos, Mexicans, and Indians, but Wilson would not permit them to fight a white enemy. Thus, untrained black National Guard units, mostly used as labor troops, took the place of trained black troops. Only two black units actually saw combat in the war: the Eighth from Chicago, Illinois, and Edwin Horne's Fifteenth from New York, "Harlem's Own."

Although the regimental colors of the Fifteenth New York were presented by New York governor Charles Whitman outside the Union League Club in the spring of 1917, and crowds cheered Jim Europe's syncopated rendition of "Onward Christian Soldiers," the regiment was not allowed to join the "Farewell to Little Old New York" parade when New York's other National Guard units, known as the "Rainbow Division," went "over there." The Fifteenth New York was told that "black is not a color of the rainbow." The Fifteenth New York went to France without a farewell, but it got both a new name and a new nickname. The old Fifteenth was now the brand-new 369th Infantry Regiment, attached to the Eighth Corps of the Fourth French Army— and the sobriquet "Harlem's Own" became the "Harlem Hellfighters." Wilson gave the 369th to the desperate French because he did not want blacks fighting for America. Wholly under French command, but permitted to carry its state colors (New York's), the 369th fought in French uniforms, with French weapons, under the French flag and became the longest-serving and most highly decorated American unit of the war. But at the end of the war, showing contempt for its own black troops, the U.S. government officially requested that the French not mention the 369th in any postwar testimonials or memorials and not permit the 369th to march in any French victory parades. Only white Americans could take part, although black Frenchmen and black

Britons marched with their respective countries. Wilson did not want the world to learn about black heroism—even though the first American soldiers to recieve the Croix de Guerre, Sergeant Henry Johnson and Private Needham Roberts, belonged to the 369th.

Black Americans without a doubt helped France win the war, and the French were grateful, though they could not show it officially without offending the U.S. government. France showed its gratitude in a deeper way, by discovering and embracing black soldiers and black music. During its February 1918 goodwill tour of the country, the famous, larger than regulation 369th Regimental Band, led by the great Jim Europe, now Lieutenant James Reese Europe, single-handedly raised French morale. The 369th introduced jazz to France and the world, and the tour of France was a huge story in America. The 369th did much more than lift the spirits of a country at its lowest ebb. It won that country's deepest gratitude by the fact that the soldier-musicians went back to the front after their tour to fight with the French army. They were the first unit of Negro Americans in combat and Jim Europe was the first Negro officer in combat. The band and the entire 369th were loved in France—explaining the French passion for black American jazz and sympathy for black Americans who sought a refuge from American racism between the world wars. The enlisted men of the 369th were all black, and except for the chaplain (Paul Robeson's brother), the legal officer, and the bandmaster (Europe), the officers were wealthy white American men with paternalistic ideas about race—not a good thing, but certainly preferable to the vicious racism of the ordinary U.S. Army officer.

In February 1919, ironically enough, the 369th led New York City's victory parade up Fifth Avenue. Two years earlier the regiment had not been allowed to march, but now the Harlem Hellfighters were the stars of the parade, famously photographed by newsreel cameras. The sidewalks were thronged with cheering New Yorkers of all races who screamed in deafening collective delight when they saw that the first regiment to come through the lower Fifth Avenue Victory Arch was the 369th. Delirium became near pandemonium when the crowd saw that the regiment marched in phalanx order, with massed blocks of men, across the avenue. The French army used the phalanx (the Nazis and the Soviets picked it up later) and, as the Romans knew very well, the phalanx could be intimidating.

The U.S. Army had discovered that the 369th Regimental Band, now considered one of the great bands of the world, could be useful and sent it on a triumphant cross-country tour. Lieutenant Noble Sissle, whom army public relations billed as "The Greatest Singer of His Race . . . America's Own 'Young Black Joe,'" was the featured star. But real tragedy struck on the last night of the tour. Jim Europe was stabbed to death in Boston by one of his musicians. His was the first public funeral for a Negro in New York City. The funeral procession, with his flag-draped coffin carried on the backs of uniformed band members, retraced the victory parade route of four months earlier. Europe was buried in Arlington National Cemetery.

Cora Horne had a new role in life. Sadly, both of baby Lena's parents deserted her before she was two. It cannot be blamed on the war. One day in 1919, Ted Horne was no longer there. Letters arrived at his workplace stating that he had to take a long trip west for his lungs. It was a surprise to his wife, too. He fled all the way to Seattle, where he took up with a widow or divorcee named Irene. There is an amazingly racy "hot cha!" picture of Ted and Irene. Apparently, he made a killing gambling in the Black Sox baseball scandal—but no one was ever certain. Lucky Ted was always on the furthest fringes of organized crime, ever since he had learned to gamble at the old Plaza, but he was never in trouble with the law. Consequently, although he deserted his wife, child, and job, he was able to send money to Cora for herself and Lena and to help his younger brothers with college. Ted now spent his time at prizefights, Negro League baseball games, college football games, and horse races. He liked to own large automobiles. He also liked to spend his time with gamblers and demimondaines. Both of Lena's wayward young parents were a disaster. After Ted went west, Edna ran away to Harlem and the Lafayette Theatre—where, to Cora's outrage and horror, she took Lena onstage as the baby in *Madame X*. Cora put her foot down, and Teddy agreed that Lena should be in Cora's custody. Since Edna essentially feared as well as disliked her mother-in-law, and probably regarded Lena as a hindrance to her career aspirations, she allowed Cora to have her way. Until the age of seven, Lena lived with her grandparents exclusively. How Cora found time for Lena is a mystery, but she did manage to take care of the important things. In April 1919 the NAACP published *Thirty Years of Lynching in the United States*, listing the names, by state, of Negroes lynched from 1889 to 1918. That year Cora enrolled her two-year-old granddaughter as a lifetime member of the NAACP. She also took her to the new office at 70 Fifth Avenue, where Lena sat on the lap of the great James Weldon Johnson and played with his telephone.

CHAPTER FIVE

South/1900–1919
THE NEW SOUTH

THE ATLANTA census of the Fourth Ward of 1900 does not list Antoine Graves as "an American success story"—it should have. It simply lists Antoine Graves and family as living at 116 Howell Street: Antoine, age thirty-nine; wife Catherine (Katie Webb), age thirty-nine; daughter Nellie, age fourteen; son Antoine Jr., age twelve; Catherine (called Kate), age ten; and Marie Antoinette, age eight. The census reported that the whole family could read, write, and speak English and they owned their own home free of mortgage. The census color listed for everyone was "B" for black. Antoine's occupation was listed as real estate agent. The South was well into the long, dark post-Reconstruction night of what Mark Twain called "The United States of Lyncherdom"—but the black Calhouns were more or less protected, because as professionals and businesspeople, they needed little from the white community except its vague goodwill—which they kept by staying out of trouble and out of politics (until their grandchildren later brought them to civil rights).

"The problem of the Twentieth Century is the problem of the color line," Lena Calhoun Smith's old friend Willie, now *Doctor* Du Bois, famously said in 1900. By then the South was solidly segregated, and the North was about to be flooded with Southern revisionism. The Old

South and slavery itself were now sentimentalized and romanticized in many ways—from movies hailing the KKK to songs about Dixie. Again, the black Calhouns were more or less protected. They lived in Atlanta neighborhoods, not isolated rural homesteads, and they were known to important Atlanta whites. Like their Northern cousins, they were able to communicate with both worlds.

On the other hand, between 1890 and 1910, more than two hundred thousand blacks left the American South, in flight from political and racial oppression. Blacks in the South were at the mercy of their region, and their region could do anything it liked to them without fear of reprisal. Parts of the North were as virulently racist and hateful toward blacks as the South, but in the North blacks could vote and had legal redress against attacks. Despite living in a fearfully hostile environment, the black Calhouns who stayed in the South stayed safe and certainly seemed happy within their close-knit community and family enclaves. Although there were working mothers in every generation—teachers or social workers mostly, married to busy professional men—they raised confident and successful children who understood the unfair and unjust nature of their society, and were smart enough not to provoke it.

By 1900 Atlanta seemed the perfect New South city. But there were definite underlying racial tensions. Negroes in Atlanta and other Southern cities began boycotting streetcars to protest Jim Crow seating. White journalist Ray Stannard Baker, in his book *Following the Color Line*, described Atlanta in the early years of the new century:

> Atlanta is a singularly attractive place, as bright and new as any Western city. Sherman left it in ashes . . . and a new city was built, which is now growing in a manner not short of astonishing . . . But this is not the whole story. Everywhere I went in Atlanta I heard of the fear of the white people . . . And yet every Negro I met voiced in some way that fear.

Baker told the story of one white woman who had been accidentally brushed on the shoulder by a hurrying "rather good-looking young Negro" and his reaction when he discovered that she was white:

> He had not seen me before. When he turned and found it was a white woman he had touched, such a look of abject terror and fear came into his face as I hope never again to see on a human countenance. He knew what it meant if I was frightened . . . It shows, doesn't it, how little it might take to bring punishment upon an innocent man!

Atlanta, like Brooklyn, metropolitan but leafy, was a black middle-class haven. Brooklyn may have had no "whites only" signs—but Atlanta was the Athens of the black South. Atlanta University was home to wunderkind "Willie" Du Bois, with degrees from Fisk, Harvard, and the University of Berlin. Du Bois first discussed the Talented Tenth in his 1903 collection of essays *The Negro Problem*. Calling his fellow former Missionary students the "Talented Tenth," Du Bois defined their job:

> The Talented Tenth of the Negro race must be made leaders of thought and missionaries of culture among their people. No others can do this work and Negro colleges must train men for it. The Negro race, like all other races, is going to be saved by its exceptional men.

The same year the prodigiously talented Du Bois established his reputation as a great American essayist with the publication of *The Souls of Black Folk*:

> It is a peculiar sensation, this double-consciousness, this sense of always looking at one's self through the eyes of others . . . One feels his twoness,—an American, a Negro; two souls, two thoughts, two unreconciled strivings; two warring ideals in one dark body, whose dogged strength alone keeps it from being torn asunder.

That July, Booker T. Washington made a speech in Atlanta to cele-brate the thirty-sixth anniversary of the First Congregational Church and the ninth anniversary of its pastor, Reverend H. H. Proctor. Some of the leading white men of the city attended, including the governor, the mayor, and the pastor of the Methodist Episcopal Church. Unlike Du Bois, Washington had no interest in the psychological problems of black people in America. His main concern was not giving any problems to white people. He complained that "idle men," North and South, who hung around street corners and barrooms were the next race problem. It would be much worse in the North, he said, because in the North "the doors of industry are too often closed against the Negro." This, of course, was true. White immigrants were hired in the North before native blacks, and except for the "Wobblies," the short-lived Industrial Workers of the World (IWW), American labor unions rejected any black members.

In 1904 Atlanta's Union Mutual Insurance Company put out a pamphlet about selling insurance that was actually a picture of black life in Atlanta—and a very polite guide to the intricacies of the Jim Crow system:

> Atlanta has a population of 132,000 people, and of this number 45,000 are Negroes. They are scattered among all the wards of the city . . . A map of Atlanta has been drawn with the particular aim of helping Negroes find their way to the wards most thickly populated by Negro residents, business houses and pleasure centers . . .

Under "Places of Amusement," for example, it was noted of the opera house and the theater, "Accommodations for Negroes Limited." In other words, do not try to attend the opera or the theater. Middle-class blacks entertained each other at home. Every house had a piano, any type from upright to grand, and somebody played it. They made their own amusement in Atlanta.

"The Negroes do not own or manage any banks," said the pamphlet, sounding vaguely apologetic. And hospitals, of course, were "Under white management." As for churches, there were seventeen Baptist, eight African Methodist Episcopal, two Colored Methodist Episcopal, one Protestant Episcopal, one Presbyterian, and one Congregational. First Congregational was the black Calhoun church. Its dynamic young pastor, the celebrated Reverend H. H. Proctor, was born in Tennessee in 1868, the son of former slaves, and attended Fisk and the Yale Divinity School. He became the first black pastor of First Congregational in 1894, at age twenty-six. The American Missionary Association stopped supporting First Congregational when Proctor arrived. From the beginning, he made the pastorate self-supporting and began missionary activities among the poor and in Atlanta jails. In 1903 Proctor was a cofounder and the first president of the National Convention of Congregational Workers, an effort to promote Negro Congregationalism.

The 1904–1905 Union Mutual pamphlet, whose aim was "to lift the moral tone of Negro business life and thereby increase the people's respect and appreciation for it," included a directory of black Atlanta businesses.

> Opportunity for employment is the most serious question . . . we are vastly more in need of Leaders of Industry and Business than anything else just now . . . we must all agree that "the man who has done something" is of much more value to the community than the one who is constantly theorizing . . .

This appears to be a dig at Du Bois and a push for Washington. The list includes a bakery on Auburn Avenue, two grocers (one on Piedmont Avenue, the other on Fraser Street where Moses Calhoun began his life in freedom), and several contractors and builders, boarding- and lodging houses, restaurants, caterers, dressmakers, tailors, shoemakers, and barbers, along with "T.E. Askew, The Only Colored Photographer."

There was Mrs. W. A. Hinton, "Business Stenographer, Typist and Accountant, telephone 8673." And there was one ice-cream parlor on Piedmont Avenue—"The public's presence is respectfully asked." There was a dentist on Peachtree Street, and a drugstore where prescriptions were "carefully Compounded Day or Night." There was a trained nurse, two orphanages, one old folks' home, and two white hospitals, Grady and MacVicar (where a basement corner was set aside for blacks). There was also Dr. T. Howard and Son, on Piedmont Avenue, undertakers and embalmers, "Oldest, Most Reliable, Best Equipped and Most Polite Service." Finally, at the end of the long list, Antoine Graves Sr. had a double-page ad:

> I sell lots of property for investment and firms
> List Your Properties With Me for Results A. GRAVES
> 121-2 Wall Street Atlanta, Ga. *A. Graves Real Estate and Loans.*

Under "Athletics," the pamphlet had remarked:

> The college sports among Negroes in Atlanta have always been free. This applies to baseball. Atlanta University has constructed an athletic park on the campus where baseball and football are played. The admission fee is 15c. The custom has been to play in the city parks, but this privilege has been denied the Negro colleges.

Healthy bodies as well as minds were encouraged at Atlanta University, as they were in all black middle-class venues. From the April 1904 *Atlanta Independent Sporting News*: "Atlanta University is playing great ball this season . . . has a great infield in Jones, Graves, Hawkins and Huggins. . . Big Antoine Graves is a great infielder."

Antoine Graves Jr., scholar, athlete, and musician, the calm center of a whirlwind of sisters, was a solemnly handsome young man whose nickname was "Judge." The gifted violinist posed for photos with his good-looking male friends, most of them smiling, but Judge always looked sober and solemn.

Black Atlanta was busy improving itself. In 1906 Reverend H. H. Proctor helped put First Congregational Church in the black by creating "Circles of Ten." He called it "an original plan of church work":

> The object of the Circles is to promote the helpfulness of the members to one another, and to unite them for Christian service. The Circles are to serve in the three following directions:
>
> 1. SERVE ONE ANOTHER by regular visitation, caring for one another in affliction, relieving in need, encouraging one another in Christian service and life, and whatever else one Christian can do for another. Read John 13:35
> 2. SERVE THE CHURCH by inviting others to it, leading persons to Christ, securing those without a Church home to join us, coming to the rescue of the Church in time of financial need . . . Read Ephesians 5:25
> 3. SERVE THE COMMUNITY of which the Church is a part by ministering to those shut in by affliction, for whom no one cares, by reclaiming the outcast, visiting hospitals and prisons, and doing whatever you think Christ would have you do. Read Matthew 25:31–46 . . .

Ten persons made a Circle, each with a specific role to play, meeting once a month:

> The meetings should rotate from house to house so that by the end of the year each member will have had the privilege of entertaining the Circle in his own home. Light refreshments add greatly to the pleasure of the meeting . . .

First Congregational was an active faith community. Antoine "Judge" Graves Jr. had his own Circle of young male friends. And his mother, Catherine (Katie Webb Graves), had her own Circle of "matron" friends. Judge's young sisters, Kate Graves and Marie Graves, made professions of faith for membership in First Congregational in March 1904.

In June 1906 young Marie (Antoinette) Graves graduated from the same Houston Street public school that had fired her father ten years earlier. Atlanta was now considered the example of how Negroes and whites could live side by side in harmony. But that same June found Georgia's new governor-elect, M. Hoke Smith, making a disturbing pronouncement: "Legislation can be passed which will . . . not interfere with the right of any white man to vote, and get rid of 95 per cent of the Negro voters."

This was the onset of a violently antiblack press crusade. Arch-racist Smith was the former publisher of the *Atlanta Journal*. Smith's rival in the campaign was Clark Howell, editor of the anti-Smith *Atlanta Constitution*. The *Atlanta Journal* was loudly pro-Smith. On August 1, 1906, it printed an incendiary racist appeal as a front-page editorial:

> Political equality being thus preached to the negro . . . what wonder that he makes no distinction between political and social equality. He grows more bumptious on the street, more impudent in his dealings with white men; and then, when he cannot achieve social equality as he wishes, with the instinct of the barbarian to destroy what he cannot attain to, he lies in wait, as that dastardly brute did yesterday near this city, and assaults the fair young girlhood of the South . . .

Now there was talk everywhere of disenfranchising Negroes. In trying to "out-nigger" each other for a political campaign, the Atlanta papers started a race war. The press offered rewards for lynching bees and urged a revival of the Klan. On Saturday, September 24, Atlanta newspapers reported four assaults on white women by Negroes. The *Atlanta News* had screaming headlines about black rapes of white women—all of which proved false. But by early evening, some ten thousand white men and boys came surging down Decatur Street attacking black men, women, and boys—and killing some—and torching and smashing black-owned businesses. The Amos Drug Store, on Auburn Avenue, was nearly destroyed. Moses Amos, who had been an apprentice to a white druggist in 1876, was owner of the first and largest of several Negro drugstores. The wealthiest Negro in Atlanta in 1906 was A. F. Herndon, president of the Atlanta Life Insurance Company and owner of the biggest barbershop in the city—all black barbers, all-white clientele. The mob went into Herndon's and dragged out all the barbers to be beaten to death, or near enough. The mob also attacked streetcars and trolleys, assaulting black women as well as black men. At least three men were beaten to death. The governor finally called out the militia at midnight, but the mob did not begin to disperse until there was a heavy rainfall around 2 A.M. Even then, vigilante mobs continued to attack black neighborhoods on Sunday and Monday. Four black men were killed in the black Atlanta suburb of Brownsville, home to black Clark College and Gammon Theological Seminary, whose president was severely beaten by the police. Instead of a mob riot, Brownsville actually saw a police riot against black citizens, who had called the police for protection. Typically, the police spent more time confiscating black weapons, leaving blacks helpless, than arresting white rioters. And the fire department had trouble getting to burning black businesses. But the mayor, as ever thinking about image, only wished the riot to end. He got the governor to call out the militia, as Ray Stannard Baker said, "to apply that pound of cure which should have been an ounce of prevention." Saloons were closed for two weeks. The police managed to arrest twenty-four white rioters, who were sentenced instantly to the maximum possible time on the chain gang. Yes, twenty-four. Atlanta wanted the whole thing to go away.

By Monday and Tuesday, city officials, businessmen, the clergy, and even the white press, which had instigated the riot, were calling for an end to violence. Not only was Atlanta's image being damaged throughout the United States, but the riot was big news internationally. Estimates ranged from twenty-five to forty black deaths—although the coroner officially listed only ten. All accounts agree that there were only two white deaths, one caused by a heart attack.

On September 24, 1906, a thirteen-year-old Negro boy in Atlanta named Walter White discovered the meaning of being black. It had not quite sunk in for young Walter because he and his family looked white. "I am a Negro," Walter wrote in his 1948 autobiography, *A Man Called White*:

> My skin is white, my eyes are blue, my hair is blond. The traits of my race are nowhere visible upon me . . . There is no mistake. I am a Negro. There can be no doubt. I know the night when, in terror and bitterness of soul, I discovered that I was set apart by the pigmentation of my skin (invisible though it was in my case) and the moment at which I decided that I would infinitely rather be what I was than, through taking advantage of the way of escape that was open to me, be one of the race which had forced the decision upon me.

The White family of seven children and their parents lived on Houston Street, and all the children attended Antoine Graves' old school. They lived in an eight-room two-story frame house that Walter's father, a graduate of Atlanta University and a mail collector, kept spick-and-span and whitewashed, with neatly trimmed grass and flower beds—in the midst of a mixed neighborhood of run-down black and white homes. (Neighborhoods in the South were often integrated.) He collected mail in a little cart that he drove from three to eleven P.M. On Saturdays, Walter drove the cart for him regularly from two until seven. Around seven o'clock in the evening on Saturday, September 24, as Walter and his father were driving toward the mailbox at the corner of Peachtree and Houston, "there came from near-by Pryor Street a roar the like of which I had never heard before, but which sent a sensation of mingled fear and excitement coursing through my body." Walter wanted to see what the trouble was, but his father ordered him to stay in the cart. On Peachtree Street they witnessed a lame Negro bootblack from Herndon's barbershop being beaten to death by the howling mob of whites. Walter and his father were safe from the mob because of their white skin. On Marietta Street they saw an undertaker's carriage:

Crouched in the rear of the vehicle were three Negroes clinging to the sides of the carriage as it lunged and swerved. On the driver's seat crouched a white man, the reins held taut in his left hand. A huge whip was gripped in his right. Alternately he lashed the horses and, without looking backward, swung the whip in savage swoops in the faces of members of the mob as they lunged at the carriage determined to seize the three Negroes.

Back on Pryor Street Walter and his father rescued an elderly black woman, who cooked at a downtown white hotel, as she ran as best she could from the mob of whites. Walter's father lifted her onto the cart while Walter took the reins and lashed the horse to speed.

The next day was Sunday. Normally, the White family walked half a block to the corner of Houston and Courtland streets to First Congregational—this morning, they did not. On the Sunday morning after the first night of the riot, most black worshippers stayed home. Late that afternoon some friends of Walter's family came to tell them that a mob was gathering to march down Houston Street to "clean out the niggers." Walter had no idea where his father got the two weapons that they now each held at the living room windows. Lights in every Negro house on the street that Sunday night were turned out early. Walter's father sent his wife and daughters to the back of the house. Walter and his father were the only males at home. They took their places at the front windows . . . Walter's father turned to him and said in a quiet voice, "Son, don't shoot until the first man puts his foot on the lawn and then—don't you miss!" Walter was wondering what it would feel like to kill a man when suddenly shots were fired from a nearby house. And the mob, armed only with torches and clubs, paused, grumbled, then suddenly evaporated and retreated up Houston Street as more shots were fired. The white mob retreated in the face of black self-defense. It was *then*, White wrote, that he knew who he was:

> In that instant there opened up within me a great awareness; I knew then who I was. I was a Negro, a human being with an invisible pigmentation which marked me a person to be hunted, hanged, abused, discriminated against, kept in poverty and ignorance, in order that those whose skin was white would have readily at hand a proof of their superiority . . .

In 1906 Du Bois had the title of professor of economics and history at Atlanta University. The former professor of Latin and Greek at Wilberforce sat all night on the library steps at Atlanta University with a shotgun, waiting for attackers who never came. He wrote a (long) "Litany for Atlanta"—one of the last lines of which was: "Sit no longer blind, Lord God, deaf to our prayer and dumb to our dumb suffering. Surely Thou too art not white, O Lord, a pale, bloodless, heartless thing?"

Northern white journalist Ray Stannard Baker, who went to Atlanta right after the riot, made an acute observation about the South:

> When I first went South I expected to find people talking about the Negro, but I was not at all prepared to find the subject occupying such an overshadowing place in Southern affairs . . . the South is overwhelmingly concerned in this one thing.

White Southerners in general were so obsessed with keeping blacks from rising that they were keeping the whole region down. They would rather have themselves and their families suffer than see Negroes have an advantage.

Respectable white Atlanta was outraged, but the mob was not made up of "respectable" white Atlantans. "The poor white hates the Negro," wrote Baker, "and the Negro dislikes the poor white. It is in these lower strata of society, where the races rub together in unclean streets, that the fire is generated." Poor whites hated blacks because during slavery, poor whites often perceived blacks as being better treated than themselves. But the white power structure was angry because Atlanta looked bad in the eyes of Yankee investors and the international press.

Thanks to Charles T. Hopkins, a prominent attorney, for the first time in Atlanta's history the city's "respectable" whites and blacks came together. It was agreed that when whites said that they "know the Negro," they meant the servant Negro, the field hand, and the laborer. They knew nothing about the "better class of Negroes," wrote Baker, "those who were in business, or in independent occupations, those who owned their own homes." Baker believed that many whites wanted the "New South" and the "old Negro"—"faithful, simple, ignorant, obedient, cheerful."

A committee of ten was proposed to raise funds for black assistance: Charles T. Hopkins headed the list, followed by the president of the chamber of commerce, the president of the board of education, the president of the Fourth National Bank, and several important businessmen. Prominent Negroes were invited to join the committee, including Reverend H. H. Proctor of First Congregational Church and four other black ministers and Benjamin J. Davis Sr., editor of the black newspaper the *Atlanta Independent*. Antoine Graves Sr., business manager of the *Independent* from 1903 to 1928, would surely have been among the black notables on the committee. Negroes discussed grievances: specifically unnecessary roughness by streetcar conductors and police. White members agreed to speak to the streetcar company and the police. Hopkins discovered that Atlanta Negroes were clearly not the "child race" he had thought them to be:

I believe those Negroes understood the situation better than we did. I
was astonished at their intelligence and diplomacy. They never referred
to the riot: they were looking to the future. I didn't know there were
such Negroes in Atlanta.

Hopkins now invited 1,500 prominent white men to join the committee. At the same time, Reverend H. H. Proctor and his committee
of Negroes organized the Colored Co-operative Civic League, which
comprised 1,500 of the "best" colored men in city. When rumors
came of another possible outbreak of violence over Christmas, new
policemen were added to the force, newspapers agreed not to publish
sensational stories, and the city was warned against lawlessness. Saloons
were closed at 4 P.M. on Christmas Eve. And there seemed to be new
harmony between the races. An integrated prayer meeting of black and
white ministers was held at the Negro YMCA.

One can only imagine the excitement in the black Calhoun household of the Graves family in the early summer of 1908. Judge Graves,
the twenty-year-old musician-athlete son of real estate broker Antoine
Graves and Katie Webb Graves, had given up baseball. He was scheduled
to give a violin recital in the first week of August. It would be a very
white recital—at Phillips and Crew's piano emporium in downtown
Atlanta, before a white audience and white critics. News of Judge's
gifts had probably spread from his teacher. There should have been
no worries for Judge, the boy who showed no emotion. As usual, he
surpassed himself. From the Saturday, August 8, 1908, black weekly
the *Independent*:

Tuesday of this week A. Graves, Jr. gave an exhibition of his musical
talent at Phillips and Crew's music hall before the best white critics
of the art in the city . . . When the critics at Phillips and Crew's parlors heard young Graves, supported by his sister, Miss Nellie, racial
prejudice gave way to talent and character. The critics forgot that the

young violinist was a negro and they were as liberal in their criticisms as if Mr. Graves were white . . . Mr. Graves feels much encouraged at the favorable comment of his home press and has decided upon a tour of the principal cities of his state . . . accompanied by Miss Nellie, his sister, a pianist of rare development and culture from Oberlin Conservatory of Music . . .

Nellie attended Oberlin College and the Conservatory of Music from 1906 to 1909. Nellie and Judge's Georgia itinerary that August included recitals in Columbus and Americus.

Judge's rave reviews were not limited to the black press. The arch-racist *Atlanta Journal* used the words "masterful," "virtuoso," and "genius." His success was not that surprising; Southern Negroes had always been allowed to make music (or prepare food), but there had clearly been a huge change of attitude since 1906. There was still a post-riot honeymoon for the New South in which *some* good things could be said about *some* Negroes. The black paper referred to the pianist as "Miss Nellie"; to the white paper she was plain "Nellie Graves." There were certain ironclad social rules in the South. A black person could be called "Doctor," "Reverend," "Professor," "Aunt," or "Uncle"—but never "Sir," "Madam," "Mr.," "Mrs.," or "Miss."

For the black Calhouns of all ages, education was paramount. In November 1908 Antoine Graves Sr. enrolled in the American Correspondence School of Law in Chicago, a three-year course. The following year his daughter Marie completed the college preparatory course at Atlanta University, where a young Edward Twichell Ware was the third president and the second President Ware. Except for industrial institutions like Hampton and Booker T. Washington's Tuskegee, by 1910 the Missionary colleges were in dire financial straits. By then the state of Georgia had withdrawn its annual appropriation to Atlanta University. It had also unsuccessfully attempted to forbid white instructors to teach there. The university depended more than ever on individual and foundation endowments from Northern liberals. Among the out-of-state contributors: Cornelius Vanderbilt, Cornelius Bliss, Edward S. Harkness, Henry Villard, Charles Francis Adams Jr., William Lloyd Garrison (the son of the great abolitionist), the Reverend Phillips Brooks, Julia Ward Howe, Richard P. Hallowell, Melissa P. Dodge, Olivia Stokes, and many educators and college presidents.

When Edward Ware was inaugurated on December 31, 1907, there was great celebration, with official greetings from Yale, since all three of Atlanta University's presidents—the Reverend Asa Ware, the Reverend Horace Bumstead, and the Reverend Edward Twichell Ware—were Yale graduates. The chancellor of the University of Georgia had excellent advice for Edward Ware:

> Don't let any theory about the race question come into your dealings with your pupils. What they need is to realize that they are individuals. Whatever you do, recognize the individual. Don't undertake to educate a race, a class, a section of a class. Educate the individual in your school. That is what I want you to do.

There is a photograph, circa 1910, of the Graves house, 116 Howell Street. It is a sturdy-looking, two-story wooden frame house. There is an ornate front porch with carved wooden posts like a colonnade and a picket fence with a gate. The two upstairs front windows are open, and fluttery curtains are glimpsed. Seated on the comfortably wide porch are Katie Webb Graves in a rocker; a friend of the family; and Katie's three daughters: Nellie, Kate, and Marie. They have been told to pose but not to smile. The composition is quite lovely. Three of the young women sit on the carved porch fence, and Nellie stands near a post. Nellie seems to be the odd girl out. She was her brother's accompanist, best friend, and possible confidante. She was also the plainest of the three sisters—though all were fetching in their white dresses and carrying flowers at various graduations. Katie Webb Graves had another portrait taken—possibly by the only Negro photographer in Atlanta. She is an attractive, well-dressed matron in a silk ankle-length dress, wearing an ostrich feather hat (a toque).

On June 12, 1912, musical Nellie became the first Graves bride when she married Noel Brown, a 1911 Oberlin graduate and son of a Mississippi doctor. They had met at Oberlin when Nellie was there studying music, and were married by Dr. Proctor at First Congregational. Nellie, who had a lovely slim figure, wore a simple and becoming white wedding dress and veil. Noel Brown seemed to suffer from the typical Southern black middle-class male problem of "finding himself." He was "in banking" in Greenville, Mississippi, from 1911 to 1913. By 1913 he was a photographer and cotton broker. From 1914 to 1915 (possibly assisted by his father-in-law) he was in real estate and insurance in Atlanta. From 1915 to 1918 he was a teacher at Jackson College in Mississippi. By 1918 he was a teacher and principal in Indianapolis public schools. Nellie and Noel would have four children and be the first Southern black Calhouns to divorce.

Later in June 1912, Nellie's brother, Judge, who four years earlier had earned accolades for his music, now earned a doctor of dental surgery degree at Howard University. Judge gave up his first love for the practicality of dentistry and opened his first dental office in Atlanta. Judge went abroad on a holiday by himself in August 1913 and sent a letter from the Grand Continental Hotel in Rome to his sister Kate. "I am leaving Rome today for Naples," he wrote. He talked about sightseeing and shopping and "not being bothered about color." He said that he had seen "6 or 7 negroes since I've been here. From Naples I go to Paris then I will sail on 30th." But he came back to a place where he would be bothered about color all the time.

Color actually took a backseat in Atlanta in 1915 when the Leo Frank case erupted. Two years earlier a white thirteen-year-old named Mary Phagan was found dead in the Atlanta pencil factory where she worked. Suspicion fell on both a black factory watchman, Jim Conley, and the Jewish superintendent of the factory, Leo Frank. Frank had been born in Texas and raised in Brooklyn, but had recently been elected head of the Atlanta B'nai B'rith (the oldest Jewish service organization). The trial took place the summer before Walter White's senior year at Atlanta University and White, like all of Atlanta, was fixated on the case:

> Under "normal" circumstances no one would have thought of accusing a white man had he been gentile and Southern. The guilt of the Negro would have been the inevitable assumption and he would have been lynched or tried, convicted, and executed. Because of Frank's religion and place of birth the case developed into a clash of prejudice in which anti-Northern and anti-Semitic hatreds had been whipped to such a frenzy that the usual anti-Negro prejudice was almost forgotten.

Frank's trial was swift and unjust—in a packed courtroom with openly armed spectators howling for a fast conviction. Most historians of the case now agree, as Atlanta police privately thought at the time, that the black janitor, Conley, who told many contradictory stories, was the real murderer. His own lawyer finally announced it, but neither the state nor the police seemed to care. Both the public and rival newspapers refused to consider Conley's possible guilt—"black brute– white maiden" was so old hat. But Leo Frank was *so* new and so much more the "other" than blacks, whom whites had known all their lives. Among the polite epithets, "Yankee," "capitalist," and "industrialist" all were anathema in the South. The trial was divided by class, with Atlanta's upper class and its paper, the *Constitution*, generally believing Frank innocent. The more downscale papers and the man in the street were vociferously anti-Frank. Atlanta's always latent mob mentality (the town was built by and for railroad workers) called for the head of Frank. Atlanta, probably for the first time, was drunk on anti-Semitism rather than simply hating blacks. Why? Atlantans were in love with the novelty of Frank. Frank himself was amazed, as he said in his court statement, that the "perjured vaporizings of a black brute" could be used against him. The Jewish community of Atlanta was the biggest in the South. Though Frank was raised in Brooklyn, he had adopted Southern attitudes about race.

On May 31, 1915, Frank pleaded to the Georgia State Prison Commission that his death sentence be commuted to life in prison. The conscientious and popular departing governor of Georgia, John M. Slaton, decided to study all the facts of the case. Five days before Slaton's term as governor was over and one day before Frank was scheduled to hang, Slaton commuted Frank's sentence to life in prison and presented a sort of apologia:

> I can endure misconstruction, abuse, and condemnation, but I cannot stand the constant companionship of an accusing conscience, which would remind me in every thought that I, as governor of Georgia, failed to do what I thought to be right . . . Feeling as I do about this case I would be a murderer if I allowed this man to hang.

The public reaction was outrage. A lynch-mad mob surrounded the governor's mansion, while state police and the Georgia National Guard led Governor Slaton and his wife to safety. The Slatons left Georgia the next day and did not return for ten years. Meanwhile, Frank was sent to a minimum-security work farm where he was slashed in the jugular by another inmate but not killed—and so was left to the hands of a group called the "Knights of Mary Phagan." On August 16 Frank was kidnapped from prison and taken to Marietta, Georgia, where the murdered girl was born, and lynched. Several photographs were made of the body hanging from a tree, surrounded by the lynching party. In typical Southern fashion, the lynching photos were sold as souvenirs in Atlanta shops for twenty-five cents, along with pieces of the rope and the nightshirt that Frank was wearing when he was taken. But local newspapers did not publish the pictures, because the lynchers could be easily identified. They included a former mayor and the current mayor of Marietta; several sheriffs, deputy sheriffs, and police officers; a superior court judge; the organizer of Marietta's first Boy Scout troop; and Joseph M. Brown, former governor of Georgia—whose mind was changed about black intelligence by Atlanta University. After Frank's lynching, about half of Georgia's three thousand Jews left the state. The lynchers were not publicly identified until 2000.

In November 1915 Booker T. Washington died. In a world with so many enemies, it was important for Southern Negroes to know that they were not completely alone—that they had white friends. The pre–Civil War friends of the Negro had been abolitionists. The postwar friends tended to be idealists and progressives with and without money. But former slave Booker T. Washington, of Alabama's Tuskegee Institute, made powerful white friends from a different category altogether. Tuskegee Institute could always depend on its white friends because Washington's message to blacks was to be apolitical, anti-intellectual, noncompetitive with whites, and skilled at manual labor. His Northern money came from the top tier of the titans of industry and conservatism. But his power would mostly die with him. On the other hand, W. E. B. Du Bois, as a young professor of economics and history at Atlanta University, would dare to question the Tuskegee policy of educating the black "hand," not the "head." With liberal white seed money, Du Bois built grassroots support for the National Association for the Advancement of Colored People (NAACP), an organization that would single-handedly, inch by inch dismantle Jim Crow through the courts and the Constitution.

The Great Migration began in 1915. Farm wages were seventy-five cents a day or less; boll weevils destroyed the cotton crop; and Jim Crow had reached the point of parody: South Carolina insisted on separate entrances, stairs, pay windows, lavatories, and water buckets for textile workers; and Oklahoma required separate phone booths. Jess Willard, finally the "Great White Hope," defeated Jack Johnson.

Rumor had it that Johnson threw the fight to relieve racial tensions and escape punishment under the Mann Act. By 1915, between Woodrow Wilson, a racist president; the movie *Birth of a Nation*; and black and white Southerners migrating to the industrial North at the same time, race relations were at an all-time low. According to statistics collected by antilynching crusader Ida B. Wells-Barnett and the NAACP, 1,100 Negroes were lynched between 1900 and 1915—and those were only the ones reported or known about.

In 1916, when twenty-three-year-old Atlanta University graduate Walter White, now working for Standard Life Insurance Company, heard that the Atlanta Board of Education planned to eliminate seventh grade for black children, he knew he had to protest. He had already turned down an offer to become principal of a Missionary school in Albany, Georgia—but he had to do something about Atlanta. He further learned that besides abolishing seventh grade for blacks, the board was planning to build a new high school for white students. Eighth grade for blacks had already been abolished two years earlier. Now education for black children would end at sixth grade. There were no high schools for blacks—although blacks paid taxes for white high schools. Blacks had fourteen grammar schools serving seventy-five thousand black children in double and triple sessions. All except one of the fourteen schools was a dilapidated wooden fire hazard. Parents who wished their children to receive a high school education had to pay tuition to Atlanta University, which was forced to keep its high school department open because the city refused to pay for a black high school. Some of the older generation recommended caution and submission, but White was part of the group that decided to write to the fledgling NAACP in New York for advice. It also decided to form an Atlanta NAACP chapter. White drafted the letter. Meanwhile, it was discovered that an informer had reported to the board of education that Negroes were planning to protest. But informing worked two ways. The protest group discovered that the board had moved up the date of the meeting to eliminate seventh grade, so that it would be a fait accompli before the protest could gather steam. So the protesters were ready for the new date. Considered "too young and hot-headed," White was not allowed to appear before the board. But he was a member of the committee that drafted the petition. The petition was not just a demand to retain seventh grade, but also a demand for academic and technical high schools, more modern grammar schools, and "educational facilities in every way the equal of those enjoyed by their white contemporaries." One of the 1906 black leaders, Dr. William F. Penn (stepfather of Dr. Louis T. Wright, future chairman of the board of directors of the NAACP), acted as chairman of the committee to present the petition. Benjamin J. Davis Sr., a newspaper editor, head of the Georgia Odd Fellows, and chairman of the Georgia State Republican Committee, was another committee member. The board of education made little effort to conceal its astonishment and resentment at the petition. But one white member, James L. Key, a future mayor of Atlanta, was on the petitioners' side:

> Gentlemen, I want to plead guilty to every word these men have spoken. We have the government in our hands, we control the finances, and we would be derelict to our duty if we did not grant their demands.

But Mayor Asa G. Candler, head of the Coca-Cola Company, jumped up and shouted angrily: "I do not agree with the gentleman who has just spoken. I do not wish to plead guilty. Let us not give way to hysteria but look at this matter in a sane manner." But Key would not be moved:

> The seat of all hysteria in this city is in the Mayor's office and the chief professor of that science is the Mayor himself. I do plead guilty, and as long as I am a member of this board I pledge my word here today that I shall fight for the rights of these men.

The black delegation never found out what was said in the executive session of the board, but a few days later, it was announced that the board had abandoned its plan to cut seventh grade for blacks and had decided to float a bond issue to improve Atlanta schools. Elation and victory were short-lived. When Dr. Penn and the committee next appeared before the board, they were told with "brutal frankness and considerable profanity" that none of the bond money would be spent on Negro schools and there was nothing colored citizens could do about it. Members of the board had been attacked by their friends as well as newspaper editorials for being "whipped into line by niggers."

Meanwhile organization of the Atlanta branch of the NAACP, with Walter White as secretary, had been sped up. All hope for school improvement seemed lost until someone thought of examining the city charter of Atlanta in order to learn the requirements for the floating of bond issues. The charter required affirmative approval of two-thirds of registered voters, not two-thirds of those who actually voted. "We counted on white voters' neglecting—in the great American tradition—to vote on an issue in which no personalities were involved," wrote White. His group now started a house-to-house campaign in the black Third and Fourth wards to get Negroes to pay poll taxes and register to vote. They had to space out their appearances at city hall, in case whites figured out that blacks were planning to vote. By the time city hall realized what was happening, it was too late to register large enough numbers of whites to override the Negro vote. James Weldon Johnson, the new NAACP field secretary, came to address the new Atlanta branch of the NAACP. He spoke to a packed house in the Negro movie theater in the Odd Fellows building of the need to wipe out race prejudice before hate destroyed both victims and perpetrators. Later he would say that "the race problem in the United States has resolved itself into a question of saving black men's bodies and white men's souls."

Walter White was called on to say a few words. Unprepared, he launched into a rousing, impassioned speech about the NAACP: "We have got to show these white people that we aren't going to stand being pushed around any longer. As Patrick Henry said, so must we say, 'Give me liberty, or give me death!' "

The audience loved these words, but White saw a look of absolute consternation and abject terror on the face of a well-known black school principal, who was doubtless realizing what would happen when word got back to the board of education. White's parents invited James Weldon Johnson to dinner after the meeting, and he paid particular attention to Walter. Walter soon got a letter from Johnson in New York inviting him to join the staff of the NAACP as assistant secretary. To accept the job meant considerable financial sacrifice. He would be paid $1,200 a year, far less than his pay at Standard Life Insurance. At the time, the NAACP had 8,490 members in seventy-six branches—ranging from 1 member in St. Joseph, Missouri, to 692 in Boston.

Florida-born James Weldon Johnson, an 1894 graduate of Atlanta University, came from Jacksonville's longtime colony of free Negroes. An educator, lawyer, diplomat, poet, and author, the first black national director of the NAACP was a Renaissance man and, in many minds, the first great black leader of the twentieth century. In the summer of 1891, as a college freshman, he taught children of former slaves in a rural Georgia district. Like W. E. B. Du Bois before him, Johnson called it the most meaningful experience of his life. He returned to Jacksonville and became principal of the city's largest black public school, where he was paid less than half of what a white would receive. In 1897 he became the first black admitted to the Florida bar exam since Reconstruction—one of the examiners walked out because he did not want a Negro admitted. Johnson worked on Teddy Roosevelt's 1904 presidential campaign, and Roosevelt appointed him U.S. consul at Puerto Cabello, Venezuela (1906–1908), and Nicaragua (1909–1913). In 1912 he was the composer, with his brother, J. Rosamond Johnson, of "Lift Ev'ry Voice and Sing," known as the "Negro National Anthem." He was also, that year, the anonymous author of the groundbreaking

The Autobiography of an Ex-Colored Man. He became a field secretary for the NAACP in 1916.

While Walter White was thinking about Johnson's offer, a "flying squadron" of patriotic young Negroes came to Atlanta to encourage Negro college men to volunteer for the new Negro officers' training camp, which the War Department, under pressure from the NAACP, was planning to open at Fort Des Moines, Iowa. For the first time in its history, the city of Atlanta permitted Negroes to use the city auditorium for a meeting to whip up patriotism. White, on the platform, was one of the first to volunteer. But he, along with two or three others with skin light enough to pass as whites, was rejected—ostensibly because German agents could be infiltrated among them and because "confusion" could occur in enforced segregation. (The same thing happened in World War II.) On January 31, 1918, White reported to the NAACP in New York City. Atlanta was still in the middle of the bond issue, but Negroes voted in sufficient numbers to defeat it. The result was the new David T. Howard High School, named after a philanthropic and greatly loved prosperous Negro, whose farm each summer was the scene of a magnificent barbecue. And the black grammar schools were patched up.

When 1917 tests of new black immigrants from Africa and the Caribbean showed that they were more literate than American blacks, this became an issue for black officers. The army assumed there were few educated young black Americans. And if they were found, the army definitely preferred that they be Southern—the army did not want Northern Negro officers giving any radical ideas to black troops. Joel Spingarn, the white chairman of the NAACP, responding to black protests against the lack of officers' training for blacks, convinced the War Department to establish the first training camp for black army officers at Fort Des Moines, an old cavalry camp, in May 1917. There were one thousand black officer candidates and instructors from Howard, Tuskegee, Harvard, and Yale. Two hundred fifty sergeants from the Buffalo Soldier regiments attended the camp, which also became a training center for black medical personnel. It was the first black officer candidate class in the history of the U.S. military. The commander of Fort Des Moines, Lieutenant Colonel Charles C. Ballou, was white. Many people thought the commander should be the highest-ranking black officer, West Point graduate Colonel Charles Young, but Young had been forced to retire so he could not become the first black general. In October the army commissioned 639 black officers. But new black officers who traveled in the South were in for a rude awakening. White Southerners hated black soldiers, but they *really* hated black officers. Whites in Vicksburg, Mississippi (according to the *New York Age*), announced "they would allow 'no nigger' to wear a uniform that a white man was bound to honor."

Both branches of the black Calhouns, North and South, had war brides and officer bridegrooms. In Texas, there were Errol and Lottie Horne. In Atlanta, Marie Graves married a young captain, Homer Nash of the Army Medical Corps. Dr. Homer Nash, who had graduated second in his class at black Meharry Medical College, opened his medical office on Auburn Avenue ("Sweet Auburn") in 1910. His certificate from the Georgia Board of Medical Examiners is dated July 25. He became a member of First Congregational Church in 1915. (He would eventually become chairman of the board of deacons.) He was at Fort Des Moines for ninety days of training as part of the medical group. He had been determined to marry Marie. It was a difficult courtship.

Here are two letters from Antoine Graves Sr. to Homer Nash at "Camp Freedom," Kansas, in November and December 1917:

11/17/17

Dear Sir,

I have not changed from my original proposition. I shall insist that before you marry Marie that you be settled down to business with a decent income . . . Respectfully, A. Graves

12/17/17

My Dear Sir,

I have given you all the best advice in my judgment, however if you can make it all right with Marie that will suit me. Personally I have no objection to you . . .

A marriage license at last: Homer Erwin Nash (COL) and Marie Antoinette Graves (COL) were married on February 6, 1918, at First Congregational Church by Dr. Proctor. ("COL" meant colored.) It was a big traditional wedding, like her sister Nellie's, awash in roses and bridesmaids, but Marie looked as if she had stepped out of the pages of *Vogue* with a daring, absolutely of the moment dress. Hinting at shorter hem lengths to come, the dress was longer in back and cut to the ankles in front, revealing beautiful satin shoes. The veil was a complicated but flattering arrangement of lace and tulle partly covering her pretty face. Captain Homer Nash, U.S. Army Medical Corps, looked very handsome in his uniform.

In 1918 Judge Graves, who had opened his first dental practice in Atlanta the year before, married a legendarily beautiful young woman called Pinkie Chaires, whose mother was a longtime clubwoman friend of his mother's. Judge's heart may not have been in it—they soon separated. By everyone's estimation, Pinkie was the most beautiful girl in Atlanta. There is a picture of her, taken some fifteen years or so later at a graduation, where her beauty just leaps out.

On January 15, 1919, Homer Nash wrote to his mother from the 366th Field Hospital in France:

My Dear Mother, I am wishing you all a happy new year and the very best of health. I am quite well and quite happy. I had a cablegram from my wife telling me of little Marie's arrival . . . I know that she is the most wonderful baby in the world. I just love her to death already. For

I am sure she is just as cute as she can be. God has been so good to us in so many ways. And I am always more than thankful to him for all his many blessings . . . Love to all, Your Son, Homer

On May 19, Valdosta, Georgia, in the southeastern part of the state near the Florida border, was the scene of one of the most unspeakable crimes ever committed anywhere outside Nazi Germany (which made a study of Southern racism). Mary Turner, aged twenty-one, was newly widowed and eight months pregnant. Her husband was one of thirteen men killed in a mob-driven manhunt to avenge the death of a white farmer. Mary Turner insisted that her husband never knew the farmer and threatened to have some of the men who killed her husband arrested. This was Turner's mistake. When she was lynched, they tied her ankles, hung her upside down from a tree, doused her in gasoline, and set her on fire. While she was still living one of the men split her abdomen with a pocket knife and crushed under his boot the nearly full-term infant who fell out. Although Walter White and others investigated and verified the full story of Mary Turner's death, and passed it on to the Northern media, only the black press mentioned her pregnancy. The racist Associated Press, which rejected black membership, wrote about people taking exception "to her remarks, as well as her attitude." (Attitude?) In April 1919 the NAACP published *Thirty Years of Lynching in the United States, 1889–1918*, listing the names, by state, of Negroes lynched.

CHAPTER SIX

North/1920s

HARLEM RENAISSANCE

SUDDENLY, IN the decade of the 1920s, the word "Harlem" began to have a specific meaning all around the world—which is why, for example, the Harlem Globetrotters did not call themselves the Chicago Globetrotters for their real hometown. The odd thing about the word "Harlem" was how *new* it was. Blacks had lived there only since 1911 or so, thanks to some brilliant real estate dealings by John "Jack" Nail and Henry C. Parker, the famous black realtors—one of whom (Nail) was James Weldon Johnson's brother-in-law. No one spoke of the Harlem Renaissance in the spring of 1921, but it was just about to happen. In June 1921 *The Crisis* published a poem, "The Negro Speaks of Rivers," by a Cleveland, Ohio, high school senior named Langston Hughes. When *Crisis* literary editor Jessie Fauset passed the poem to W. E. B. Du Bois, she wrote a note saying, "What colored person is there, do you suppose, in the United States who writes like that and is yet unknown to us?"

If the *literary* Harlem Renaissance began in June 1921 with a Cleveland teenager, the *theatrical* Renaissance began a month earlier on May 23, 1921, at the Cort Theater on West Sixty-Third Street in New York City with a revolutionary new musical revue called *Shuffle Along*. Both the teenage poet and the musical put Harlem on the map forever.

The title of the show may have been regressive, but the show itself was progressive in the extreme. Produced on a shoestring, *Shuffle Along* had a wonderful score written by two young men, Noble Sissle and Eubie Blake, both of whom had played with Jim Europe. Noble Sissle, aged twenty-two in 1921, had been through the war with Europe. There was even a Cleveland connection. Though born in Indianapolis, Sissle was raised in Cleveland. His mother was a teacher and his father a preacher who played the organ. Sissle had played the violin since childhood and had been a soloist in Cleveland's integrated Central High School chorus. Considered one of the best public high schools in the country, Central High School was actually more desegregated than integrated—out of 1,500 students, six were black. Sissle had a very successful high school career. Butler University, where Sissle wrote college songs and cheers, gave him a scholarship, but he transferred to DePauw, earning money for his education by organizing a small dance band. But he left college at nineteen to become part of the Royal Poinciana Sextet, the first black dance band to play full-time at the exclusive Palm Beach hotel of the same name. The country and the world were dance mad—and blacks were making the music. In 1916 the sextet played the Palace in New York City, the first black act to work the Palace wearing dinner jackets and without burnt cork. That year Sissle was invited to join Jim Europe's famous Society Orchestra. Eubie Blake was a member of the orchestra.

Baltimore-born Eubie Blake, the son of two former slaves, was a musical child prodigy who received music lessons from a neighbor. Blake's father, John Sumner Blake (note the middle name), had been secretly taught to read and write by the daughter of his owner. Eubie, the youngest of eleven children and the only one to reach adulthood, never knew his brothers and sisters. As a child, he sang on the street for change with three friends. Later, at age fifteen, he played in a sumptuous white brothel, having climbed out the window at home after his parents went to sleep. Blake composed his "Charleston Rag" the same year as Scott Joplin's "Maple Leaf Rag." In 1912 Blake began playing with Jim Europe's orchestra. When Europe and Sissle went to war, Blake put music to the words Sissle sent from France. After the war, Sissle and Blake became vaudeville's "Dixie Duo," playing the Palace in New York once again without blackface.

Two years after the victory parade, Sissle and Blake produced the show that not only revolutionized the American theater, but specifically marked the beginning of a decade of black achievement in the arts and entertainment. West Sixty-Third Street was actually closer to San Juan Hill, the prewar "Harlem," than to the Broadway theater district. Despite the title, *Shuffle Along* was a fast-paced semi-revue that became an overnight smash thanks to unanimous praise from the critics. It was *revolutionary* because the characters were not cartoons or stereotypes (except for one pair of blackface comics, without whom the audience probably would have walked out). Besides bringing blacks back to the Broadway stage after ten years of banishment, *Shuffle Along* made Broadway history by featuring a pretty ingenue and a handsome young leading man who sang a romantic—not a comic—love song, "Love Will Find a Way." Above all, audiences left the theater humming another song that became a sensation. The plot concerned an election in a small Southern town, where a chorus of pretty dancers sings the campaign song, "I'm Just Wild About Harry." Sissle and Blake had an overnight hit song as well as a hit show. *Shuffle Along* was also a fashion forerunner. The *Variety* critic commented:

> Broadway may not know it, but the fashion of wearing the feminine head with the bobbed hair effect has more fully invaded the high browns of the colored troupes than in the big musical shows. All the gals in "Shuffle Along" showed some sort of bobbed hair style, principals and chorus alike.

Younger black women performers were known to almost slavishly follow *Vogue.* Skirts were inching their way up and waists were uncorseted.

The show also fostered young black talent, such as Josephine Baker in the chorus. Other wonderful black performers got their start in subsequent productions of the show, which ran for over a year in New York and two years on the road—including London and Paris. Yes, there was ethnic comedy, but there was also sophisticated humor and costumes that were simple, flattering, and not grotesque. Everything was very modern. It was about the 1920s, not the 1850s. Heywood Broun of the *Evening World* loved the cast:

> We don't suppose the members of the cast and chorus actually pay for the privilege of appearing in the performance, but there is every indication that there is nothing in the world which they would rather do. They are all terribly glad to be up on the stage singing and dancing. Their training is professional, but the spirit is amateur. The combination is irresistible.

Actually, if they could have, the cast members would certainly have paid to perform on Broadway after having been barred from performing there for ten years. The show was such a success that there were special midnight performances on Wednesday nights so that other performers could see it. Sissle and Blake were invited to join ASCAP—a rarity for black composers. "I'm Just Wild About Harry" alone made Sissle and Blake well-off for the rest of their lives. Alan Dale, in the *New York American*, perceptively called the show "a semi-darky show that emulates the 'white' performance and—goes it one better." Of course, Sissle had to be a "semi-darky" to be the success that he became at Central High School. This was the secret of Noble Sissle's success. His was always "society orchestra" music—black musicians playing "white" music. Standing halfway between uptown and downtown, *Shuffle Along* was a fabulous hybrid.

All of this was *before* an enchanting young dancer-singer named Florence Mills stepped into the ingenue lead in September 1921, after the show opened. Unlike any black dancer-singer before her, Flo Mills was "Dresden china" who "turned into a stick of dynamite." The daughter of former Virginia slaves, Mills had been a six-year-old cakewalk champion. The wildly popular cakewalk, a high-stepping Reconstruction dance famously captured on film by Thomas Edison, was named for the fact that the best dancers won a cake. ("That takes the cake!") As an adult, Mills was still a waif, a genuine gamine, a magical dancer with a sweet, heartbreaking soprano voice. From 1921 until 1927 she made audiences and critics in America and Europe fall madly in love with her. Just as an army band made the French love black American music and musicians, *Shuffle Along* in London, with Flo Mills, made the British people fall in love with black American music and musicians. Noël Coward, icon of the 1920s, saw the show two or three times a week when he was in New York; the Prince of Wales, another 1920s icon, did the same when the show went to London. Dancers from the company taught the younger royals how to Charleston. The *Shuffle Along* company was the toast of London high society. Several novelists of the period refer to it. (In the movie *Gosford Park*, an ironic and constantly on the move footman, played by the inimitable Richard E. Grant, suddenly says, apropos of the bossy butler, "Shuffle along everybody, here he comes." This is a tip of the hat by writer Julian Fellowes to what was of the moment in popular culture among the upper classes and their betters belowstairs.) *Shuffle Along* started a decade-long series of copycat musicals that at least put a lot of talented black performers to work.

Florence Mills starred in several hit shows and became an international star, featured in *Vogue* and *Vanity Fair* and photographed by Edward Steichen. In 1923 she was a guest star in *The Greenwich Village Follies*—the first black female star to appear in a white revue. In 1924 she turned down an offer from Ziegfeld, but starred in *Dixie to Broadway* and became the first black star to headline at the Palace. In 1925 she starred in another Sissle and Blake hit, *Chocolate Dandies*, and in *Blackbirds* of 1926, which the Prince of Wales claimed to have seen eleven times and which made her a superstar. It was her last show. After taking it to London and Paris, she died on November 1, 1927, at age thirty-two, in New York of what was described as complications from appendicitis. Thousands attended her funeral, including Noël Coward, and a flock of blackbirds was released over her grave. Her signature song from her last show was "I'm a Little Blackbird Looking for a Bluebird." When she came onstage singing it in her little runaway newsboy costume with her slim little legs and a bundle on a stick, there was rarely a dry eye in the house. Sissle and lyricist Andy Razaf wrote a tenderly beautiful ballad, "Memories of You," in tribute to Florence Mills.

While Edwin Horne was the black Calhoun bon vivant in New York who would have seen *Shuffle Along* more than once, Cora Horne, miles away from Broadway, was in the real world of Brooklyn. Working with the organization since its beginning in 1917, Cora had been named a director of the national Big Brothers and Big Sisters Federation. She was a founder and chairperson of the Black Big Sisters of Brooklyn, which, by 1923, had fifty Big Sisters. Edwin and Cora were on separate tracks. At no point now did their lives interconnect. They were not even going in the same direction.

To say the least, baby Lena Horne, who would be called "another Florence Mills," came from a dysfunctional family. In a way, it was dysfunctional because it was Northern. Perhaps there were too many choices in the North. In the North, unlike the South, her father could *choose* to live on the edges of the "rackets" and her mother could *choose* to be an actress. If Teddy Horne had grown up in Atlanta there would have been no *choice* except to be a doctor, lawyer, small businessman, or postal employee (a very good black middle-class job). And Edna Scottron would have had no *choice* except to be a housewife, teacher, librarian, or social worker. The dysfunction started before Teddy and Edna. It started when Edwin, Lena's grandfather, *chose* to have an affair with a white magazine editor who looked like Cora when she was twenty-two. And Cora, who basically divorced Edwin without bothering the state of New York or arguing over a stick of furniture, *chose* not to forgive him. She had several good reasons not to forgive. Ingratitude, for example, though Cora would never admit this to herself. She had married Edwin when he was mourning two wives and as many babies and had presented him with four healthy sons. They had been married for twenty-five years and she had spent many of those years alone in Brooklyn with the boys, while he had enjoyed the nightlife of Manhattan as a Tammany man. From Edwin's point of view, maybe Cora *was* a bit of a shrew. Her anger made her sharp with everyone, especially Edwin. It was her tone—her icy, modulated sarcasm. Cora took secret pride in never raising her voice. At the same time she could reduce healthy young males to tears. Lena never forgot seeing a teenage Burke, Cora's youngest son, standing outside his mother's closed door in utter dejection, weeping after a tongue-lashing.

Edwin, on the other hand, was a boulevardier. It was not necessarily Edwin's fault that in 1912, when he was winning elections for Tammany, he was so incredibly attractive to women, with his silvery hair, sad blue eyes, old-fashioned manners, and love of music and poetry. Blacks would always be locked out of much of Northern life because they were Negroes—but they still lived in the midst of a broader, more seductive world of choices than their Southern cousins.

Lena, who began to accompany Cora to meetings almost as soon as she could walk, was always a solemn baby—as if she understood that she had been orphaned by two living parents. This is clearly seen in the picture taken in the NAACP office the day she met James Weldon Johnson. She is wary—but also brave and poised. Toddler Lena apparently managed to keep her aplomb at Cora's various meetings. She learned her meeting manners early: shake hands, look people in the eye, sit still, and do not speak unless spoken to. Cora loved Lena dearly, but she believed that her own role in life was to be a teacher—even to her only grandchild.

Cora had retired from the marital bedroom around 1912 or 1913—over the *Vogue* editor, one presumes. She retired from the kitchen circa 1914, when Burke went into high school, and immediately threw herself into social work, war work for the YWCA, and Republican women's circles. Blacks in the North still had a home in the GOP. When the Nineteenth Amendment finally gave Cora the vote, she chose the straight Republican ticket, ignoring the siren song of Edwin's Tammany Hall. Meanwhile, she was the mayor's appointee to the Brooklyn victory committee, secretary of the Brooklyn Urban League Board, president of the Big Sisters Club, vice president of the Brooklyn Charity Club, chairman of the big sister department of the National Association of Colored Women, a director of the Katy Ferguson Home (the only home for unwed black mothers in America), a director of the Big Brothers and Big Sisters Federation, a member of the International Council of Women of the Darker Races, statistician of the Greater New York Federation of Churches (for social workers), and editor in chief of the New York State Federation monthly. And these were the quiet years. She did not get really busy until 1923.

It is hard to imagine Cora—such a delicate, small-boned woman—with enough stamina for the life she had chosen, but apparently she was a dynamo. Paul Robeson said she was known as the "Tiny Terror." This Carrie Nation of Harlem truancy would swoop down on street-corner boys, demanding to know why they were not in school. It would be easy to believe that all her energy and stamina came from anger—a powerful source of adrenaline. Cora had decided to hold on to her anger forever, but did not show it in her public smile. She had her picture taken in Washington as part of a group of Big Brother and Big Sister directors visiting President Harding. (When asked about his rumored black ancestry, Harding had memorably replied, "How should I know? Maybe somebody jumped the fence.") Cora wore her steel spectacles all the time now. She was vain only about her small feet and always wore beautiful shoes; otherwise she had no interest in clothes.

After her son Errol died, she wore only black. When she came home from her busy day, she went directly to her chaise longue and left it only for her bed. Burke brought tea and toast on a tray, while Lena lay on the floor looking at picture books. Evenings before bed were light reading times for both Cora and Lena. Lena always remembered that it took her grandmother forever to read *The Forsyte Saga* because she read it before bed—otherwise she read only her committee paperwork. One evening Lena knew she herself could read when she was lying on the floor in Cora's room looking at *Little Orphan Annie* in the funny papers and read the word "asylum."

Cora had planned Act III of her life. Act I had been raising her boys. Act II was living in sorrow, over Errol's death and Edwin's betrayal. And Act III was discovering her talents for organization and activism and putting them to work for the greater good. Act III was going to be *her* time. The nest was essentially empty. Errol was gone. Teddy was transitory. And Frank had just followed his namesake uncle into his Chicago ophthalmology practice, where he planned to stay at least two years. Burke would soon be ready for City College. Cora certainly had not planned on dealing with a baby. So Lena, pretty baby that she was, was never a baby to be loved and adored—she was more like a favorite pupil. It was Edwin who gave all the love that Lena's mother, father, and grandmother seemed unable to give. It turned out that Grandfather Edwin was the warm, maternal figure in Lena's life. She thought of him later as "a mother and father rolled into one."

Thanks to Tammany, Edwin had a pension and all sorts of fire department perks. He had security for himself and his family, but he was disillusioned and bitter. He had wound up a clubhouse pol. Politics had betrayed him at every turn—but it had also rewarded him. He should not have expected anything better from Tammany. He was tired of the battle—happy for a gentle life with his little granddaughter. He loved strolling around Bushwick with Lena or taking her to the botanical gardens.

By the time Lena was born, the house still belonged to one family—but it was definitely divided. The ground floor, kitchen, and third-floor former marital bedroom belonged to Edwin; Cora had the entire second floor front and back parlors, one of which Lena slept in; Burke was on the top floor now that Ted and Edna had moved out. Burke was teasing and sweet, but obviously had little time for Lena. Burke moved between his parents, taking trays to Cora, who ate like a bird, while patronizing the German delicatessen on Bushwick Avenue for himself, Edwin, and Lena, who was being taught to enjoy "bachelor" food. But now Edwin had to be a grandfather-grandmother-father-mother to little Lena, and he made her oatmeal religiously every morning. Beyond "Good morning, Mrs. Horne" and "Good morning, Mr. Horne," Cora and Edwin still did not speak. Longer communications came from notes via Burke.

Lena's particular block on Chauncey Street had been desegregated by the Hornes—not that the neighborhood cared. There were clusters of middle-class black families in Brooklyn on what was basically the border of Bushwick and Stuyvesant Heights (now Bedford-Stuyvesant). Typically, the black families lived on the economic high end of their streets. The Hornes lived in one of four identical single-family brownstone row houses, built in the 1890s, each with an iron fence and a stoop. Across the street were old-style wooden tenement apartments, populated mostly by Irish. In winter the brownstones looked forlorn next to an Irish-owned farm on one side and a Swedish-owned livery stable cum garage on the other. Boys Welcome Hall, a gymnasium on the corner, was where the Horne brothers grew up playing basketball. But Lena had no playmates: she could not play with the farmer's children, because they were boys; and she could not play with the livery stable children, because Cora feared dirt and automobile oil—not to mention horse manure. As for the Irish across the street in the tenement apartments—Cora said they "did not speak well." One little boy from the Chauncey Street tenement, a year older than Lena, grew up to be Jackie Gleason. Lena certainly would not have been allowed to know him. With the terrible elitism of the Talented Tenth, and the old Southern Negro way of looking down on poor whites, Cora was almost as prejudiced as the Southerners in her worst nightmare.

Edwin might be the father-mother figure, but evenings before bed-time always belonged to Cora, who was moving spiritually from Ethical Culture to Bahá'í. Considered by some to be a non-Christian cult, Bahá'í advocated racial equality and held integrated meetings throughout the United States. Lena went to Bahá'í meetings with Cora. Cora was a serious spiritual pilgrim. Although she had given up Catholicism for Ethical Culture, she still heard Lena's Hail Marys and Catholic prayers nightly. All of Cora's children had been baptized and raised as Catholics. As a pedagogue, she probably admired the firm but gentle discipline and strong sense of morality that nuns tried to instill in even the youngest child.

Lena had been baptized at Holy Rosary Church on Chauncey Street, but Cora sent her to the Brooklyn Ethical Culture nursery school. Either Edwin or Burke took Lena to nursery school and picked her up. One of her classmates was little Betty Comden of future Broadway fame in the duo Comden and Green. There was a lost photograph of Lena and Betty side by side. Lena was wearing a paper crown and grinning happily. Allowed to play at last! But enough of liberalism—Cora sent Lena to kindergarten at St. Peter Claver School. Father Bernard J. Quinn was the white pastor of St. Peter Claver, a pioneer black Catholic ministry in Brooklyn. Father Quinn built a parish center so that neighborhood people could have a place to showcase their talents. Father Paul Jervis, pastor of St. Martin of Tours parish in Bedford-Stuyvesant and author of *Quintessential Priest: The Life of Father Bernard J. Quinn*, wrote that young Lena first performed in front of an audience at St. Peter Claver: "She is remembered as a child singing in the children's choir of St. Peter Claver Church, then making her debut as a fledgling singer on the basement stage." For his work among black Catholics, Father Quinn is being considered for sainthood in the Roman Catholic Church.

Lena wore a key around her neck and had a Hershey bar and an apple waiting for her on the kitchen table after school. She also had many dolls, all gifts from her father, needing her attention. No one thought anything of leaving an obedient child of six or seven at home alone in the afternoon for an hour or so. In nice weather, she always played in the garden in the back under the cherry tree. Soon Burke would appear and then disappear. More often than not, Edwin met her at school and they would walk hand in hand to Bushwick Avenue for some nice delicatessen for supper. Edwin smoked slim aromatic cigars, very elegant in photographs. From time to time an expensive doll or a rabbit fur coat would arrive for Lena from Teddy. Once or twice a year Ted himself might appear out of the blue. Lena was happy at home on Chauncey Street with Granddad and Grandmother. Still, she kissed the small photograph of her mother, Edna, every night.

Twice, Cora allowed Lena to visit her mother. Both visits were disasters. The first involved taking Lena onstage, and the second, in the South, involved fleeing the site of a lynching that was about to happen and that Lena had nightmares of long after.

Teddy, meanwhile, was on the West Coast having a fabulous time. He met up with his cousin Frank Smith Jr., who was living in Los Angeles and working as a photographer. When Teddy died he left a trunkful of photographs and scrapbooks. There were many pictures taken by Frank Smith Jr.—mostly of fun times at the beach with pretty girls and boxer Joe "Baby" Gans, the lightweight champion of the world. The National Negro Baseball League was founded in 1920—Ted would have been very happy. He also must have been pleased to see the 1923 birth of the Rens, the first full-salaried black professional basketball team, named for Harlem's Renaissance Ballroom, where they played. Originally from Brooklyn, and direct heirs of Teddy's Smart Set teams, the Rens became the iconic black basketball team—ahead of the Harlem Globetrotters. Teddy Horne lived the "sporting life" to the max. The photos with Irene, who became his second wife, say everything about his pose as a dandy and a lothario. In reality, he was more interested in talking than acting. He was about as unromantic and unsentimental as a person could be, but he was superconfident and certainly pleased with himself. He always looked younger than his age and never allowed himself to be bored. How nice for him that his semi-illegal activities would involve spending all his time at sporting events—with hundred-dollar ringside seats on July 4, 1923, at the Jack Dempsey–Tommy Gibbons fight in Montana, for example. He kept a wonderful record of his 1920s with his collection of speakeasy cards. He belonged to the "Exclusive Social Literary Club" (Detroit), "Citizen's Progressive Club" (Pittsburgh), and "Pullman Athletic Club" (Chicago). My personal favorite among Teddy's speakeasy cards was the "certificate of membership" issued to "Mr. Teddy Horne" in October 1924 to the Fifty Club (city unknown) with the expiration date listed as "never."

In 1922 Cora went to Washington for the meeting of the International Council of Women of the Darker Races. But 1923 and 1924 were Cora's busy years. In 1923 the National Association of Colored Women selected her to represent New York, among other prominent women. As usual, she was also a director of the Big Brothers and Big Sisters Federation, which had black as well as Jewish Big Brothers and Big Sisters. According to George L. Beiswinger's *One to One: The Story of the Big Brothers/Big Sisters Movement in America*:

> Mrs. Edwin F. Horne, an Urban League leader . . . was a director of the Big Brother and Big Sister Federation of 1923. She was an authority on the special problems encountered in black Big Sisters work, which was just getting underway during the early 1920s.

Cora also became a Republican Party activist. During the 1924 Calvin Coolidge campaign she was a national organizer and secretary of the eastern division of the National Republican Women's Auxiliary.

This was a big deal for a black woman. The black press sought her out. From the national edition of the *Chicago Defender*, October 31, 1925:

> Mrs. Cora Calhoun Horne, corresponding secretary of the eastern division of the National Republican Women's auxiliary, Y.W.C.A. and Red Cross worker, statistician, editor and social organizer, is one of Brooklyn's busiest figures. During the last presidential campaign she was on the national speakers bureau of the Republican party.

The 1924 Democratic National Convention, held in New York City, was integrated, but the Republican National Convention, held in Cleveland, was segregated. Besides failing to integrate its national meeting, Cora's party did nothing about the Immigration Act of 1924, which severely restricted the number of "Negroes of African descent" allowed to enter the United States. It was typical of American racial paranoia that just when the United States wanted to reject "Negroes of African descent" the rest of the civilized world was clamoring to welcome them. It started with the war—and the capture of West African art from the former German colonies. Always receptive to the "exotic," Paris had responded to the exhibit of African art as it had responded to the Russian ballet before the war—with wild enthusiasm. Cubism was born when Picasso changed the faces of *Les Demoiselles d'Avignon* to look like African masks. The French love affair with black Americans, which began in World War I with the celebrated valor of Edwin's "Harlem Hellfighters," continued throughout the 1920s. This time, instead of the 369th Regiment, it was Josephine Baker, who had started out in the chorus of *Shuffle Along*.

The nonmusical theater was also interested in black stories. Eugene O'Neill's *The Emperor Jones*, starring the great black actor Charles Gilpin, opened in November 1920 at the Provincetown Playhouse in Greenwich Village. It moved uptown in January 1921 and Gilpin received a Drama League Award. O'Neill was at his most controversial in 1924. *All God's*

Chillun Got Wings starred Paul Robeson as an educated black man and Mary Blair (Mrs. Edmund Wilson) as his abusive white wife. When it was learned that the drama required that Blair kiss Robeson's hand, there were editorial demands that the play be banned. The play finally opened to decidedly mixed reviews—but thanks to the controversy, both young O'Neill and young Robeson were no longer unknowns. (Robeson was already known by fans of college football as a "Walter Camp all-American" player, one of the best in the country.) And the hottest ticket on Broadway for 1920 was a black play, *Miss Lulu Bett*, from the novel by Zona Gale, which became a Broadway smash with white actors in blackface and starred the extraordinary white actor Henry Hull as a totally believable black man.

Prohibition was a bad thing for America, but very good for Harlem. During Prohibition, Harlem was as close to Paris as America got. "Gentleman" Jimmy Walker, the mayor of New York City, a charming rogue, put Harlem after dark at the top of the VIP tourist list. The Cotton Club was used to royalty, who got the same chop suey as everybody else. The married mayor had a girlfriend in the *Follies*—everybody knew, nobody cared. Gentleman Jimmy was up to his neck in Tammany shenanigans—nobody batted an eye. He was the right man for the times, and he certainly knew nightclubs, having spent almost every night of his mayoralty in them. Harlem had everything a tourist with plenty of money and a thirst for illegal pleasures could desire. As long as he stuck to the expensive places, he would be more or less protected. The Cotton Club was, of course, the jewel in the crown of New York's up-all-night life. After the theater, rich tourists and celebrities went to the midnight show to have a chop suey supper and hopefully see a gangster. The Cotton Club, big and garish, put on a swinging black show for whites only in the midst of a black neighborhood. The shows always had famous bands, terrific singers and dancers, comedians, songs from Tin Pan Alley greats, and beautiful girls in every color except very dark. They worked three shows a night. Everyone who was anyone went to the Cotton Club. An exception to the no-blacks rule was always made for certain black celebrities or gangsters—certain Harlem numbers kings, for example. They were always seated near the kitchen. Very near the Cotton Club there were other popular nightclubs where blacks and whites actually mingled—there were even some clubs that would not admit whites. But all night, everywhere along Harlem's broad Parisian boulevards, there was laughter and music and traffic that stilled only toward dawn.

Harlem did have a daytime life, however; twenty-five-year-old Dr. Frank Smith Horne, a Harlem ophthalmologist, could attest to that. Frank, a graduate of Boys High School, and a winner of letters in track and field at City College, was known as the smartest Horne brother, the intellectual. He had practiced ophthalmology for two years with his uncle in Chicago before returning to New York in 1923 to open his Harlem practice. Frank and his cousin Dr. Antoine "Judge" Graves Jr. opened practices in Harlem at more or less the same time. Neither young doctor was doing what he really wanted to do. The cousins both tolerated their day jobs. Frank wrote poetry and essays on the side while being an eye doctor; and Judge, the violinist cheered by Atlanta's white critics, was a dentist. As young middle-class black men, they were both lucky to have work that brought them security. Frank threw himself into extracurricular activities. As a joiner, he was not that unhappy to be a second-tier, part-time, younger member of the Harlem Renaissance. But poor Judge threw himself into alcohol and a sad private life.

In 1924 there were basically only two outlets for young black writers: the NAACP's *Crisis* and the Urban League's *Opportunity*. That year *Opportunity* published Frank's review of a black poetry anthology. He titled the review "A Call to Makers of Black Verse":

> Your task is definite, grand, and fine. You are to sing the attributes of a soul. Be superbly conscious of the many tributaries to our pulsing stream of life. You must articulate what the hidden sting of the slaver's

lash leaves reverberating in its train—the subtle hates, the burnt desires, sudden hopes, and dark despairs . . . Sing, O black poets, for song is all we have!

In 1925 Frank won poetry prizes given by both *Opportunity* and *Crisis*. Under a pseudonym he submitted *Letters Found Near a Suicide*, a collection of eleven poems, to *The Crisis* for the Amy Spingarn poetry award. It won the second prize (thirty dollars). First prize was won by Langston Hughes—the Cleveland teenager had become a grown-up New Yorker. Frank's long poem "Letters Found Near a Suicide" is unique in New Negro poetry—these are intimate, semi-mysterious farewells to young college friends without a single reference to race. Frank may have had other things on his mind. Sometime after college, Frank, the college runner, contracted polio. He recovered, except for one leg. He walked with a cane and obviously would never run again. One of the "Suicide" notes concerned a college runner:

At your final drive
Through the finish line
Did not my shout
Tell of the
Triumphant ecstasy
of victory . . . ?
Live
As I have taught you
To run, Boy—
It's a short dash . . .

But Frank was a popular member of Harlem's young intelligentsia, with cosmopolitan friendships and many girlfriends. Women loved his soft voice and gentle manner. Too many Harlem Renaissance writers were "befriended" by creepy white patrons. Frank was never in danger.

As a part-time, second-echelon Renaissance poet with a bachelor of science degree, he would have little or no chance for sponsors. But the ophthalmologist by day was a founding member of the KRIGWA Little Theatre Movement, the serious Harlem amateur dramatics club, and wrote book reviews for *Opportunity*. He got into big trouble, however, when he panned Walter White's second novel. According to David Levering Lewis' wonderful *When Harlem Was in Vogue*, "In substance, the NAACP demanded an apology from the Urban League."

Unlike the Cotton Club clientele, Frank actually belonged to the part of Harlem after dark that *did* mingle with whites. Frank's Harlem nightlife had its own white tourists—artists and intelligentsia bringing their own motives and baggage. Frank was certainly a popular second-tier figure. He won the *Opportunity* prize for criticism and *Opportunity* literary prizes in 1924, 1925, 1926, 1927, and 1932. Although Walter White never forgave Frank for his withering review of White's novel, Frank also won *Crisis* literary prizes in 1925, 1926, and 1928. Critic Ronald Primeau divided Frank's poetry into three types: "quest," meaning athletics; black heritage; and Christianity, using Christian images to connect black religion, black spirituality, and black militancy. Many of Frank's poems are included in anthologies, and two were translated for inclusion in a 1929 German anthology.

But Frank was about to experience culture shock when he agreed to become acting dean of students at Fort Valley High and Industrial School (later Fort Valley State University) in Georgia. He actually became an instructor, dean, acting president, and track coach—despite the polio.

In the fall of 1924 Cora Horne was seldom at home; she was busy with her first election year. Burke and Edwin, more than ever, were Lena's companions and babysitters. Edwin was lonely Lena's beau ideal. She later said that he gave her "companionship on a grave and adult level." They took walks all over Brooklyn. They went to the museum, to Prospect Park, and to the public library to borrow books. And they went across the bridge. Edwin took Lena to see Marilyn Miller in *Peter Pan*. She was more excited by having traveled so far with her grandfather than she was by the show.

Lena had seen her mother twice in four years. One afternoon that busy election season, Edna essentially "kidnapped" Lena—snatching her via a cousin from the Chauncey Street garden. As usual, Lena had been playing after school under the cherry tree in the back garden with her dolls, when an unknown white woman appeared to say that she was a friend of Lena's mother and that Edna was sick and wanted to see Lena. The woman was actually one of Edna's actress cousins who lived in Chelsea and passed as white. The mother-daughter reunion was tearful. Here was the mother whom Lena had longed for, whose picture she had kissed every night. Lena did not really understand what Edna meant when she told her that Teddy planned to "kidnap" her. Actually, it was Edna who did the "kidnapping." Teddy clearly had absolutely no interest in living with his seven-year-old offspring.

Whatever the pretense, Edna did a terribly cruel thing. She took Lena away from the only home she had ever known and took her South, where she had never been, to leave her with sometimes brutal strangers in places like Miami and Atlanta—so near and yet so far from her second cousins, whom Edna refused to see because they were Cora's relations. Lena should have been adored and doted on, the family pet. Instead, she was pulled here and there, North and South, mostly for spite, in the private war between Edna and Cora. In all things, Edna and Cora were sworn enemies. Life with Edna, the original drama queen, was all emotion. Life with Cora was all reason, discipline, and logic. Despite the fact that Cora was austere and lacking in affection, Lena loved her grandmother. She felt safe with Cora, who was there every night for bedtime prayers. Cora did not believe that children should be free to find God on their own. She thought they should be *given* God—and then be free to reject the whole concept. Cora, patient and steady as a rock, never raised her voice to Lena. But Edna was unconditionally loved, despite "kidnapping" hysteria, abandonment, and sadistic beatings, because Lena had dreamed about her and longed to see her for such a long time. Edna had never been a *person* to Lena; she was the small picture that Lena kissed every night. Edna appeared to love her daughter extravagantly—unless she needed to strike out at her and punish her for being born. What does an actress do with a child? Two of Edna's cousins were currently acting and passing as white. Edna knew it would be impossible to pass with little Lena. Teddy and Lena, both copper-colored, were the darkest members of the Horne family.

So Lena was periodically returned to Brooklyn whenever she interfered with Edna's itinerant passing. Otherwise, she boarded with strangers whose kindness and hospitality usually rose in inverse ratio to their bank accounts. Young as she was, Lena understood that Chauncey Street was her only home. That wandering with Edna was not home. Despite that sense of *home*, however, Lena did not believe that the Chauncey Street household was ever a real family unit. How could it be when Cora refused to speak to Edwin? Lena was raised with no other children except whomever she ran into in nursery school and kindergarten. In the 1920s Burke, the only brother still at home when Lena's parents ran off, was more like a big brother than an uncle to Lena. Lena did not have a real family, but at least she had a *home*. The house on Chauncey Street was a beacon for Lena for the first quarter of her life. She was naturally a stranger in the white world—but also a stranger in the world that most Negroes inhabited. She never stayed long enough in either world to put down roots. The house on Chauncey Street represented roots. It told her who she was—Lena Horne of Chauncey Street.

CHAPTER SEVEN

South/1920s

TERROR

THE NEW decade opened with the masks of comedy and tragedy. The birth of Catherine Graves Nash, future family historian of the black Calhouns, on May 12, 1920, was a delight to her family. Tragedy came three months later, on August 13, when Catherine's "big" sister, Marie, aged one year and eight months, was pronounced dead of what was called "Cholera *infantum.*" The medical report stated that she was "last attended by doctor 8/10/20" and "last seen alive on 8/13." Adored and adorable baby Marie, the image of her pretty, big-eyed, dimpled mother, was doted on by all—especially her father. Homer Nash had written to his mother that he adored the baby sight unseen. Baby Marie was possibly the victim of contaminated drinking water in Atlanta in August. What her namesake mother might have been feeling! All the guilt, horror, and despair, plus a needy three-month-old. Homer, her doctor husband, could not give his wife a sedative because she was nursing. But she knew if she gave in to grief she might never get out of it. It was not Catherine's fault that she came along after everybody's little angel. As is typical with a firstborn, there were many pictures of baby Marie: with her mother and grandmother, at baby birthday parties, sitting in her father's shiny new automobile. There seem to be *far* fewer pictures of Catherine than Marie.

The decade began with joy and heartbreak—and life went on. Middle-class black Atlanta was optimistic about the future. There was no Harlem Renaissance in Atlanta, but there was a flourishing middle-class culture of self-improvement. Middle-class self-improvement in the South was very different from the Northern variety. One has only to compare the scope and political heft of Cora Horne's "club" life (granted, an extreme case) with that of Katie Webb Graves and her daughter Marie Graves Nash. If Cora had lived in Atlanta and pursued her normal interests, she might have been lynched. Atlanta self-improvement was decidedly safe and sane.

"Self-improvement" was, of course, part of the Talented Tenth credo—but it was also a big 1920s fad. "Every day, in every way, I'm getting better and better," said Émile Coué, an early pop psychology guru. Katie and Marie were part of an Atlanta Chautauqua Circle in 1926 and 1927. A history of Chautauqua reads:

> The Chautauqua Literary and Scientific Circle (CLSC) was started in 1878 to provide those who could not afford the time or money to attend college the opportunity of acquiring the skills and essential knowledge of a College education. The four-year correspondence course was one of the first attempts at distance learning . . . the CLSC program was intended to show people how best to use their leisure time and avoid the growing availability of idle pastimes, such as drinking, gambling, dancing and theater-going, that posed a threat both to good morals and to good health.

The Chautauqua founders were Methodists.

In *A Handbook of Information for Negroes* someone, possibly Katie or Marie, had written in pencil, "Our Doubts are traitors." The motto of their Chautauqua Circle, which met once a month from four to six P.M. at the home of a member, was "Keep moving: A standing pool becomes stagnant." The Circle colors were green and white, and the Circle flower was the carnation. Every meeting opened with the Lord's Prayer.

On "February 17," no year given, the topic for discussion was "Birds," followed by a vocal solo "Hark, Hark the Lark" and a "Schubert Discussion, led by Mrs. Graves." Similarly, the month before, the subject had been "Nature" and the vocal solo was Beethoven's "The Glory of God in Nature." In June (again no year) Katie Webb Graves was hostess and the subject was "Books." In October, the vocal solo was "'The Negro National Anthem,' sung by Mrs. Cater" and the subject was "Travel"—Mrs. Johnson discussed "My Trip to Europe." In a change of pace, in November "Mesdames Thomas, Green, Lawless and Nash" gave a "Tacky and Paper Bag Party for Our Husbands." In December, of course, the meeting subject was "Christmas," and "Marie gave a reading of Paul Laurence Dunbar's 'Christmas in the Heart.'" And so on. The directory of Circle members listed fifteen regular members and six "Honorary"—including Mrs. Antoine Graves at 522 Auburn Avenue and her daughter Mrs. Homer E. Nash at 982 Simpson Street NW. Women of Atlanta's black middle class handled the indignities of Jim Crow with as much personal dignity as possible. Otherwise, they lived in their own secure world in which there were no white people and where other, poorer black people worked for them.

For most blacks, of course, the South was still a fearsome place. During a thirty-year period, between 1890 and 1920, more than two million Negroes migrated north. In 1920 there were sixty-one lynchings—reason enough for emigration. In 1920, 85 percent of all Negro pupils in the South were enrolled only through fourth grade, and 26.3 percent of Southern Negroes were illiterate—compared with 5 percent of Southern whites and 8 percent of Northern Negroes. That year Georgia was the scene of a secret meeting between black back-to-Africa proponent Marcus Garvey and the imperial wizard of the Ku Klux Klan. Garvey, who hated middle-class blacks, considered the NAACP to be his archenemy. The NAACP countered that Garvey, despite his vaunted concern with the African diaspora, did not care about Haiti, for example, while the NAACP did. Du Bois won the 1920 Spingarn Medal for founding and calling together the first Pan-African Congress.

In September 1922 Antoine Graves Jr. was commissioned a first lieutenant in the Dental Officers' Reserve Corps of the U.S. Army. Judge was now practicing dentistry in Atlanta—in suite 207 of the Odd Fellows Auditorium, the primary black office building. That Christmas, his card, featuring snow and evergreens and a wintry village, read, "May good cheer be with you this Christmas Day and happiness attend you through the New Year. Dr. Antoine Graves." His wife's name was not on the card. Judge and Pinkie Chaires (considered the most beautiful girl in Atlanta) had been married in 1917. They had no children. The marriage ended in 1921 or 1922 and Judge left Atlanta for New York in 1923. (Without any corroboration whatsoever, I am convinced that Judge was gay and could not deal with that in his hometown.) Shortly after he moved to New York, he sent a sad Father's Day greeting to Antoine Sr.: "I thank you for the good example you have always set before your children and wish that I had proved more worthy of it. Judge."

Six months later, he wired holiday greetings to his parents: "Merry Christmas couldn't make it love to Browns and Nashes. Judge." The wires to his parents and messages to his sisters Marie Nash and Nellie Brown (his musical accompanist) are so sad. In family photographs of handsome Judge he never smiles. Poor Judge, with so much talent, felt so unworthy, insecure, and full of self-hatred. It is no wonder that he had to get out of Atlanta. Getting away from the prying eyes of Atlanta was a good idea in one way and a bad idea in another. In Atlanta, someone might have been able to stop him from drinking himself to death.

Meanwhile, the Graves-Nash clan continued to seize every opportunity for education and self-improvement. In May 1926 Catherine Graves Nash received her kindergarten teaching certificate. Two years later Catherine's aunt Kate Graves earned her certificate from the Atlanta

University School of Social Work with "very satisfactory" marks in human behavior, social evaluation, social psychology, community organization, home hygiene, social casework, and social hygiene. In 1928 young Catherine and her aunt Kate Graves visited their second and third cousins Frank Horne and his niece, Lena Horne, in Fort Valley—halfway between Atlanta and Macon. They traveled by Jim Crow train, sitting in the blacks-only car—this was safer than going by automobile.

When Lena and her mother went South together for the first time, they went by train, and Edna was sick and mostly asleep the entire trip. Thanks to Woodrow Wilson's resegregation of Washington some dozen years earlier, the South began in the nation's capital, when suddenly all the white people in the car disappeared and were replaced with black people. But something quite wonderful happened. If her uncle Frank and W. E. B. Du Bois had "learned" about being black because of Southern white horror, Lena learned about being black from her introduction to Jim Crow—and the kindness of black people. The new passengers, uniformly dark, immediately started caring for Edna and treating Lena as one of their own, sharing their food and letting her play with their children.

This was seven-year-old Lena's first train trip. When they arrived at their destination, Miami, where Edna was scheduled to appear in Negro-only tent shows of popular dramas, Lena received the first beating of her life—the first of the many she would receive in the South. Edna was still so sick that she needed nursing care. The nurse took it upon herself to beat Lena for making noise. Lena and Edna lived in a three-room frame house, and Lena went to a one-room five-grade schoolhouse, where she was immediately put ahead a grade. Her schoolmates hated her. Fortunately, they were in Miami only a few months when Edna deposited Lena with a nice family in Jacksonville. Birthplace of James Weldon Johnson, Jacksonville had a stable black middle-class community that had existed since before the Civil War. The local blacks had, in fact, invented the famous cakewalk dance. There,

Lena and her hosts were on their way to see another tent show when they nearly collided with a lynching. A black man stopped them on the road. "There's going to be a lynching," he shouted. "Turn around!" Lena did not know what a "lynching" was, but she never forgot the atmosphere in the suddenly speeding automobile. Her nightmares began that night, and Lena believed she would have them forever.

After Jacksonville came a short period in Birmingham, as Edna followed the tent show circuit and Lena got scraps of education. It was an awful childhood—a time of terrible loneliness and self-protectiveness, broken occasionally by the hope that somehow she might be allowed to settle down in one place permanently.

There was the doctor's house in southern Ohio, where Lena had her own room for the first time since Brooklyn. She read late into the night to stave off nightmares. The family's maiden aunt had the room next to Lena's and comforted her when she cried in the night. Lena next lived with two old ladies in Macon, a mother in her nineties and a daughter in her seventies, whom Lena actually loved. The daughter worked in what she called the "white folks' kitchen" and brought home treats. The mother, who was thin and spry, dipped snuff, told Bible stories, and made Christmas fruitcakes to sell. Lena was allowed to help. When Lena got rickets, the mother's home remedies eased the terrible pain and her Bible stories helped her sleep. Despite the rickets, Lena loved Macon and loved her school—bigger and better than the black school in Miami. She became the teacher's pet and, once more, was hated by the other children. Every few months or so Edna and Lena would move to another base on the circuit where, when her mother was not around, Lena often went to bed hungry. The tent show circuit was all black—Edna did not pass as white, but her complexion guaranteed leading roles. Since blacks could not attend the theater in Southern towns, tent shows were the only theatrical entertainment that they had. The shows were usually adaptations of older standard Broadway favorites.

In Atlanta, only a few blocks from the cousins Lena had no idea existed, Edna left her with a crazy woman whom she had hired to take care of her house and daughter. The woman made ten-year-old Lena do all the housework, then beat her, claiming she had a "demon" in her when she failed to pass "inspection." When Edna returned, neighbors told her about Lena's screams. Drama queen Edna made it all about herself—half guilt, half shame. "Why do I have to learn about this from other people?!" she said to Lena. Edna's beatings were worse than any others because they were always followed by tears, remorse, and kisses. But now Lena was sent back to Brooklyn for an extended visit. Edna was beginning to understand that Teddy meant what he said about money. Unless Lena spent a specified number of days in the year with Cora and Edwin, Edna would get no money. Even Teddy knew that his child would be better off with his parents than with her mother—so his financial support of Edna and Lena depended on Lena spending more time with Cora than with Edna.

Fortunately, Lena's blighted and almost Dickensian Southern childhood had been broken at intervals by trips back to Chauncey Street, where she dropped into and out of proper schools and had friends who were always happy to see her, and where Cora tried to exorcize her Southernisms. Lena no longer minded Cora's nagging; she lived at home now with her own room upstairs, with people she knew who never raised their voices to shout at her or their hands to beat her.

In 1927 Lena returned to Miami. Edna was sharing a house with her friend Lucille, an actress who passed as white. Lena was under strict orders to stay in the room and read, and not make a peep, when her mother and "Aunt Lucille" had "cocktail parties." Lena now devoured all the works of Frances Hodgson Burnett. The only decent thing Edna did for Lena, other than producing her, was to provide her with the best late nineteenth- and early twentieth-century children's books. When Edna was in a good mood, she was charming and wonderful— otherwise, be careful. Despite her earlier leading roles at the Lafayette,

Edna now found that traveling in summer tent shows in the South was the only work she could get.

In 1927 Edna was obsessed with staying out of the sun even though she was secretly planning to go farther south than Miami. She had met a white Cuban military officer and, unbeknownst to Lena, was on her way to glamorous Havana. Once again, Lena's world was turned upside down. Her mother disappeared from her life as suddenly as she had eight years earlier—but not before depositing her with the nice old ladies from Macon. (I wonder if she chose the old ladies in Macon because she knew they would be kind to her daughter, or because they were cheap.)

Edna had a good reason to go to Havana. It turned out that she and the woman whom Lena was instructed to call "Aunt Lucille" were not simply entertaining touring actors at their "cocktail parties"—but were illegally "entertaining" strange men. Somehow, Lena had an accidental guardian angel who was aware of the situation. Her angel, the father of her lifelong Brooklyn friend Llewellyn Johnston, was the second-generation owner of a family field glass company with concessions at all eastern stadiums and racetracks, including Miami. Now Johnston called both Cora and Ted to say, "Get that child out of there!" Teddy then called Edna and ordered her to deliver Lena to his brother. Edna, busy packing for Cuba, had already taken Lena to stay with the Macon ladies—which was where Frank Horne found her. Lena had looked up from playing in the Macon yard to see a man who was vaguely familiar, but who she thought was white. "Hello, Lena," the man said. "I'm your uncle Frank—I've come to take you to Fort Valley with me."

While not in the league of James Weldon Johnson, Frank Horne, practicing optometrist, poet, essayist, and educator, could also be called a black middle-class Renaissance man. He had suffered the slings and arrows of racism only collectively—as part of an excluded black group. Frank by himself could have spent his life passing as white. Even when he was a scoutmaster, some of his black Scouts thought he was white.

In many ways, Frank was a typical middle-class second-generation New Yorker, but instead of coming from a foreign country, his parents were immigrants from the American South. He was also the typical product of a completely integrated education—from parochial school to Brooklyn's excellent Boys High School to City College. The only time he purposely and publicly passed as white was to go to the Illinois optometry college where his uncle and namesake had passed as "Cuban." Privately, rather like his father, he might do whatever was convenient at the moment. In 1926 Frank went south for the first time to find himself in a school that he would later recognize in Ralph Ellison's *Invisible Man*. Fort Valley High and Industrial School was an excuse for free labor for canning peaches. Traditionally, until Frank arrived, the president had been white. I suppose the administration thought that Frank's wavy brown hair, intelligent gray eyes, and quiet confidence stemming from having been a leader since boyhood made him white enough. Because he walked with a limp and used a sturdy cane, people assumed he had a war wound. Clearly, he could no longer run; but he found that he was expected to coach both the boys' and the girls' track teams—as well as be dean of the college and acting president at a salary far below that of a white in the same position. Frank and Lena had similar Southern experiences, all bad and all new. Lena, a skinny ten-year-old kid with bad legs from a case of rickets that she got in Macon, had experienced personal cruelty. And Frank, aged twenty-eight, had discovered and experienced the casual cruelty of Southern racism. He wrote: "I am initiated into the Negro race . . . From now on I am the Enterer of Side Doors, and Back Doors, and sometimes No Door At All."

If she could not be back on Chauncey Street with Cora, Uncle Frank was the next best thing. As far as Lena was concerned Fort Valley was about two schools—one a blessing, the other a curse. The school where Lena *lived*, where Uncle Frank ruled, was heaven; but the one-room schoolhouse across the road for ages six to twelve was hell. By 1927 there were nearly two thousand Rosenwald Fund schools in the South, continuing the work of the nineteenth-century Missionaries. As usual, Lena was the teacher's pet—but the hatred of the other children seemed more virulent than ever. It was not whites who were the racial tormentors (Lena never interacted with Southern whites); it was little black children of all ages in rural Georgia. Everything about Lena was wrong: color, accent, hair, clothes (courtesy of Teddy's largesse), and life experience. It was in Fort Valley that Lena had her first Florence Mills moment. The teacher had arrived in a somber mood because Florence Mills had died. She asked if any of the children had heard of her—and Lena was the only one to raise her hand. Invited to the front of the room to speak about Mills, Lena proceeded to the blackboard and, not saying a word, executed a perfect split—one of Flo Mills' famous dance moves. On the other hand, her life at Uncle Frank's college was so wonderful that it almost made suffering at the hands of classmates worth it. Lena was finally a happy child. For the first time since she went south three years earlier, she felt safe at night with no need to worry about the next beating or bite of food. She was with her family. She had been neglected and endangered until Uncle Frank dropped into her life and rescued her. It was just like *A Little Princess*, her favorite Frances Hodgson Burnett book.

Lena was the pet of the girls' dorm, where she lived next door to Frank's fiancée, the glamorous Frankye Bunn of Philadelphia and Brooklyn. Frankye was an English teacher—fun, kind, and beautiful. To Lena, she was also the essence of "flapper." She had the perfect boyish flapper figure, the perfect flapper slouch, and the perfect flapper gestures with her cigarette. Lena adored dorm life. She did not have to speak—she merely listened and looked, making herself small in a corner. Imagine the amazed delight of a ten-year-old girl permitted to look as an intimate into the minds of sixteen- and seventeen-year-old young women.

Easter 1928 saw a wonderful and rare Fort Valley Horne family reunion. Teddy Horne had been in a bad car accident and came to stay with Frank to recuperate. As dean and acting president of the college, Frank lived in a substantial brick-and-stone house. Ted had stunned the locals when he arrived in Fort Valley in a great big Cadillac or Packard with a driver-bodyguard. Edwin also traveled south for the first time in years, arriving in Fort Valley with two Brooklyn boyhood friends of Ted and Frank's to join Ted and Lena and Frank and Frankye. Only Cora and Burke were missing. Lena was in seventh heaven. It was probably the happiest moment of her young life. There were all of her favorite people: her beloved grandfather, her irresistible father, and her knight-in-shining-armor uncle. There is a picture of Lena, grinning from ear to ear, bursting with happiness in Fort Valley, at the idea of a family and people who did not ever wish to hurt her.

What can you say about Ted Horne? Men called him "Ted." Women, including his mother, called him "Teddy." He was everything that his mother hated: he worshipped money; he was a gambler, a rake, best friends with the demimonde, and on speaking terms with every major gangster, black or white, especially Owney Madden, Legs Diamond, and whoever fixed the Black Sox baseball scandal. Ted's best friend was Bub Hewlett, a former middle-class college man and World War I army officer, now the black numbers king of Harlem. Cora would have been sick at the idea of his friends and his women. It was not just that she was extremely puritanical; she was really sickened by the waste of it all. Where did the education go? Where was the *uplift*? In principle, Ted Horne had received a good Catholic education. In reality, the devil, in the form of the old Plaza hotel, began competing early with that education. It was not about *immorality*—it was about the root of all evil. Teddy fell in love with money—*real* money, such as no black man in America could ever hope to pursue by legitimate means. Then, in 1918, he looked up Bub Hewlett and somehow got hooked into the Black Sox scandal. So he was able to leave Edna, with her tantrums and fantasies, for good; to leave Cora money for Lena; and to get to Seattle to meet the widow Irene, matronly even in 1921 as she posed next to the slim 1920s sheikh. Then as now, gangsters were dapper dressers—and black gangsters were probably the most dapper of all.

When he came back into Lena's life at Fort Valley, Ted neither mentioned nor explained the ten years in which they had basically missed each other's company. Ted behaved as if he had been gone a week and started drilling her about math, at which, having been taught to gamble as a tot, he was naturally very good. Since Lena was terrible at math these sessions were agony. Sometimes Frank or Frankye had to tell him to let it be. Cora had ruled with an iron tongue, but she never struck any of her sons, and Lena knew that Teddy would never brutalize her the way her mother did. So she minded less and less that the Southern children bullied her mercilessly. She also went hatless in the sun so she would get darker, and she exaggerated her Southern accent. She would have to shed both habits when she finally went back to Cora in 1929.

CHAPTER EIGHT
North and South/1930s
LENA AND FRANK

T HE 1930s were transitional years for America—overnight, it went
from the mindless 1920s to the catastrophic 1930s. The 1930s
were only partly redeemed by the New Deal, which, while
feeding the starving millions, specifically denied Social Security benefits
to farm laborers and domestic workers—representing at least three-
quarters of all the black, brown, red, and yellow people in America.
Moreover, government relief allotments were distributed by the states,
and this meant that Negroes in the South were denied their fair share.
Georgia was among the states where blacks automatically received less
relief money than whites. Negro illiteracy was 16.3 percent—and 93.6
percent of that figure lived in the South. The average Southern school
district in 1930 spent $44.31 per white child and $12.57 per black
child. The racists were not all in the South. Approximately twenty-two
major unions officially discriminated against Negroes; that is why blacks
did not trust the labor movement, or socialism in general.

The Great Depression and the New Deal brought politics into
urban, educated black American life. FDR had a "Brain Trust," a term
coined by *New York Times* reporter James Kieran for the academics from
Columbia University whom Roosevelt, a former governor of New York,
induced to work for the government. There was even a black "Brain

Trust" in Roosevelt's so-called Black Cabinet (an informal group of black educators and activists who advised FDR on racial issues). The Depression changed the Negro emphasis in literature from race issues to class oppression. In 1930 the Communist Party USA organized the League of Struggle for Negro Rights with Langston Hughes as president. Twenty Negroes were lynched that year. In 1931 W. E. B. Du Bois rejected Communism in the pages of *The Crisis*. But he gave the Communist Party the cause célèbre of the decade when the NAACP decided that the Scottsboro Boys, nine black youths accused of rap- ing two white girls, were not that important and let the Communists take over their defense. (The last Scottsboro "Boy" was not freed until 1950, although the girls had long ago recanted.) Eighteen Negroes were lynched between 1931 and 1932. Negro unemployment for men and women in nineteen major cities was at 25 percent or more. The following year was a very bad one in the South for cotton, thanks in part to the New Deal's Agricultural Adjustment Administration (AAA) curtailment of production and destruction of surplus—programs that also forced out many sharecroppers and tenant farmers. Twenty-four Negroes were lynched in 1933, a year that found 25.4 percent of urban Northern Negroes on relief. Unlike other black communities, Harlem found some fun in adversity with "rent parties." And, unlike other communities, Harlem was lucky to have a generous, creative mayor in Fiorello La Guardia, elected in 1933. In 1934, the year that fifteen blacks were lynched, the NAACP began formulating a plan for a "systematic coordinated legal assault on discrimination in the schools." In 1935 eighteen blacks were lynched; 1936 and 1937 each saw eight blacks lynched. There were six lynchings in 1938, but only two in 1939—possibly because racists were counting on the efficacy of Mississippi senator Theodore G. Bilbo's Greater Liberia Act (a back-to-Africa bill) for American blacks.

The 1930s were also a period of transition for the Horne family. Lena and Frank finally left the South. The older generation passed away. Frank went to work for the federal government, and Lena, now a young wife and mother, started on the path to the recognition that would make her the best-known, but not necessarily the most important, member of the black Calhouns.

Meanwhile, the years 1929–1931 were the second happiest of Lena's young life. They were two years of good friends, a good school, her own room, club meetings, and parties—none of them under Cora's roof. Cora was only a few blocks away, but she seemed to love Lena best from afar. Lena was staying with Cora's good friend Laura Rollock, a widow with no children, who loved having Lena to spoil and made her dresses. Mrs. Rollock was active in the NAACP, the Urban League, and amateur theatrics, namely the *Junior Follies*. In Mrs. Rollock's house Lena was allowed not only to have Junior Deb club meetings, but to have her own radio—two pleasures Cora had discouraged.

Cora had not meant to be away when Lena arrived from Georgia, but her "grand tour" had been planned for a year. The grand tour, with her other good friend Mrs. Minta Trotman, a fellow NAACP activist, was a gift from Ted, who knew how to stay on his mother's good side. On September 30, 1929, Cora wrote to Burke from the small French liner *De Grasse* (I would first sail to Europe on that ship in 1950): "I obeyed Ted's instructions and we own the boat . . ." Ted's instructions to Cora were to tip every hand she saw. And how clever of him to choose the French Line, which never let a passenger's complexion come between itself and money. She never would have been shown similar courtesy on an American liner.

Cora remembered Lena in her letter to Burke: ". . . I forgot to leave money for her music but I hope you paid it as Dad will surely return it to you . . ." Cora's favorite city on her grand tour was Berlin—"so clean." In January 1930 she sent a card from Vienna, saying that she had heard from Lena, who was excited about Christmas. "She is a dear little girl," Cora said.

Lena was thrilled because she remained a paying boarder with Mrs. Rollock when Cora returned from Europe—although she still attended Bahá'í and Republican women's meetings with her grandmother. While Cora gently but constantly sought to stretch Lena's mind, in Laura Rollock Lena had a devoted adult who helped her through adolescence by caring about everything *except* the mind. Despite her Southern education, Lena did well in school. She was a teacher's pet wherever she went in the South, and this meant that teachers always gave her *their* best. She loved Girls High School—like its counterpart, a venerable Brooklyn institution, and practically around the corner from Chauncey Street. Boys and girls of the black middle class went to separate high schools, but they got together once a month at *Junior Follies* rehearsals with Mrs. Rollock. There were boys Lena liked but she was mostly too shy and too busy to make friends with them. Despite her peripatetic Southern childhood, she got good grades, especially in English and history, in her Northern schools. This was a result of Cora's influence.

Lena resumed her outings with Edwin. Sometimes they went to downtown Brooklyn to the movies. The best excursions, of course, were the ones across the bridge to Broadway. They saw Eva Le Gallienne's *Alice in Wonderland* and Fred Astaire in *The Gay Divorce*. Lena was in love with Fred Astaire. She asked for and was permitted to take dancing and singing lessons. Mrs. Rollock was grooming her to star in the *Junior Follies*, whose amateur theatrics for charity were always covered as social news in the black press. Cora approved of the lessons in terms of "accomplishments." At fourteen, Lena was becoming a performer— singing "Indian Love Call" at all the Junior Deb teas.

Then, in 1932, two terrible things happened: Edna returned from Cuba and Cora died. Not only did Edna turn up like the bad penny she was, but she was accompanied by a white Cuban husband who spoke no English. Edna's Cuban husband, an officer exiled by the Machado revolution, was named Miguel and called "Mike." Lena was horrified. Worse, now Edna insisted that Lena live with her and Mike in the

Bronx. Cora's death in September 1932 brought the total collapse of Lena's happy new world. Obituaries revealing Cora's spiritual seeking appeared in the *New York Amsterdam News, Baltimore Afro-American,* and *Chicago Defender.*

The *Amsterdam News* of September 14, 1932, reported:

Mrs. Horne, Civic Leader, Succumbs. Funeral held for woman who served in numerous movements in city and nation—rites private. Cora Calhoun Horne, prominent over a period of 27 years in the civic and social worlds of Brooklyn, died Thursday (September 8) from natural causes at her home, 189 Chauncey Street. She was 68. Burial of the body was made in Evergreen Cemetery on Monday. Her funeral services . . . were conducted by A.C. Holley of the Bah'ai, a religious cult, assisted by the Rev. Dr. H.H. Proctor, of Nazarene Congregational Church, and the Rev. George Frazier Miller of St. Augustine P.E. Church . . . Mrs. Horne . . . was educated in the public schools of Atlanta and at Atlanta University. She became the wife of Edwin F. Horne of Birmingham, Ala., in 1887. Migrating to this city, she began her public career in 1913. During the late World War she organized and directed a Y.W.C.A. unit for the American Red Cross, and in recognition for her work in this connection was appointed a member of the then mayor's victory committee.

The deceased is survived by her husband, an inspector in the department of combustibles of the New York Fire Department; a sister, Mrs. Frank A. Smith of Chicago; three sons, Edwin F., Jr. of Pittsburgh; Dr. Frank S., dean of the Fort Valley Normal School of Fort Valley, Ga., and John Burke, a graduate pharmacist of this city. All were present for the internment.

All of Cora's spiritual homes were represented, except for the Catholic Church—and all of her family was there except for Lena. Edna, at her worst, forbade Lena to attend Cora's funeral. For the first time in her life, Lena rebelled and had a screaming fight with Edna, insisting that she was going to Cora's funeral anyway and running several blocks to the funeral home with Edna chasing behind her and making a scene at the door. Edwin announced that Edna was a "skunk" and refused to have anything more to do with her. Unfortunately, Lena had no choice. The *Pittsburgh Courier*, the highest-circulation black newspaper, by the way, made Ted the center of the story: "Ted Horne's Mother Buried in Brooklyn."

Edna did two more cruel things, which Cora would never have permitted, to Lena in 1932. After refusing to allow her to attend Cora's funeral, she made Lena drop out of Girls High School and go to Wadleigh Secretarial School in the Bronx so that she could earn money to support her mother and stepfather. Taking the long view, it was a very good thing that Lena dropped out of Girls High School—if she had not, she might never have become "Lena Horne." At the time, however, it felt like a double bereavement. Her grandmother and her friends, the ones who had stuck by her always, were her only constants—and her friends were all at Girls High. Now, once again, she was being wrenched away from everything she knew—this time, however, it was only to the Bronx. Recognizing possible benefits, Edna let Lena continue her singing and dancing lessons (which Ted paid for). Early in 1933 Lena starred in the *Junior Follies*, singing Cole Porter's "Night and Day" and Harold Arlen's "I've Got the World on a String." That same year, when the Anna Jones Dancing School played a week at the Harlem Opera House, Lena sang as well as danced with scarves (and electric fans in the wings) to Arlen's Cotton Club hit "Stormy Weather." (Lena would sing Arlen's songs for the next fifty years or more, and he would become a dear friend.)

Edna now made a decision. Lena would have the theatrical career that had eluded *her*. Besides, they needed the money. Edna knew the dance captain at the Cotton Club from her Lafayette Theatre days. After an audition with some overenthusiastic spinning, very pretty

Lena was hired. Thanks to Bub Hewlett, the numbers king, word went out almost at once that the sixteen-year-old was "protected." Lena was also informally protected by members of the Cab Calloway band, who treated her like a little sister and called her "Brooklyn." Besides being famously pretty, girls from Brooklyn were famously chaperoned. Edna sat in the cramped chorus dressing room every night, pointedly ignoring the other girls and saying no when Lena pleaded to be able to just *once* go Lindy Hopping at the Renaissance Ballroom. But Lena was denied those innocent pleasures by Edna, whose constant presence ensured her daughter's virtue. As for Teddy Horne, he was one of the few Negroes allowed in (at a table near the kitchen, of course) when Lena appeared in the chorus of the *1933 Cotton Club Review.*

Many people believed that the repeal of Prohibition, more than the Depression, killed Harlem. Without illicit alcohol, and happy, well-dressed "natives," there was no reason for white tourists to visit Harlem—which seemed to change almost overnight from a lively tourist mecca into a derelict slum. Harlem jobs utterly depended on the downtown economy. When the stock market crashed, downtown jobs disappeared almost overnight—and Harlem had no financial cushion. Harlem by day, once a place of colorful street life and cheerful banter, was now a place of breadlines and political harangues. Night was better. The Cotton Club, still big and noisy, still lured celebrities and tourists. In 1933 the star was Cab Calloway, who sang about "Cocaine Lil" and was a merry proponent of "reefers." Arguably the first hipster, he was certainly the first zoot-suiter. Rich white tourists had departed, but younger and poorer white tourists had returned for the music: Count Basie, Ella Fitzgerald, Chick Webb, and so forth. Lena did enjoy one Cotton Club outing, even though Edna went along. The club did a free show at Sing Sing prison, where Owney Madden was under temporary protective arrest on tax charges, as all the other mobsters were killing each other for control of New York rackets. The band, the stars, and the chorus girls went up the Hudson in two buses and had a sumptuous free meal, provided by the Cotton Club, in prison.

Harlem itself was no longer a happy place. In 1934, presaging the White Citizens' Councils of the 1960s South, Blumstein's department store on 125th Street formed the all-white Harlem Merchants' Association in order to keep its staff lily-white. Blumstein's was adamant in its refusal to consider hiring Negro employees on the main street of a Negro community. Yet the 1935 Harlem riot against police brutality and the refusal of Harlem stores to hire black employees shocked and surprised the city.

Black Communists and black fascists were both busy in 1930s Harlem. Frank Horne's good friend Langston Hughes was openly a Communist. James Ford, a former Missionary college football hero, was the perennial Communist Party vice presidential candidate. Paul Robeson, harassed by Nazis in Germany and white American tourists in England, went to Soviet Russia and was treated like a king. An admirer of the "colored" empire of Japan ever since the Japanese defeated the czar's navy in the Russo-Japanese War of 1904–1905, Dr. Du Bois had very different political sympathies in the 1930s. Du Bois was widely criticized in 1936 for suggesting that the Chinese look on the Japanese as liberators. That same year, however, he went to Berlin and stated that Nazi persecution of the Jews was "an attack on civilization, comparable only to the Spanish Inquisition and the African slave trade." The Nazis admitted that most of their racial laws were borrowed from the United States. Although Du Bois reported that German academics had shown him more respect than his American colleagues, he soon gave up fascism.

James Weldon Johnson continued to encourage Frank Horne to write more poetry. Frank had appeared in Johnson's 1930 *Anthology of Negro Poetry* and was included in a 1929 German anthology, but he was still dean and acting president at Fort Valley—which meant he did *everything.* He was also a newlywed. Frank and Frankye were married in New York in August 1930 at the Actors' Chapel, St. Malachy's Church, the "Little Church Around the Corner." Everyone, North and South, was very happy. Frankye was warm, outgoing, and full of charm. Slender and chic, she actually looked like a young Coco Chanel. Frankye brought a sense of Paris wherever she went—even Fort Valley, where she was now the official "acting" first lady. She was the first Negro first lady, but it seemed to be OK because she looked *almost* as white as Frank did. She moved out of the girls' dorm and into Frank's "acting" president's house and continued teaching. The students loved her because she had a sense of fun. The teachers liked her because of the weekend parties that she and Frank gave—with plenty of moonshine and Louis Armstrong records. The other teachers were a mixture of Southern and Northern middle-class blacks stuck in rural Georgia Klan country. In 1932 Frank and Frankye finally had a decent honeymoon, when Frank took a leave of absence to get his master's degree at the University of Southern California. They met up with Ted Horne for the Los Angeles Olympics. In pictures they look so happy—partly from love and partly from being away from the South.

In Atlanta in 1933, a nineteen-year-old black Communist named Angelo Herndon was sentenced to twenty years on the chain gang for leading a hunger march to petition county commissioners for relief for Negroes. He was defended by a young black Harvard Law graduate, Benjamin J. Davis Jr., whose father was the chairman of the Georgia Republican Party and the former editor of Atlanta's black newspaper, the *Independent*, whose business manager had been Antoine Graves. During the Herndon trial, the judge turned his back and read a newspaper whenever Davis spoke—and refused to address him as anything but "nigger." Davis' response was to join the Communist Party himself as soon as the trial was over.

In 1933, of the 24,536 people said to be members of the Communist Party USA (CPUSA), no more than 2,500 were black. Two years later many of those black Communists left the party when it was revealed that Russia was selling oil and wheat to Mussolini, whose airplanes were killing barefoot Ethiopians. It was hardly likely that there would be many black Communists in America anyway, since black Americans thoroughly despised the American labor movement. Except for the Wobblies, the fabled, integrated, short-lived Industrial Workers of the World, blacks were barred from all labor unions, as well as all productive work opportunities. They could be janitors—but they were never allowed on the factory or shop floor. In 1934 the American Federation of Labor (AFL) once again rejected A. Philip Randolph's plea to integrate. The AFL wanted separate black and white unions. The integrated Congress of Industrial Organizations (CIO) was born the following year. The CIO was no second-tier group—it represented big steel, automobiles, factories, and mines. This was a time of bloody labor battles featuring outnumbered workers against brutal, armed police. Young Walter Reuther of the United Automobile Workers and older, charismatic John L. Lewis of the United Mine Workers of America were important CIO leaders.

In 1935 Du Bois published his book on Reconstruction:

> If the Reconstruction of the Southern States, from slavery to free labor, and from aristocracy to industrial democracy, had been conceived as a major national program of America, whose accomplishment at any price was well worth the effort, we should be living today in a different world.

That year Negroes were lynched at the rate of one every three weeks—and the NAACP withdrew support from FDR because, needing Southern Democrats to pass his New Deal legislation, he refused to support the Costigan-Wagner antilynching bill (although Eleanor encouraged him to support it). Meanwhile, fifteen blacks were lynched in 1934. The South remained the South. In 1935 in Atlanta the median income for blacks was $632 and for whites was $1,876. The Southern states as a whole spent an average of $17.04 that year on each black pupil and $49.30 on each white pupil. Frank Horne knew very well how ill-funded black schools were. He was beginning, in fact, to see the true extent of the perils of applying Jim Crow to formulate an industrial "education." In 1935 he wrote a much-talked-about piece in the Urban League magazine, *Opportunity*:

> As factors in training Negro youth to earn a livelihood in industrial America of today, the industrial schools of the South, except in a few rare instances, could practically all be scrapped without appreciable loss to any one . . . In the midst of this teeming, complex, kaleidoscopic economic world, the Negro industrial schools of the South sit as though sublimely oblivious . . . We are fiddling with "man-and-plow" agriculture in the face of the gang-plow and the tractor; our home economics girls are in bodily danger in a modern kitchen; the language of collective bargaining, company unions and cooperatives is so much Greek to the ears of our industrial students.

The following year Frank got a call from Mrs. Mary McLeod Bethune, inviting him to join the New Deal. Thank God, he and Frankye could leave the South.

After two years at the Cotton Club, Edna had decided that Lena could do better. She conceived a plan to spirit Lena away to Boston to join Noble Sissle and his Society Orchestra. Edna and Lena actually left between shows, bundled into a taxi by a cohort of chorus girls, while stepfather Mike, after being roughed up by some of the "boys," stayed in New York.

Recognized as a war hero in Boston, where Jim Europe died, Noble Sissle led the first black band to play the Ritz-Carlton Hotel. To honor the occasion, Sissle decided to redo Lena. Fortunately all of her "Cotton Club–isms" were put on, not innate. This was the era of the debutante "torch singer"; Sissle seemed to have that in mind when he renamed Lena "Helena Horne" and assigned her to sing slightly plaintive ballads. She sang "Blue Moon" at the Ritz-Carlton and acquired a Harvard fan club that returned night after night. Lena and Sissle were a big success in Boston. In fact, the Ritz-Carlton's manager was so impressed that he called young New York jazz impresario John Hammond, Benny Goodman's brother-in-law, to say, "There's a terrible band on the roof called Noble Sissle, but the girl singer is so beautiful, she belongs in New York." Later that year, en route to a well-publicized engagement at the huge whites-only Moonlight Gardens dance hall outside Cincinnati, Sissle was in a bad car crash. It was headline news. When Lena saw him in the hospital, Sissle told her that *she* must lead the band. "It's the only way to keep the band alive," he said. He told her not to worry about the music. The band would play what it always played—all she had to do was wave the baton around and pretend to conduct. A terrified Lena, wearing her band "uniform" of red sequin tailcoat and white crepe bell-bottom trousers, went on for Sissle at the Moonlight Gardens to cheers from the audience and raves from the Cincinnati papers—such was the novelty of a young, pretty female leader of a band. All the places that had canceled when they heard about Sissle's accident now wanted the band with Lena. Reporters came backstage looking for interviews. They invariably mentioned Lena's "modesty," which was actually distress. She had no idea what she was supposed to say or do in an *interview*—though Sissle had always been a stickler for details and gestures onstage. After a long Southern tour—equal parts fear, exhaustion, and harassment ("Look at the New York niggers!")— Lena realized that she hated what she was doing. She was tired of "show business" and tired of her mother pushing her around as if she were a commodity—while fiercely guarding the virginity that Lena was less and less interested in protecting. In fact, she was tired of her mother altogether—which is why she married my father.

In early 1936 Lena decided to go to Pittsburgh to visit Ted, who owned a small hotel with a quiet gambling den upstairs. Ted's best Pittsburgh friend, Gus Greenlee, another World War I officer, had political control of the city's Democratic black Third Ward and also ran the local numbers racket—another enterprise in which whites allowed blacks to succeed. When Lena came to visit, Ted introduced her to his younger friend, Louis Jones, whom he referred to as a "college man." One of four children of a Louisville, Kentucky, minister, Louis Jordan Jones, a graduate of West Virginia State, had a Democratic patronage job as registrar of the coroner's office. The Jones siblings all lived in Pittsburgh, where Louis' older brothers were Third Ward lawyer-politicians. Pittsburgh was a blue-collar city, with white and black workers up from the South competing for the same jobs. But it produced the most important black newspaper, the *Pittsburgh Courier*, and a great black baseball team, the Crawfords, owned by Ted's pal Greenlee. Pittsburgh's black middle class was almost as insular as its white superrich. The Loendi Club, where Louis took Lena on her first date ever with a man, was known as the "favorite gathering-place of Negro Pittsburgh's most exclusive set."

Lena, who had never had a date or a boyfriend, wanted to run away from show business and her mother. Why not marriage? Louis was twenty-eight and Lena was nineteen. Lena's virginity when she married Louis had been a subject of great amusement among Louis' married friends, all older than Lena and, in her mind, extremely condescending. Besides playing high-stakes bridge and treating her as if she were stupid, Louis was extremely controlling and jealous of Lena's career. He also would not let her spend money—although he spent plenty. On top of everything, in a moment of *folie de grandeur*, he quit his job and borrowed a huge sum because he intended to run for a seat on the city council. He lost.

In the 1936 election, the Democratic platform did not mention Negroes, but two South Carolina delegates—Senator Ellison DuRant "Cotton Ed" Smith and the mayor of Charleston—walked out of the Democratic convention when a black minister began to give the opening prayer. Smith refused to support "any political organization that looks upon the Negro and caters to him as a political and social equal." Typically, the Republicans had a decent, if modest, civil rights plank:

We favor equal opportunity for our colored citizens. We pledge our protection of their economic status and personal safety. We will do our best to further their employment in the gainful occupied life of America, particularly in private industry, agriculture, emergency agencies and the civil service. We condemn the present New Deal policies which would regiment and ultimately eliminate the colored citizen from the country's productive life and make him solely a ward of the Federal Government.

The Communist platform was even more decent and much showier:

The Negro people suffer doubly. Most exploited of working people, they are also victims of Jim Crowism and lynching. They are denied the right to live as human beings . . . We demand that the Negro people be guaranteed complete equality, equal rights to jobs, equal pay for equal work, the full right to organize, vote, serve on juries, and hold public office. Segregation and discrimination against Negroes must be declared a crime. Heavy penalties must be established against mob rule, floggers, and kidnappers, with the death penalty for lynchers. We demand the enforcement of the 13th, 14th, and 15th Amendments to the Constitution.

In 1937 Burke Horne, a practicing pharmacist, collected medicines for the Spanish Republic. In March Salaria Kee, a twenty-year-old nurse from Harlem Hospital, arrived in Spain to become the only black nurse in the Fifteenth International Brigade of the Spanish Civil War. The heroine of two critically praised documentaries, she was an excellent propaganda tool for the Communist-backed Spanish Republicans. She and Captain Oliver Law, the black commander of the Abraham Lincoln Brigade, the first black American to lead whites in battle, were reason enough for black Americans in general to support the Spanish Republic—as was Paul Robeson's magnificent album of Spanish

Civil War songs. Even though they lost the war and were destroyed as a military unit, veterans of the integrated Lincoln Brigade were proud to have been among the first Americans to fight fascism—for which their own government would severely punish them.

There was actually some good news for American blacks in 1937. The Supreme Court upheld the legality of picketing firms that refused to hire Negroes. The NAACP successfully challenged the attempt to exclude black Boy Scouts from the great Scout Jamboree to be held in Washington that summer. And, in the best sporting news since Jesse Owens' four gold medals at the 1936 Olympics, Joe Louis, a young Alabama Negro, became heavyweight champion of the world when he defeated the white boxer James J. Braddock.

In Atlanta in June 1937, Kate Graves had a new job at the Fulton County Department of Family and Children Services. She was a social worker and, technically, a maiden aunt—but she was also a fashion plate with a model-sized figure. She dressed like a "career woman"—and inspired her nieces, especially namesake Catherine Nash, who had graduated from Atlanta University's Laboratory High School that same June.

I have one page of a letter or report that Kate wrote about her work that is a perfect example of the Reconstruction spirit:

My field of work is dealing with social problems and social case work. The greatest difficulty that confronts me is the lack of cooperation among people who are able to give their aid and assistance but will not; seemingly they have not the interest of the race at heart enough to help uplift struggling humanity . . .

In August, Kate's brother, Judge, died in New York City of acute alcoholism. Poor Judge: he should have stayed with music, in Europe or New York, and been true to himself. He could, at least, have been a professor of music somewhere; but dentistry was chosen for security—in everything but spirit. There was one saved letter of condolence addressed to "Mr. and Mrs. A. Graves, and family, 115 Howell Street, Atlanta Georgia" from Joseph D. Bibb, attorney at law, 3507 South Parkway, Chicago: "Dear Friends: Permit me [to] express my deepest sympathy in the passing of your dear son and my old pal, Judge. Sincerely yours. Joseph D. Bibb."

Bibb was an old black Georgia name—the original Bibb must have had many slaves. Joseph might have been one of the good-looking young men who posed with Judge in the 1904 photograph. Among Judge's papers was Frank Horne's Los Angeles address.

For Lena, the first real shock of color in Pittsburgh came in December 1937 when she was in labor with me. Her very social Negro doctor drove her to the hospital, then told her for the first time that he could not practice in the white hospital—that a strange white doctor would deliver her baby. Meanwhile she would be put in the basement where the colored babies were born. To say that Lena sustained a culture shock is putting it mildly. She became hysterical and had to be sedated. Who would have thought that Pittsburgh was part of the Deep South?

A few months after I was born, Lena got a call from her sometime agent to say that she was wanted in Hollywood to make a movie. The picture, called *The Duke Is Tops*, was intended for the Negro market and starred popular black actor Ralph Cooper. Lena took a terrifying flight to the coast because Teddy said it was the only way to go, but she swore never to fly again. Then she was almost sent home because everyone said she was too fat (my fault). So she starved herself through the shoot. However, the fact that she never got paid had nothing to do with weight. It was typical of the producers, the notorious actor-stiffing Popkin brothers. After Lena became known, *The Duke Is Tops* was rereleased as *The Bronze Venus*—still, no pay. But Louis, looking to show that he was boss, forbade her to attend the Pittsburgh NAACP benefit opening of the picture. He might let his wife work because he liked the idea of money—but he did not like the idea of her having any recognition.

The same thing happened a few months later when Lena was asked to come to New York to be one of the stars of the new revue *Blackbirds of 1939*. The original 1920s *Blackbirds* had made Florence Mills a legend in her lifetime. The new *Blackbirds* was a flop, but Lena got good personal reviews.

Brooks Atkinson of the *New York Times* wrote: "Among those present is a radiantly beautiful sepia girl, Lena Horne, who sings 'Thursday' and 'You're So Indifferent' in an attractive style, and who will be a winner when she has proper direction . . ."

Richard Watts of the *Herald-Tribune* wrote: "Miss Lena Horne . . . is a young woman of . . . pleasant singing ability and attractive stage presence. She should go far, even if her vehicle doesn't accompany her a great distance."

And *Women's Wear Daily* commented: "Lena Horne makes a very attractive little star, and her stage personality is definitely on the positive side. She sings and dances throughout the evening and the audience seems quite favorably disposed toward her."

Typically, a few days after the opening, Louis forbade her to attend the closing night cast party.

Lena had only one friend among Louis' crowd, an older, talented pianist named Charlotte Catlin who made money playing after-dinner music for Pittsburgh's iron, steel, and ketchup magnates. Now Lena joined her for this easy and not unpleasant form of entertainment. Even Louis approved. Lena and Charlotte would arrive after dinner in evening clothes. Charlotte would play and Lena would sing "The Man I Love" and "Sunny Side of the Street" and other favorites, with some of the guests sitting on the floor around the piano. Afterward, Lena and Charlotte would be given dessert and coffee, and guests would tell them how much they enjoyed the performance. Money never changed hands—a generous check would be delivered to Charlotte the next day.

Lena and Louis' marriage would have been over sooner than it was— except that they had a second baby. Lena wanted to leave Louis after

Blackbirds, but Little Teddy, my baby brother, born February 7, 1939, was the "reconciliation" child. Even adorable Teddy could not help Lena overcome her fury when she discovered that Louis had hidden a brand-new pair of shoes for himself at the back of the closet after they had a screaming fight about *her* spending. Lena said it was the final straw—though the real final straw was realizing that she was the only person who did not know that Louis had never stopped seeing his long-time Pittsburgh girlfriend, a member of their set. The marriage lasted about four years, and the only good things about it were my brother, Edwin Fletcher "Little Teddy" Jones, and me, called "Gail"—instead of Catherine, Cora, Lena, or Nellie.

In 1938 Dr. Frank Horne became a new member of FDR's Black Cabinet. First known as the Federal Council of Negro Affairs, the so-called Black Cabinet was an informal group of Negro public policy advisers. By mid-1935 there were forty-five blacks working in New Deal agencies and federal executive departments. Frank had signed on as assistant director of the division of Negro affairs, in the National Youth Administration, under Mary McLeod Bethune, a good friend of Eleanor Roosevelt's. Mrs. Bethune, an *ur*-black matriarch known as "Ma Bethune" behind her back, was the only female member of the Black Cabinet, which comprised activists, community leaders, scholars, and advisers. It included Walter White, William Hastie (in 1937 the first black federal judge), and Robert C. Weaver (future head of the Department of Housing and Urban Development). The president approved of the cabinet, but the first lady was the driving force. Former Republican Mary McLeod Bethune, founder of Bethune-Cookman College, created the National Council of Negro Women in 1935 and delivered many votes to FDR. From 1936 to 1944 Mrs. Bethune, the first black woman ever to head a federal agency, was Roosevelt's special adviser on minority affairs. There is a photograph taken in 1938 that I accidentally came across in the 1980s at the old Smithsonian in Washington, where I had gone to look at my favorite machine in the world—the red McCormick reaper. Having seen the beautiful machine, I turned a corner and there, blown up on the wall, was a photo of Bethune and nineteen members of the Black Cabinet. Frank, looking very "white," stands front and center, next to Mrs. B., very dark.

Actually, 1938 was a terrible year for Frank. In Washington during the week working for the New Deal, every weekend he went back to New York to see Frankye, now very ill at the Tuberculosis League Hospital. To great family sorrow, beautiful Frankye died in the hospital a year later. Frank now went to work on minority housing issues for the U.S. Housing Authority. He eventually became director of the Office of Race Relations. During this time he advised FDR's administration on racism in public housing. Blacks liked FDR, but were becoming more and more suspicious of the New Deal. No matter what policies came out of Washington, they still had to be implemented by local, often racist administrators. Once again, the very poor were denied a sense of future or old age security. By the end of the decade, the New Deal would be known among some blacks as the "Dirty Deal."

At Easter 1939, thanks to Eleanor Roosevelt, Walter White, and Secretary of the Interior Harold Ickes, Marian Anderson famously sang spirituals on the steps of the Lincoln Memorial after the Daughters of the American Revolution (whom Langston Hughes called "Aryan hussies") barred her from Constitution Hall. That same spring, Mississippi senator Theodore Bilbo introduced a back-to-Africa bill to get all blacks out of America. In the 1930s Germany planned the "final solution" for the "Jewish problem" and boasted that the Nuremberg race laws were based on American Jim Crow. According to historian C. Vann Woodward, white Southerners in the late nineteenth century had referred to the Jim Crow system as the "final settlement" of the "Negro problem." Black Americans would understand the irony during World War II. "Negroes did not need us at the NAACP to tell them that it sounded pretty foolish to be against park benches marked JUDE in Berlin but to be *for* park benches marked COLORED in

Tallahassee, Florida," Roy Wilkins, then editor of *The Crisis*, would write. The NAACP remained public enemy number one in the South, and Jim Crow flourished in the North as well as the South, despite the coming war. The *meaning* of Jim Crow was the complete separation of the races and the total oppression of blacks as a people. Fortunately, there were no death camps in America.

Edwin Horne, a man of the nineteenth century, died in September 1939—a sad, lonely, bitter, prejudiced old man who complained that Chauncey Street had become "Africanized." Edwin had lived so many lives: the Indiana prodigy; the middle border Republican activist; the Tammany star pamphleteer (after a change in party affiliation). He had seen the birth and death of Reconstruction, and he had seen the enemies of black freedom go from strength to strength. One can only wonder if he ever regretted having *chosen* to be a Negro.

CHAPTER NINE

North/1940s
MOVIE STAR YEAR

THIS IS the point in the history of the black Calhouns when my mother, Lena, the second "Lena" and fourth generation in the family, unavoidably becomes the star of the story. She was the pride and joy of all the black Calhouns. And she was particularly beloved by black women in the days before everyone realized that "Black Is Beautiful." She was a brand-new image for black women—certainly preferable to Aunt Jemima, say. She was a beautiful and dignified Negro woman who made speeches. Because she was simultaneously a *token* (in the movies), a *symbol* (to the world that the United States, unlike the Axis powers, was not a racist country), and a *forerunner* (how difficult it is to be the *first* anything), and because she was also an enormous moneymaker for nightclubs, she had a triumvirate of protectors: the black center (that is, the NAACP and the Pullman porters); the white Left, which would heavily woo her; and the Jewish Mafia that owned the nightclubs.

In 1943, Lena's "movie star" year, only four black people had any place in the national consciousness: Marian Anderson, who made the Daughters of the American Revolution look very bad when they refused to let her sing in Constitution Hall; Paul Robeson, remembered as a nationally known college athlete, now a great singer-actor starring on

Broadway in *Othello*; Sergeant Joe Louis, heavyweight boxing champion of the world, now the number one army public relations asset; and twenty-six-year-old Lena Horne, known as the first black movie star because she had signed a long-term MGM contract and was not relegated to servant parts. Though she would ultimately make few movies, in 1943 Lena had three movies released between January and June, and she broke nightclub revenue records in New York and Chicago. A year later she became the first black to be on the cover of a movie magazine. She was known as a star because of the way she looked (gorgeous), because of the way she sang (sweetly), and because America was at war. Black GIs needed a pinup and Lena was the one and only—they were not permitted white pinups. She christened Liberty ships, toured black army camps, and danced with black GIs at the Hollywood Canteen, which, unlike the USO, was integrated. Above all, Lena was expected to almost single-handedly give proof to the Allies that America, unlike the Axis, was not racist—even though 1943 alone saw four major and bloody race riots, mostly between poor Southern blacks and whites colliding over defense industry jobs. The Nazis and the Japanese had a propaganda picnic. After the war, however, Lena confounded people of both races by marrying Lennie Hayton, a white man. But before all this happened, my mother had to divorce my father.

By 1940 Lena and my father, Louis Jones, were officially separated. Leaving the children in Pittsburgh with Ted and her stepmother, Irene, Lena went back to New York to look for a job. She took a room at the Harlem YWCA. Her stepmother gave her some nice dresses and money to tide her over. She ate her meals at lunch counters and her basic entertainment was the radio. She fell in love with Artie Shaw's recording of "Stardust." She had no idea, of course, that she would soon be singing with Artie Shaw. She called her old agent from the *Blackbird* days and tried to find a job. Everywhere she went with the agent, she heard the same refrain: "She doesn't look like a Negro," "She's not black enough"—meaning she was not a stereotype. Or, "Make her Latin and

I'll put her in the show." After several months of humiliating interviews, Lena almost gave up. But her luck had not run out.

One afternoon she decided to forget about herself and go to the movies. Suddenly, there was a commotion in the aisle of the Loew's Victoria at 125th Street. An usher with a flashlight, accompanied by Clarence Robinson, the dance director of the Apollo, beckoned her out of her seat. She was to run to the Apollo immediately, because Charlie Barnet needed a girl singer right away. With no time to fix her hair or makeup, she did as Robinson ordered. "Wow! Who are you?" said Barnet when Lena came in. She sang two songs and his next question was "You want to work in the next show?" So she got the lucky break and her first job as a band singer with saxophonist Charlie Barnet, whose band was known as the "blackest" of the big white bands. (In the 1940s "big bands" had all the impact on young people that rock and roll groups had in the 1960s.) Charlie, who idolized Duke Ellington and Count Basie, had a huge hit that year in "Cherokee," one of the best big band recordings ever, which all the Harlem jitterbugs adored for its compulsively danceable beat. Ted Horne, however, did not adore Barnet—the very thought of his daughter traveling around the country with fifteen or twenty white men infuriated him. Lena ignored him—it was a very good job, everywhere but in the South and at certain very snooty girls' schools. Charlie Barnet, four years older than Lena, was the "bad boy," jazz-loving son of a vice president of the New York Central Railroad. As a rich "good guy," he kept Lena on full salary when she stayed north while the band toured the South with a white singer.

Obviously, Ted had not complained when she toured with Sissle because Sissle was a friend of Edwin's—and he was black. Unlike his younger brother Frank, Ted had no white friends (except for gangsters). Nonetheless, Lena played a famously successful gig with Barnet and band at the Paramount Theater on Broadway. Lena *never* kissed and told, so I have no idea if she had a romance with Barnet, but he was apparently a very likable guy, with no racist attitudes, and she always smiled when she spoke of him. Charlie would eventually marry *eleven* times and retire from music in 1949 because he was tired of it. Singing with Charlie brought Lena musical attention. Charlie had no problem with Lena recording with Artie Shaw when the Barnet band went south. Barnet, Shaw, and Benny Goodman were the only white big bands to feature black singers or musicians. Lena soon had two hit records: "You're My Thrill" (1941, Bluebird Records), with Charlie Barnet and His Orchestra; and "Don't Take Your Love from Me" (1941, Victor Records), with Artie Shaw.

But before this, in late 1940, Louis Jones had told Lena that she could have "the girl," but he would keep "the boy." So Lena returned to Brooklyn with me, and, at Teddy Horne's suggestion, Cousin Edwina, daughter of Lena Calhoun Smith, came east to help take care of me. Lena was happily installed on Chauncey Street, hoping to make some more records and to find a New York job with no touring. She now asked John Hammond, a wealthy white liberal friend of Frank Horne's who had followed her career since the Noble Sissle days in Boston, for help, and he was instrumental in getting her a job at Café Society— Greenwich Village's relatively new, totally hip nightclub.

Barney Josephson, Café Society's young owner, gave Lena a chance, although she did everything wrong at her audition by singing two wildly politically incorrect songs: one was racist ("Sleepy Time Down South"), and the other ("Down Argentina Way") hinted that she was "passing." (Although Lena was one of the "darkest" members of her family, her looks were such that she could have been all sorts of nationalities—and her vocal style was definitely not what was called "black." But "passing," except for the briefest pragmatic reasons, was never a black Calhoun thing, even for the "whitest" members of the family.) Josephson now told her to sing "Summertime" and think of her children—and to ask Billie Holiday about how to sing the blues. Lena's repertoire at Café Society included Billie Holiday's "Fine and Mellow" as well as songs by Jerome Kern and Kurt Weill. Radio beckoned. She replaced Dinah Shore as the featured vocalist on *The Chamber Music Society of Lower Basin Street*, NBC's popular jazz series, and starred on WOR's *Cats 'n' Jammers* show. Josephson, to John Hammond's disgust, had renamed Lena "Helena," telling her that "Lena" reminded him of his Jewish aunt.

By the time Lena went to work at Café Society in the spring of 1941, it had become above all a *political* nightclub. It was also the only integrated nightclub outside Harlem, with mixed dancing (blacks and whites of opposite sex). Being in Greenwich Village, Café Society was allowed a certain leeway. It was an open secret, however, that the whole concept was a way of making money for the CPUSA. Josephson, the nominal owner, had been a young Communist shoe salesman who loved jazz and whose brother, a heroic casualty of the Spanish Civil War, had been a friend of Hemingway's. When his brother was killed in Spain, the CPUSA asked Josephson if he would like to run a nightclub and gave him $200 to rent a place. Except for the jazz musicians, who were of no interest to red-baiters, every performer who ever appeared at Café Society was later blacklisted. At the time, however, the club represented the birth of radical chic: future right-winger Clare Boothe Luce gave the club its name, younger *Vogue* editors "discovered" it, one or more of the Roosevelt boys (FDR's sons) were there nearly every night, and members of the new integrated National Maritime Union got free beer at the bar.

For Lena, it was "the best job" she ever had. Making seventy-five dollars a week seemed like a fortune. She lost much of the fear and prejudice against white people that she had learned in the South. Now, she had conversations with white people; or rather she listened to them. Marshall Field III, a committed progressive on race who owned the afternoon tabloid *PM*, saw that "Helena" got plenty of publicity. She was a new Village "star." Best of all, Louis allowed Little Teddy to have a long visit. She loved that the children could play under *her* cherry tree and stay safely in Brooklyn in *her* family home, while she took the subway back and forth to Sheridan Square and her great new job at Café Society.

After Barney Josephson, Lena's second left-wing mentor was Paul Robeson, now a political and theatrical icon, who told her stories about his own mentor, Cora Horne. "She was a mother to me when I needed one," he said of Cora. Half-joking, Paul said that Lena was "too self-centered," had "too much of a temper," and obviously liked "nice things" too much to be an effective militant—but she could still work to change this. Paul told her that the battle could never be won through anger or bitterness; it could be won only through pride and a belief that the cause was just. Paul, a loving and generous man who was fond of Lena's family, obviously saw that she was politically naive, needing protection as well as instruction. Like everyone else, Lena adored Paul and loved his attention—as she loved the attention of all these serious Café Society "grown-ups." She found herself wooed by Broadway as well as the left wing—George Abbott and Vincente Minnelli came to see her about a musical version of *Serena Blandish*. And now she was also wooed by Hollywood.

In the early summer of 1941, Lena, Edwina, and I took a train to California. Lena had been asked to be one of three stars to open a new Hollywood nightclub, the Trocadero. The opening acts were scheduled to be Duke Ellington and his orchestra, Katherine Dunham and her dancers, and Lena. Pearl Harbor ended the dream of a brand-new big nightclub—now they settled on a small one, the Little Troc, and Lena was the only star. She became, almost overnight, the toast of the town, with lines literally down the street—unheard-of in Hollywood. Achieving her extraordinary MGM contract was really not that difficult. She actually had two very clever Hollywood agents: Harold Gumm and Al Melnick of the Louis Shurr office, who advised her to sing the haunting ballad "More Than You Know" because they knew that MGM was planning a movie version of Vincent Youmans' *Great Day*, in which the song appears. She sang it twice: once for Arthur Freed, master of all

MGM musicals, and then for Louis B. Mayer himself. The big man cried, which meant that Lena's contract was a shoo-in. It helped that Lena had arrived in Hollywood just as NAACP head Walter White and former Republican presidential candidate Wendell Willkie were trying to convince movie executives and producers to show more respect to people of color who were America's allies in the war. It also may have helped that Teddy Horne himself arrived to assist in brokering Lena's contract and made it perfectly clear that both he and Lena were basically indifferent to Hollywood. He told Mayer that since he could afford to hire a maid for his daughter, he would not appreciate her playing one in the movies. Surprisingly, Mayer agreed—and Lena's contract stipulated "no maids" and no jungle denizens.

Lena's "movie star" year was 1943–1944. She was always told by MGM that she was a movie star, and MGM treated her like a star (all perks and little money was the MGM way) to make up for the fact that she did not really make movies. But in 1943, twenty-six-year-old Lena, with three movies in release, *felt* like a movie star. She was the first Negro to be signed to a long-term Hollywood contract. But 1943 to 1944 was basically the beginning and end of her so-called movie career. She would be stunned to find out that all of her singing scenes in presumably all-white movies would be cut out when the pictures were shown in the South. The editors simply removed her from the films. Unless the films had an all-black cast, Southern censors refused to show blacks in any roles except as servants.

Lena actually became a star in New York instead of Hollywood, and it happened before any of her major movies were released. In the same week of January 9, 1943, *Time*, *Newsweek*, and *Life* all featured stories about her—and *Life*, arguably the most popular magazine in the world at that time, produced beautiful pictures as well as glowing words:

Each year in New York's after-dark world of supper clubs there appears a girl singer who becomes a sensation overnight. She stands in the middle of a dance floor in a white dress and a soft light, and begins to sing. The room is hushed and her voice is warm and haunting. Her white teeth gleam, her eyes move back and forth, and her softly sung words seem to linger like cigaret smoke. This year that girl is Lena Horne, a young Negro who has been appearing at the Savoy-Plaza's Cafe Lounge . . .

Life magazine was read by almost everybody. Arthur Laurents, a Cornell student who fancied himself a sophisticate (and later wrote *West Side Story* and *Gypsy* for Broadway), read about Lena and went to New York to try to see her. Many years later, in his book *Original Story*, Laurents described his first memory of Lena and the Savoy:

> On a weekend vacation from college, I heard Helena Horne, as Lena Horne was then known, sing so sweet in that room. I had despaired of getting in, then suddenly, magically, there she was, floating toward me in flame-colored chiffon. I told her I had driven all the way from Ithaca just to hear her sing. She was so beautiful, I believed my own lie.

Laurents, a gay man who developed an enormous crush on Lena, got it slightly wrong. She was Lena Horne at the Savoy and Helena Horne at Café Society. Laurents and Lena would meet again a decade later and become close friends.

So much about the Savoy-Plaza Hotel was important—including the lounge's acoustics and the location. The acoustics were so perfect that Lena did not use a microphone. Because there was no microphone, she used her hands to underscore the lyrics. Because there was no artificial amplification of her voice, she was able to establish a gently mesmerizing atmosphere (Lena's typical cabaret audiences always seemed to sit in silent rapture, indeed holding their breath). The audience was hypnotized by her lovely face, form, and hands—and by her lovely voice, which she had just learned to "open up." The poet Sterling Brown said that Lena had a "clarinet" voice. As for location: Lena had performed uptown and downtown, in Harlem at the Cotton Club and in Greenwich Village at Café Society—with the Savoy-Plaza she finally reached *midtown*. (FAO Schwarz, the toy store, long stood where the Savoy-Plaza used to be.) From the Cotton Club to the Savoy-Plaza had taken a decade, with a marriage and babies in between. Lena was very busy polishing her craft. She had learned from every job she ever had. From the Cotton Club she had learned to keep smiling and that the show must go on; from Noble Sissle she had learned about elegance and enunciation; from after-dinner entertainment for Pittsburgh's steel magnates she had learned how to appeal to the carriage trade (they liked Cole Porter and amusing insinuation); from Charlie Barnet and Artie Shaw she began to learn, gently, to *swing*; and from Café Society's left-wing teachers she learned not only how to express feelings in her songs, but what it "meant" to be a Negro. "You are a Negro—and that is the whole basis of what you are and what you will become," Paul Robeson had said to Lena sometime in 1940 at Café Society. "When you live and learn some more you will be Lena Horne, Negro."

Of course, Lena knew what it "meant" to be a Negro. It meant second-class citizenship. And, of course, she knew what they did to Negroes in the South. But coming from middle-class Northern parents, she had escaped the Negro *condition*. She had caught glimpses of that condition as a child in the South, but never for a sustained period of time. She had certainly seen racism in action when she toured with both white and black bands. With white bands, *she* was the problem; with black bands, they were all problems. Lena hated always being a "problem." Like Du Bois and her uncle Frank Horne, two Northern Negroes who essentially learned they were black when they went south to teach, Lena had led an integrated life since childhood. But as a middle-class black female child whose grandparents had migrated to the North, and whose parents had been born in the North, she had never come into personal contact with white Southerners. Her only contact with whites was in the North. Her Brooklyn Catholic church had a white pastor;

she had white classmates and teachers at her Brooklyn Ethical Culture nursery school; she attended Cora's integrated club meetings; and her favorite teachers at Brooklyn's Girls High School were white. Lena actually learned to be a Negro during World War II in Hollywood. She learned from visiting training camps for black GIs what black people in general could expect from America. In 1943 black men in America had to be prepared to fight racism at home as well as fascism abroad every day of their lives.

Happily, thanks to the 1941 Supreme Court decision in *Mitchell v. United States*, the Pullman Company desegregated its sleeping cars just in time for Mother and Cousin Edwina (Cora's niece) and me to go to California on the Super Chief—alone in our blackness, except for Edwina, who looked white. Some of the porters, old-timers, might have known Grandpa Ted Horne. And some of the waiters, traditionally all college graduates, probably knew Uncle Frank. Pullman prided itself on hiring only the most intelligent of Negro men, all of them answering to the generic name "George," which was Mr. Pullman's name. Pullman's employees had Lena's back from the beginning of her career. "Don't forget the people down the line," Paul Robeson had said at Café Society, specifically citing the Pullman porters.

Robeson was right about the Pullman porters; but he was not necessarily correct about Lena. Being a Negro was not "the whole basis" of what she was and would become. Certainly many Negro men felt this way—that all of life was about color. Until World War II, I do not believe that my mother really thought that much about being a Negro—it was simply a fact of life. She thought much more about being a woman. I believe this to be true of most women, no matter what color they are.

Describing Lena as "a light-brown, soft-spoken young Negress who came to Hollywood straight from Brooklyn, the Cotton Club, Noble Sissle's Band and Café Society Downtown," the *New York Times* took notice of Lena at the Little Troc in an article by Barbara Berch in November 1942:

She opened quietly at the Little Troc, a few months ago, in a plain white dress and one soft light. She came on without an introduction and started to sing without even announcing her number. Everybody stopped doing nothing and listened . . . She just sang "The Man I Love" and "Stormy Weather" and a few other daisies that had been laid away by singers long before Lena ever got out of Girls High School . . . She stayed at the Little Troc for weeks, and people who never went to nightclubs pushed their way into the place four or five times a week to hear Lena Horne sing straight versions of a lot of numbers they'd been hearing for years . . . She lives in a five-room duplex in Beverly Hills with her four year old daughter and an aunt. And singing offers come in faster than she has time to refuse them . . . She [is now at] the Savoy and is . . . the first Negro girl to play the room.

Lena opened at the Savoy on November 26, 1942. The opening night audience included Cole Porter, Ethel Merman, and Richard Rodgers— Broadway giants. It was Thanksgiving—the town was full of visitors. On January 9, 1943, *Time* wrote:

Manhattan's quietly swank Savoy-Plaza Café Lounge was last week doing the biggest business in its history as a nightspot . . . No opulent floor show was packing in the customers. The attraction was the face and the shyly sultry singing of a milk-chocolate-colored Brooklyn girl, Lena Horne . . . Flashing one of the most magnificent sets of teeth outside a store she seethes her songs with the air of a bashful volcano. As she reaches the end of "Honeysuckle Rose" . . . her audience is gasping . . .

By March, she was back in Hollywood. By June, three of her movies— *Swing Fever, Cabin in the Sky,* and *Stormy Weather*—were released. By the end of the year she had become the highest-paid Negro entertainer in America.

The first Hollywood party that Lena was invited to, early in 1942, was an afternoon pool party at Cole Porter's for the integrated touring cast of the Broadway show *This Is the Army*. Naturally, Lena revered Porter—a sad man with lovely non-racist manners. She knew she would have to sing for her supper, but the mere fact that Porter liked the way she did "Just One of Those Things" made it all worth it. She had a problem, however, with one of Porter's other guests—the white Southern actress Miriam Hopkins, in the waning days of her stardom. Not the nicest of women at the best of times (as Bette Davis found out in so many movies), that afternoon, with her face frozen in a fixed smile and her voice dripping honeyed venom, forty-year-old Hopkins cornered twenty-five-year-old Lena to tell her how "different" she was from "the others," dissecting her features one by one. Lena froze—the proverbial pinned butterfly. She had never experienced racism up close before. She had no defenses. She was literally speechless. Later, of course (blaming the victim), Lena was angry with *herself*. She probably replayed the moment, imagining all sorts of horrible revenge. She had a sort of revenge, however, by soon becoming the toast of the town, singing at the new nightclub, the Little Troc, with *real* movie stars like Greta Garbo and John Barrymore, who lined up to see her more than once. To hell with Miriam Hopkins! Strangely enough, very soon some of the people she would love best in Hollywood would be gay white Southerners, who had suffered themselves at the hands of their compatriots.

Color was a complicated concept. While color mattered a bit for a band singer, it was never *everything*. Artie Shaw had two band singers of color, Billie Holiday and Lena Horne, without audience complaint. And no one boycotted Benny Goodman over Lionel Hampton or Teddy Wilson. Color in nightclubs was idiosyncratic—it depended on the owner and the audience. In the movies, however, color was *everything*. And color would have everything to do with Lena's movie career. (It would also have everything to do with the initial years of her second

Moses Calhoun, patriarch of the Black Calhouns,
in his prime as the "wealthiest colored man in
Atlanta," c.1885

Cora Calhoun at eighteen,
a belle of Atlanta

Lena Calhoun at sixteen, the
great love of W. E. B. Du Bois

Edwin Horne, Cora's husband, the "Adonis of the Negro press"—an Indiana Republican who became a New York Tammany man

Frank G. Smith, Lena Calhoun's handsome husband, was a Fisk graduate, physician, and high school principal—W. E. B. Du Bois was heartbroken when she married him.

Teddy Horne is top row, far left, of the Smart Set Athletic Club's champion basketball team, c. 1910.

Nellie Graves, who became Mrs. Noel Brown and the first Black Calhoun divorcee

Marie Graves, who became the wife of the great Dr. Homer Nash

Antoine Graves, the husband of Katie Webb, was an 1880s civil rights hero and successful businessman—the first black real estate broker in Atlanta.

Catherine (Katie) Graves, cousin of Cora and Lena Calhoun

Cora Horne at the height of her do-good-uplift career—
member of the board of directors of the Big Brothers
and Big Sisters Federation and Republican Party activist

Errol Horne, Cora's oldest son, who
died in World War I

Here is Ted Horne, Lena's incredibly
dapper dad in the 1920s.

Cora Horne's granddaughter Lena at sixteen, just beginning in the Cotton Club, c. 1933

Cora Horne's granddaughter Lena and her first husband, Louis Jones, as young Pittsburgh marrieds in quasi costumes, c. 1936

Lena Horne and her second husband, Lennie Hayton, in Baja California, c. 1943

Lena Horne at MGM, leaving her personal "movie star" trailer, c. 1943

Lena Horne as the "sweetheart" of the Tuskegee Airmen and "Queen" of the Ninety-Ninth Pursuit Squadron

Lena Horne's son, Teddy Jones, in his teenage years

Little Teddy Jones

Frank Horne, seated, bottom row on the left, with almost every important black man in America in the 1950s—including Ralph Bunche, William Hastie, Roy Wilkins, and Robert Weaver

I flew to Paris after my 1959 Radcliffe graduation
and thought I was never coming back to America.

marriage because she was committing a crime.) The war changed her, made her much more aware of injustice. I was six or seven when I received my first civics lesson from my mother, a tearful accounting of her singing "America the Beautiful" for a Nisei war veteran who had lost both his legs in the war and had his house burned down because he was Japanese American. But the real color shock of World War II for Lena was how badly the U.S. Army treated black GIs.

She actually learned a lot during World War II. She learned how to sing. She learned how to raise the morale of black GIs by listening to them. She learned about being Lena Horne, Negro. She also learned about Lena Horne, star. But she did not learn a lot about being Lena Horne, parent. It was absolutely not her fault—she did the best she could. She was loving and affectionate—but she was a single mother breadwinner. I have finally processed something important about Hollywood that I probably learned during the war. It was terrible to be a child star, and it was also terrible to be the child of a star. The first had no childhood and the second had no parent.

That said, I adored my mother completely. She sang "The Owl and the Pussycat" and read *Winnie-the-Pooh* whenever I asked. She taught me to link my fingers and say, "Here is the church and here is the steeple, open the doors and see all the people." She took me to Mass and let me light candles. I never felt anything less than loved, protected, and indulged when I was with her. She was a doting parent—I just never knew when she would be there, or when I would be with her. Since my brother mostly lived with our father in Pittsburgh and I lived with our mother in Hollywood, I was basically an only child with rare playmates. Actually, most of my playmates were adults. I have only one unpleasant memory of my babysitter Cousin Edwina, who once made me sit all morning before an uneaten bowl of Wheaties. I have always hated Wheaties.

I saw my mother briefly once or twice a day. I would kiss her good-bye early in the morning in my pajamas at the top of (aptly named)

Horn Avenue, a steep little hill off Sunset Strip that ended in sort of a cul-de-sac, while she waited for the cab that would take her to the studio. She refused to learn to drive—it was part of her instinctive anti-California bias. I would then go to the kindergarten down the hill where my schoolmate asked me why my arm was "so brown." I had no reply. "I don't know," I had said. I was the only "brown" child in the class, but I have no memory of that bothering me. I remember being happy in school, although I had few playmates. I did have a sometime neighbor, a little French refugee named Olivia, who taught me to say *"poupée."* Fortunately, like my mother, I learned to read early and found enormous companionship in books. One of the great gifts my mother gave me was to sit me on her lap and teach me to read. Besides books and dolls, I loved music on the radio. I danced around our small Hollywood living room to the Andrews Sisters' "Rum and Coca-Cola" and "Don't Sit Under the Apple Tree (with Anyone Else But Me)."

Lena's color was both a hindrance and a help in her career. It was a hindrance because there were no parts for her to play. It was a help because it made her stand out, which meant that she was less likely to be randomly exploited, or to fall victim to the kind of predators who ruined the lives of young Hollywood women, black and white. Too many people were aware of Lena—or had her back. Besides the Pullman porters, there was the NAACP. In 1942, when Walter White and Wendell Willkie complained to the studios about the undignified stereotyping of Negroes in film, Lena had no idea that she would soon become a *dignified* stereotype. Both White and Ted Horne thought that Lena could establish a new kind of image for black women.

Walter White, like James Weldon Johnson before him, was an Atlanta University graduate and the right NAACP leader for the times. He was also a man of boundless enthusiasm, energy, and imagination. Immediately after Pearl Harbor, the NAACP had called on all Negroes to give wholehearted support to the war effort. White (like Eleanor Roosevelt) certainly seemed to be everywhere during the war: popping up in the South Pacific to defend black GIs against American racism; popping up in Mississippi to investigate a lynching; popping up at the White House to confer with the president; and popping up in Hollywood to "take charge" of Lena's career and tell her how to dress. He did not actually "take charge," but he certainly promoted her career by telling Louis B. Mayer how much America needed someone like Lena in the movies. He oversaw her wardrobe to the extent that he scolded her for wearing a dress that had "good luck" written on it in several languages. "Never wear a dress with writing on it," he said.

James Weldon Johnson, a true Renaissance man (poet, composer, diplomat, author, educator, and more), had been admired and respected by important whites as well as blacks. Johnson knew many of America's most powerful people, but White knew *everybody*. When Lena met White he let her know that he knew her entire family, North and South, and intended to oversee her future. It is no wonder that members of the old black Hollywood basically regarded her as an undercover operative for the NAACP, which they disdained and feared because having no more "undignified stereotypes" could mean less work for the small "club" of black actors who controlled black extras' employment. The last thing Lena expected when she signed her contract was to get into trouble with her own race. The anti-Lena crowd called a meeting to denounce her "no stereotyping" contract. Hattie McDaniel, the 1939 Oscar winner for her performance as Mammy in *Gone with the Wind*, was the only person to defend her. "Do what's best for you and your children," said the kind and gracious McDaniel when she invited Lena to tea. (I gained new respect for Margaret Mitchell, author of *Gone with the Wind*, when I learned that she had written an admiring fan letter to McDaniel after she saw the picture.) But by now, Lena was totally fed up with Hollywood, and so desperately homesick, that she flew back to New York to make a decision about quitting the whole MGM thing entirely. She knew she always had a job with Barney Josephson.

It was Count Basie who made the difference. As she was crying about how much she hated California, Basie said, "They never choose *us*. But they've chosen you. You have to go back so that other people can have your opportunities."

Lena was incredibly lucky that Vincente Minnelli, a New York acquaintance, had arrived at MGM about the time that she had. Minnelli would direct Lena not only in *Cabin in the Sky* but also in the first two movies that preceded it—*Panama Hattie* and *I Dood It*. Minnelli, aged forty, had treated Lena as a sort of muse ever since he saw her at Café Society. He was learning to be a director and Lena, she supposed, was learning to be a movie star. Her singing bits were produced by MGM's best talents in costume, hair, makeup, and music. MGM was basically the Buckingham Palace of studios.

Waiting for *Cabin in the Sky* to finally be made, Lena made her actual movie debut in *Panama Hattie*. Because she sang a Latin song, some blacks accused her of trying to pass. Perhaps to avoid confusion, in her next film bit directed by Minnelli, *I Dood It*, she was scheduled to sing "The Battle of Jericho," a rousing Negro spiritual ("Joshua fought the battle of . . ."). She not only learned to *really* sing on *I Dood It*, but also found a friend. Tall, blond, and chic, Kay Thompson, who came to MGM after Lena, worked on a vocal arrangement for "The Battle of Jericho" at Minnelli's request. Kay had a genius for vocal arrangements that she had honed as assistant to Fred Waring—once known as "America's Singing Master" or "The Man Who Taught America How to Sing."

Lena and Kay became instant and long-lasting friends. "As naturally friendly as a puppy," Kay recalled Lena to Sam Irvin, author of the biography *Kay Thompson*: "All in all, she is one of the few completely *real* people in Hollywood." Lena called Kay the "best vocal coach in the world" and said that the most important thing Kay had taught her was breath control. "We were working on her arrangement of 'Jericho' and it really extended me and I was hitting notes I didn't know I could," she later elaborated. Kay was also working with a large integrated choir.

"Jericho" could not be kept under wraps. Word got back to Jack Cummings (Mayer's nephew). "Jack came down," Kay remembered, "and we knocked him over with great joy." The number became the high spot of an otherwise dull movie. So far, the only moviemaker Lena knew was Vincente Minnelli. She and Minnelli were like kid sister and big brother, working on their first movies together. Lena loved working with Minnelli, who made sure that she always looked and sounded wonderful, even if Southerners were going to cut her out of the picture. Thanks to Lena, the makeup department had finally created her look: Max Factor's "Light Egyptian"—which the department now used on any white actress who had to look vaguely "native."

According to *Black Women in America*, edited by Darlene Clark Hine, Lena's small scenes actually mattered:

> The guest spots had a tremendous impact. Her job, as Walter White had seen it, was to change the American image of black women, and she did. She fit white society's standard of beauty as well as the most beautiful white women did, but she was clearly a woman of color; she was also a woman of great charm and dignity who was conscious of her position as a representative of black America—her choices about the way she presented herself were influenced by that role . . . It seemed important at the time to show that a black woman did not have to sing spirituals or earthy, overtly sexual laments; Horne sang Cole Porter and Gershwin. It seemed important that a black woman could be cool, glamorous, and sophisticated; Horne always looked as though she had stepped out of the pages of *Vogue*. "The image that I chose to give them was of a woman who they could not reach."

My mother never gossiped about people's love affairs—except for the time that she had the compartment next to Marlene Dietrich and Jean Gabin's drawing room on the Super Chief and they never came out of their room during the entire cross-country journey. It seemed the height of both glamour and romance. She enjoyed hearing salacious stories about the high and mighty, but she never repeated them. Nor did she believe in kissing and telling. Other people told me about her romances. She was very cryptic. John Hammond, for example, told me about my mother and Joe Louis. Orson Welles was an exception to her own rule, possibly because he was such an incredible wunderkind. America was not yet into its youth craze. The stars of the day—Bette Davis, Joan Crawford, Myrna Loy, William Powell, Clark Gable—were all grown-up sophisticates. But Orson Welles, in his twenties, became one of the most famous people in the world when he pulled off the greatest Halloween prank in history with a radio drama purporting to be on-scene reporting of the Martian invasion of New Jersey. Enough Jerseyites believed the brilliantly executed concept that Welles, basically just a super-talented kid, was instantly (literally overnight) famous around the world. To most Hollywood "grown-ups," Welles was a brat and a pain in the backside. He had turned radio upside down. *Would anyone believe a live radio news report again?* His first movie was a masterwork. *Would any other mogul or tycoon be safe again?* He was so incredibly young, so full of himself, and so very successful, it's almost as if he *had* to self-destruct—which of course he did. Welles was two years older than Lena. She thought he was amazing; he knew everything and was always learning. In any case, it was not a long-lived romance. Welles soon moved on to Dolores del Rio.

Ted Horne, who had introduced his daughter to her husband, began the new decade by introducing her to another important man—namely Joe Louis, the *married* boxing champion known as the "Brown Bomber." Edna had upbraided Lena after the first Joe Louis–Max Schmeling bout when Lena was inconsolable over Louis' loss. "Why are you so upset?" Edna had asked. "You don't even know this man." Lena, between sobs, could only blurt out, "Don't you understand? He belongs to *us*." This was a very perceptive remark on the part of young Lena. The romance with the famous, sweetly inarticulate Louis lasted on and off for a year. Lena did most of the talking, which she loved. There is a photograph of Lena and Joe together in a rowboat sometime in early 1941 at Louis' training camp. The picture, taken by Carl Van Vechten, is basically of Louis' bare, beautifully sculpted, muscular back as he rows the boat. And Lena, all long hair and long legs, wearing slacks and a striped T-shirt, is opposite him talking away. Louis did not appear to be a boastful or conceited champion; that was why everybody, black or white, liked him. And blacks, collectively, loved him. Every time Louis won, Harlem would erupt in spontaneous New Year's Eve–like joy. Police let it happen because everyone was happy. Louis was heavyweight champion of the world from 1937 to 1949. Lena and married man Joe "dated" periodically from 1941 through 1942. The romance ended on a sour note when Lena discovered that her married boyfriend was having simultaneous "romances" with her friend Lana Turner and figure skater Sonja Henie. Lena and Joe remained publicly cordial but basically never spoke again after 1942.

By 1943 Lena was becoming an important symbol in the war effort. Blacks had only a few: General Benjamin O. Davis Sr., the first black brigadier, and his son Colonel Benjamin O. Davis Jr., leader of the Tuskegee Airmen; Joe Louis; Dorie Miller, the heroic navy cook at Pearl Harbor, first hero of the war, who manned a forbidden-to-blacks gun and brought down a Japanese airplane; and Lena. Despite their failed romance, Louis and Lena must have been gratified when two of the brand-new 155-mm artillery guns used in the Pacific by the first black marines were named *Lena Horne* and *Joe Louis*.

Lena was supposed to represent a new image of the American Negro. American movies had been criticized by Allies of color for demeaning portrayals of nearly every racial group. Most important, she was supposed to raise the morale of black GIs. They finally had a pinup—though Lena definitely hated being the only one. She was also the pinup of some white GIs, including the wonderful actor Richard Basehart, who told her he had carried her picture all through the war. Granted, the military was a Southern institution, but Lena had no idea of the depths of America's institutionalized racism until she learned about it from black GIs. The surest way for a young black man to learn that he was a Negro in America was to join the U.S. Army and to hear the N-word, and every other form of insult, every single day of his military life. Imagine the culture shock to young Negro recruits from the North and the West sent to basic training in the Deep South to encounter naked, regional racial hatred for the first time. It could be a terrifying experience.

Nelson Peery, author of *Black Fire*, a personal history of a black GI in World War II, wrote about Lena's visit to his camp:

"Lena Horne's walking around talking to the men." It was true. She came toward us with Warrant Officer Mays, leader of the band. With a few words for this soldier, a smile for that one, she came toward our tent—the dimples, the sparkling white teeth . . .

"Are you going to invite me in?" . . . She glanced around our neat tent and, gracefully crossing her legs, sat on my cot. "I want to thank you for coming out here—I mean talking with the enlisted men," I said . . . "I don't need any thanks. I think I know what you common guys, you GI Joes, are going through. You're the ones who do the fighting and dying. If my singing and talking helps—"

"Would you? I mean, sing one verse—just for us?" . . .

She stood up humming. The Lena Horne on-stage smile brightened the squad tent. "Don't buy sugar . . . you just have to touch my cup." She pressed her fingertips to her lips and blew the kiss to us. Dreamlike, she disappeared from the tent, leaving five black soldiers in love with her forever.

Hollywood was a bustling, confident place during the war. There was a new appreciation for the movies as a vital industry in the war effort. Movies were almost as important as ships and planes in waging the propaganda and morale war. Besides movie-movies, Hollywood also made training films for GIs and documentaries that explained the war to civilians. There was a new sense of heightened excitement in a normally rather sleepy place. Now Hollywood was a wartime capital—perhaps not as exciting as Washington, but more exciting than New York, which did not live under the expectation of imminent Japanese "invasion." Movie stars sold war bonds. Aged six or seven, I was aware of the excitement. Most exciting of all was that Lena's uncle Burke, Ted Horne's youngest brother, became engaged to one of the first black WAVEs, Lieutenant (Junior Grade) Harriet Pickens, a Brooklyn neighbor. A graduate of Smith College, Harriet was the daughter of NAACP field secretary William Pickens—a legendary NAACP figure. William Pickens became the most illustrious graduate of Alabama's Missionary Talladega College in 1902 when he won a scholarship to Yale, was elected to Phi Beta Kappa, and won the 1903 Henry James Ten Eyck Prize. Between 1911 and 1923 Pickens actually wrote *two* autobiographies. Highly visible in the NAACP in the 1920s and 1930s, especially in the campaign to support Ethiopia over Italy, he would be charged as a subversive in the 1950s because of his friendship with Socialist leader Norman Thomas. But now his daughter Harriet was one of the first two black WAVEs. (The other young woman was only an ensign, so Harriet was number one.) She looked amazing in her dazzling white uniform by Mainbocher, an expensive and exclusive American designer that did not sell in department stores. The WAVEs were the best-dressed women's service. I was committed to doing my bit, collecting silver foil, growing my victory garden, and hoping the war would last long enough for me to become a WAVE. Hollywood had a *good* war—unless you were conspicuously Japanese, Negro, or Mexican.

By mid-1944 Lena was known to a moviegoing audience that did not live south of the Mason-Dixon Line, where she was liable to be cut out of the picture. That she had as many Southern white fans as she did is amazing. (A white Southern woman friend, my contemporary, had two favorite paper dolls, Sonja Henie and Lena Horne.) In October 1944 *Motion Picture* made Lena the first person of color to be on the cover of a movie magazine. She was in three less than memorable 1944 movies: *Boogie-Woogie Dream*, *Broadway Rhythm*, and *Two Girls and a Sailor*. Kay worked with Lena on "Paper Doll" (a boy's song, Lena rightly insisted) for *Two Girls and a Sailor*. Lena looked incredibly beautiful in the black-and-white film, in a simple, long black dress. Later Kay worked on several *Ziegfeld Follies* segments, including what Sam Irvin called "Lena Horne's powerful rendition of 'Love,'" composed by Hugh Martin and Ralph Blane and conducted by Lennie Hayton:

> One day during rehearsals, Lena "protested she could not reach high C in a certain passage." "My voice isn't that good," Lena insisted. "Better put it down at least one key." On the next run-through, Horne hit the note pitch-perfect. "You see?" Lena said. "B-flat is my limit." "I see." Kay nodded knowingly. "For your information, I didn't change the key, and you can hit high C right on the nose as long as you think it's B-flat!"

Kay often spoke of Lennie as the best conductor on the lot. He was Arthur Freed's favorite, but Lena disliked him because he was a friend of Rags Ragland, a comedian who had told a racist joke in her hearing at a party. Lena assumed that Lennie was a racist, too. But Kay convinced her otherwise. Somehow, Lennie began to turn up whenever Lena was around. Thanks to matchmaker Kay, a romance did indeed develop after many nights of his playing and her singing with the gang at Lucy's restaurant, the favorite Freed Unit hangout. One night the gang all went home and it was just the two of them. An interracial love affair was not easy in those days. They had to be extremely discreet. The laws of California prohibited marriage between the races and so (one presumed) did the laws of MGM. They had romantic weekends in Baja California and elsewhere in Mexico.

When I got to know Lennie, he let me bang on the piano and gave me silver paper from his Camels to add to my collection of foil for the war effort. He was totally indulgent. He would become my stepfather— and I adored him. I have no memory of ever hearing Lennie raise his voice. He was everything a stepfather should be: kind, gentle, loving, and funny. He was actually already a stepfather. He was a widower with another stepdaughter when my mother married him. His stepdaughter was a teenager, whom I also loved, called Peggy Husing. Lennie had been married to the ex-wife of radio disc jockey star Ted Husing of *Make Believe Ballroom*. Lennie's wife had died suddenly of a cerebral hemorrhage. "I have a terrible headache," she said one day—and then she was gone.

Louis B. Mayer now asked Lena, as a personal favor, to sing at a friend's Chicago nightclub, Chez Paree. It was a barn of a place that was losing money, but people lined up around the block to see Lena. Because she broke every house record, and he heard that she liked star sapphires, the club's owner gave her a huge ring at the end of her run. Lennie, half as a joke, asked if she had "wiped the blood off." Lena realized that nightclubs, despite being mob-run and rejecting black customers (except for *very* special friends of Lena), were a great fallback to a movie career that might not be going anywhere.

Lena was now used to crowds and big audiences, but when she appeared at the Great Lakes Naval Station near Chicago, this was like nothing she had ever seen. Wearing a midriff dress and a hibiscus in her hair, and escorted by an incredibly handsome black naval officer, who turned out to be an old friend from Brooklyn, she heard the roar of thousands of black sailors and GIs and finally felt like a movie star. I think it was a twofold roar of approval: one roar for Lena and her midriff and hibiscus, and the other for her escort, Ensign Reginald

Goodwin, one of the first thirteen black navy officers (known in the black press as the "Golden Thirteen"). Anyway, it was a very movie star moment. Lena was always treated like a movie star in army camps. Because she basically had no movie roles to play and no parts to learn, she had time to visit army camps for the USO; time to become the first Negro member of the board of the Screen Actors Guild; time to work for the Fair Employment Practices Committee, which investigated hiring discrimination, with black California assemblyman Gus Hawkins; and time to work with the Hollywood Independent Citizens Committee of the Arts, Sciences, and Professions (HICCASP). It was HICCASP, with its liberal attitudes about race, that would get Lena and others into very hot political waters in the red-baiting late 1940s and early 1950s.

Not only was Lena learning about politics; she was learning to be tough. When she went to sing at an army camp in Arkansas and discovered that the German prisoners of war were seated in front of black GIs for her performance, she thought at first to walk past the Germans and sing only to the blacks. But she refused to sing at all and demanded to see the NAACP. The Arkansas NAACP was a single courageous woman, Daisy Bates, who later led black Little Rock high school students through their desegregation ordeal. When Lena returned to California, she was essentially kicked out of the USO for refusing to sing for the Germans. Meanwhile, the Justice Department threatened sedition charges against black newspapers for headlining stories of injustices against black GIs. Everywhere that Lena went, she heard horrendous stories from black GIs—not about enemy depredations, but about American ones.

She also made weekly appearances at the integrated Hollywood Canteen (as opposed to the segregated USO) to dance with black GIs. The Hollywood Canteen was founded by Bette Davis and John Garfield. Their combined liberal spirits—Yankee-abolitionist and Jewish-left-wing—guaranteed that the Canteen would be integrated. As far as race relations went, the nicest people in Hollywood were either gay or left wing. Other than gays and left-wingers, there were very few white Americans beyond the Freed Unit who would open their homes to Lennie and Lena. On the other hand, a group of mostly liberal stars could be counted on to be friendly, respectful, and even hospitable. Lena considered them to be the "decent" people of Hollywood. There were probably other nice people, but these are ones I remember my mother speaking of. Besides the Freed Unit ("decent" to a man and woman), her list included: Bette Davis, Myrna Loy, James Cagney, Katharine Hepburn, Charlie Chaplin, Rosalind Russell, Barbara Stanwyck, Gregory Peck, Edward G. Robinson, Robert Benchley, George Cukor, Joan Crawford (yes), Humphrey Bogart and his divine fourth wife, Betty (Lauren) Bacall, and the first Mrs. Frank Sinatra, who went out of her way to be nice by bringing one of her beautifully dressed, white-gloved daughters to tea. The "indecent" included everyone at Paramount and Republic.

I never met Louis B. Mayer. But I did meet his daughter, Irene Mayer Selznick, with whom he was always politically at odds, and her son Danny on the Super Chief. She was a charming, attractive woman who became the producer of *A Streetcar Named Desire*. Danny and I, who were about the same age, nine or ten, had a grand adventure exploring the train—each car was named for an Indian chieftain. Danny and I would meet again in Cambridge as Harvard and Radcliffe freshmen.

Although Lena had bonded with "the girls" in early-morning makeup—Ann Sothern, Kathryn Grayson, Lana Turner, and Ava Gardner (the latter two had giggled with Lena like sorority sisters over Artie Shaw)—she saw herself as isolated. Old black Hollywood hated her and most of old white Hollywood ignored her. She had few friends—and few people with whom she felt safe besides the Freed Unit. Although Lena was basically barred from most Hollywood restaurants, she and Lennie were welcome at Romanoff's, Hollywood's most expensive eatery. "Prince" Mike Romanoff proved that "White" Russians could be just as non-racist as "Reds." I had no idea that some of our Horn Avenue neighbors had passed a petition to have us removed. The petition was stopped in midcirculation by our air-raid warden Humphrey Bogart.

The "Battling Bogarts" (Bogie and his alcoholic, argumentative third wife, Mayo Methot) lived across the street on Horn Avenue. He was a very strict air-raid warden—as Teddy and I discovered the night we stayed up late, on November 9, 1944, to listen to Lena on the best radio program ever, *Suspense*. I think she played a singer somewhere in South America chased by Nazis. I remember being scared—as I was when I saw *Cabin in the Sky* and had to be taken, weeping, from the theater during the storm scene. Now, in 1944, there was a loud knock on the door. "Close that curtain!" shouted Warden Bogart. Cousin Edwina had not properly closed the blackout curtain.

The Freed Unit was like the slightly crazed, very funny family Lena never had. The members really liked one another. By now she had met the "decent and interesting friends" she had once despaired of finding in Hollywood—the people who made her feel safe. She had vowed never to go to big Hollywood parties. That was more or less true. But she did seem to spend most of her Hollywood life either going to or giving *small* Hollywood parties where people sat on the floor, their plates in their laps, with the latest jazz on the record player. When we dined *en famille*, Lennie put on classical music—but it was always jazz for parties.

My mother liked everything that did not remind her of California. She especially liked Betsy Blair, Gene Kelly's wife, who also went out of her way to avoid living or looking like a Californian. Adorable Betsy, who had been a child model, wore bobby socks and no makeup and looked about sixteen. She would not have a swimming pool because she was sincerely socialist. At the actual age of sixteen, living in New York and dancing two shows a night as a chorus girl at the Diamond Horseshoe, she had joined a Marxist study group.

Fred Astaire was the sublime king of poetry in motion, but Gene Kelly, who was not half as romantic as Astaire (or half the dancer), was wonderfully athletic and peppy in his sailor suit in *On the Town*—for which Lennie won an Oscar for musical direction. (Lennie did not bother to go to the awards ceremony, since he did not believe in the concept.) Gene was sort of a dancing cartoon; the bubble over his head said "Energy!" Betsy and Gene had left New York at the height of their combined personal success. He was the toast of Broadway in *Pal Joey*, and she, having graduated from the chorus line to acting, was an overnight success as the ingenue in William Saroyan's play *The Beautiful People*. MGM was grooming Gene to be big. The couple could have joined the old prewar Hollywood crowd: playing polo in Beverly Hills, spending weekends in Palm Springs, sailing at Catalina, and dancing at Ciro's. Those people expected to be photographed every hour of the day. But in spirit, Gene and Betsy and their friends basically never left the Times Square drugstore where all the young actors hung out. They defiantly belonged to the "New York" crowd. Betsy, who wrote *The Memory of All That*, the story of her life, absolutely refused to "go Hollywood." Gene didn't care. Gene cared only about Gene's career. He wanted to make "important" movies like *The Pirate*, with Judy Garland. Lennie was the music director on *The Pirate*. The music was by Cole Porter. The picture was a turkey.

Lena had clearly evolved since Miriam Hopkins. She could now fight at least some of her own battles. In the words of Paul Robeson, she was learning to be "Lena Horne, Negro." In 1943 Robeson was at what his biographer Martin Duberman called "the apex of his fame." In October he opened on Broadway in *Othello*. His costars were Uta Hagen and José Ferrer. It was an unqualified smash hit. According to *Variety*: "The tremendous ovations given to Paul Robeson, the star, are ample indication that these times are when the sweep and majesty of artistry and a democracy must encompass racial barriers."

Paul Robeson's *Othello* at the Shubert Theatre ran for 296 performances —a record for Shakespeare on Broadway. Eleanor Roosevelt went to see a performance in November and wrote about it in her newspaper column, "My Day," describing the play as "tense and moving" and "beautifully acted and produced." Robeson came to California after the run, and the Kellys had a party for the NAACP with Robeson as the guest of honor. Betsy described the evening:

"After he sang, he spoke, 'Must I tell my children to tell their children to tell their children that someday things will be better? We will not wait any longer. We cannot wait any longer.' His words burned into the hearts of everyone in the room. We raised a lot of money."

Marxism was probably at its most popular in America in 1943. The siege of Stalingrad had great recruitment value. Benjamin J. Davis Jr., the young Atlanta lawyer in the Angelo Herndon case ten years earlier, whom the judge had called "nigger," was elected that year to the New York City Council on the Communist Party ticket. Davis, whose best friend was Robeson and whose father, former chairman of the Georgia Republican Party, was a lifelong friend of the Calhoun cousins, would be reelected in 1945 and become a member of the Communist Party's National Committee. Meanwhile, in Hollywood, Lena was being politically wooed by Carlton Moss, a black writer and rumored Communist Party member. Moss was taken seriously by Lena and others because he was the screenwriter of the acclaimed Frank Capra documentary *The Negro Soldier*. One night, Moss drove Lena to the top of the Hollywood Hills. At the sight of the famous Hollywood lights below, he suddenly announced, *"All this can be yours if you join the party."* Lena thought he sounded so corny that she started to giggle. Besides, she thought that the whole purpose of socialism was the concept of sharing the wealth, not one person having it "all." Since at that point Lena believed that everyone, even a man she did not particularly like, was smarter than she was, she kept quiet. Soon after, however, she asked Robeson if she should join the party. His advice, in no uncertain terms, was "Absolutely not!" Robeson may well have been thinking about his mentor, Cora Horne, who would indeed have reeled in her grave. Cora wanted a better America, not another Soviet Union.

Lena's Hollywood friends were actually divided between the super politically attuned and the apolitical. Most of the Freed Unit gang, Betsy Kelly aside, was apolitical. Kay Thompson, in particular, was certainly too self-involved to be political. She never had a political thought, but professed to be anticommunist because she had once been fired by a well-known Broadway "Red." Kay, like so many others in Hollywood, was actually hiding deep personal disappointment. Sam Irvin wrote:

> In his unpublished memoir, jazz composer Alec Wilder observed that after Kay had been in Hollywood for a while, "a tougher, harsher, more cynical person" emerged. She had reason to be cynical. Bolstering the careers of others was a bittersweet endeavor for someone who craved the spotlight so intently.

Playwright Arthur Laurents, who fell in love with Lena when he first saw her at the Savoy-Plaza, and rediscovered her at the Kelly house, saw the same attitude in Lena. She had to be feeling deep personal disappointment because she had finally realized that she would probably be glued to a pillar for the rest of her movie career, interacting with no one, for the sake of the white Southern market. Laurents saw Lena evolve, through her anger at the system, into a totally different performer:

> It happened overnight, not in pictures—she was the wrong color for pictures—but at a downtown club called Slapsie Maxie on the night it opened . . . There is such a thing as cabaret history and it was made at Slapsie's in one night. Everybody lucky enough to be there (I was one of them: the Kelly group went to support Lena) saw fireworks explode twice. First from the heat of Jack Cole and His Dancers: three highly sexual males, three highly sexual females, dancing unlike any dancers anyone had seen anyplace before. The first number, "Spy," set to Benny Goodman's "Sing, Sing, Sing," fixed the tone—intense

and erotic—and the style—angular, slashing, knee slides, tipping hats, twisting torsos and pelvises. That tone, that style, the moves and steps themselves, unseen until then, became a permanent part of the choreographic language of the Broadway musical. Bob Fosse is credited but it all began with Jack Cole in a town that drained and discouraged and finally destroyed him . . .

The closing act at Slapsie Maxie's was Lena Horne with a trio led by Lennie Hayton. She wasn't Metro's Lena Horne, she wasn't the Helena Horne I remembered from the Savoy-Plaza, she wasn't the Lena who sat removed and bemused at the Kellys'. The voice deeper, the lyrics almost bitten and spat out, the eyes glittering, this was a new Lena. This Lena was angry sex . . .

In the early Sixties, when we were so close, I asked her what was in her head when she came out on the elegant floor of the Waldorf in New York or the Fairmont in San Francisco. She bared her teeth in the smile those expensive audiences waited for.

"Fuck you," she said. "That's what I think when I look at them. Fuck all of you." She meant it figuratively, they took it literally.

The new Lena Horne was not about "angry sex." She was far too much of a romantic to be that interested in sex. Since Lena loved dancers, and adored the strange, "angry" genius Jack Cole, she may well have been influenced by Cole's dancers, famous for their intense erotic energy and the fact that they never grinned when taking bows. Lena's smile was always dazzling and gracious, but Lena, like Cole, was "angry." She was angry at her career. She had changed the public image of black women, but she was still the definition of tokenism—all alone in a white world with nothing to do. And she hated nightclubs.

Lena's anger, like Jack Cole's, was elegant, contained, and controlled by intelligence. She treated her audience with deference and courtesy. But she never *gushed* and was never sentimental. She let audiences know that while they might be getting the singer, they were not getting the woman. As the first black to appear in so many of the clubs she worked, she had built a wall between herself and the audience—mostly because she had no idea what her reception might be. She spoke very little beyond "thank you" and introducing her musicians. She was also too "tasteful" to be obviously "sexy"—if anything, women in her audience loved her as much as, or more than, men for her looks and gowns. Graciousness aside, unlike most performers, Lena never sought the audience's approval—but the audience seemed to seek hers. There was always absolute hushed silence when she sang, and not an ice cube tinkled unless she wanted laughs. The beat of silence, then rapturous applause, as audiences, mesmerized by her seemingly "aloof" self-absorption, as well as her voice and face, begged her to love them. This creative tension helped make her the highest-paid female international nightclub star throughout the 1950s and early 1960s.

At Slapsie Maxie's Lena was announcing that she was no longer a saccharine ingenue or a dignified token. She was taking her career and her life into her own hands. As for Lena's profanity, while Cora Horne would have been shocked, in many circles it would have been considered the appropriate response to the Miriam Hopkinses of the world.

Once the war was over Lena remained a musical star, but she was never again a movie star. She always hated Hollywood and hated the way she had to make movies. Unless the picture had an all-black cast, Hollywood wanted her only to sing, never to speak—all for the sake of the Southern market. It is clear, some seventy years later, that her MGM contract was purely a wartime propaganda gesture. Without the war, Lena would probably never have made a movie. But in World War II she was propaganda gold—proving that America, unlike Germany and Japan, did not oppress racial minorities. Lena was, in a sense, a human "perfect storm." As a stand-in for all minorities, she was portrayed with so much "dignity" that she was practically paralyzed. Within a decent interval at the end of the war, Lena and MGM parted ways. Despite her unhappiness with her so-called movie star career, MGM and Lena actually did well by each other. Thanks to Lena, MGM did its bit for the United Nations, as the Allies were called, and thanks to MGM, Lena learned to really sing (as well as make up her face). MGM also helped her to become a nightclub superstar before television began to keep nightclub patrons at home.

CHAPTER TEN

South/1940s

WAR BRIDES

B Y 1940 a black Calhoun, Antoine Graves Sr., a handsome and imposing white-haired figure beloved in Negro Atlanta, and the first black man to receive a real estate broker's license, had been in business for fifty-five years—longer than any other Atlanta broker, white or black. Dealing with the city, the state, and the white power structure, he became one of the best-known and most important black businessmen in Atlanta. From his real estate offices in the Kimball House on Atlanta's Wall Street, a street otherwise occupied by white businesses, he brokered the deal for the sale of the land for the Georgia State Capitol. A man of many firsts besides his broker's license, he was the first to envision an upscale residential Negro neighborhood in Atlanta—a wild success. Earlier in the century he had been responsible for building the first Negro schools. And he was forever known as the hero of 1886, for losing his job as principal of the Gate City Public School when he refused to march in a mandated parade honoring the remains of Jefferson Davis.

In September 1940 the ailing Graves received a note of appreciation from a local woman doctor:

Dear Sir:

I have known of your confinement to your home for some time and being a physician I have hesitated to come to see you. The rest you are taking I hope you will continue to take long enough to fully restore you to your former self, because Atlanta wants you as long as possible in its midst.

Your outstanding qualities of manhood wherever it was involved has endeared you to the real people of Atlanta. I shall never forget how you exerted it while you were principal of Gate City School. I hope you remember.

Sincerely yours,
B.B.S. Thompson, M.D.

Dr. Blanche B. S. Thompson, physician and surgeon, of 161 Hilliard Street NE, was unusual not only in her gender, but in her profession. In 1940 there were only 3,939 registered Negro physicians and surgeons in the United States (an increase of 740 since 1910) and there were 1,175 lawyers (an increase of 396 since 1910). There were probably more physicians than lawyers because doctors, unlike lawyers, did not get into political or civil rights issues. In white thinking, a few black doctors were probably necessary—black lawyers were not.

On March 10, 1941, Antoine Graves, aged seventy-nine and about to retire, was summoned to serve as a grand juror in the city of Atlanta. In many parts of the South, blacks were forbidden to serve on juries at all. On March 16, the day he officially retired from active professional work, he learned that his wife's much-loved cousin Lena Calhoun Smith had died in Chicago the day before, aged seventy-two. On March 21 Antoine Sr. died in his sleep of heart failure.

The following obit must be from a Negro paper because the honorifics "Miss" and "Mrs." are used:

The deceased handled some of the biggest real estate deals in the city's history. At one time he sold the Governor's mansion to the state. To his union with Miss Kate Webb were born six children . . . At one time, Mr. Graves was prominent in the Republican party. He is a past grandmaster of the Odd Fellows . . . Internment will be in the family mausoleum at Oakland cemetery. His body will be cremated and the ashes of his son, Antoine Graves, Jr., which were kept in the father's room up until the time of the latter's death, will be interred at the same time.

The Graves mausoleum was the only mausoleum in the black section of Oakland cemetery. It is touching that Antoine Sr. kept the ashes of his only son, Judge, in his room. There is a photo of Antoine Sr. and Katie Webb Graves circa late 1930s. They are a handsome, dignified old couple—the way old people *used* to look. They both have white hair. Still slim and erect, Antoine actually looks like a dark "Kentucky Colonel" in his three-piece linen suit and with his little white goatee. After seventy-something years and six children, Katie Webb Graves no longer has a waistline, but she is not overweight. Her posture is good. She is still elegant. She wears a light dress and good shoes and shows slim ankles. In another picture, she wears a pretty, entirely age-appropriate evening gown and, fresh from the beauty parlor, sits on a settee waiting patiently for a party to begin.

If the New York branch of the black Calhouns was a patriarchy, with Edwin Horne and his four sons forcing their feminist mother to fend for herself and make her own life, the Atlanta branch, the whole Brown-Nash clan, was a matriarchy that became a sorority. There were two sets of sisters and cousins, all slightly younger than their distant cousin Lena Calhoun Horne, who were also best friends. The Browns and the Nashes were the grandchildren of Katie Webb and Antoine Graves Sr. The Browns, three daughters and a son, were the children of Nellie Graves and Noel Brown. There is a picture, probably taken in the late 1930s, of the three Brown girls: Kathryn, Antoinette, and Nellie. The Nashes, four daughters and a son, were the children of Marie Graves and Dr. Homer Nash. The Nashes were Catherine, Helen, Harriet, Dorothy, and Homer Jr.

As a solitary child, I always loved reading books about big families and cousins who were best friends. But there were so many sisters among the Atlanta Calhouns that the women may have sucked up all the air. They were Southern women, after all, with an endless supply of small talk. The sisters and female cousins, fortunate in their parents, became strong, independent wives, mothers, teachers, social workers, librarians, and physicians. Most would have long-lasting marriages and many children and grandchildren.

On August 6, 1941, Antoine Graves' granddaughter, the dimpled, sweet-faced nineteen-year-old Kathryn Brown, was up at three A.M. typing out some verses (a few almost rude) about her cousins and sisters. "The Nutt Family as Written by Nutt No. 5" relied on family slang, inside jokes, and sister-cousin secrets. The tone is teasing, but what is very clear is that these young women clearly enjoyed one another's company—and their very comfortable, insular lives.

This is an abridged version of Kathryn Brown's much longer poem:

> Listen, my dears, and you shall hear
> (And please don't question what)
> The story of that famous family clan—
> The Graves clan of Nash-Brown Nutt.

She opens with the older relatives:

> The eldest Nutt in this family of Nutts
> is a lady frail and dear
> She makes us shout—she makes us scream
> Because she cannot hear.

The "eldest Nutt" is Katie Webb Graves, Kathryn's grandmother.

> Mrs. Nellie Brown Nutt is next in line
> And a nutty nut is she
> She has great big eyes (and she uses them too)
> And a family of devils three.

Kathryn is one of the "devils three" and Nellie is her mother. She soon moves on to herself and her sisters:

> Kathryn Brown Nutt is a tempestuous Nutt
> Who dearly loves a spat—
> Her gaits uncertain, her language rude
> And—well, we don't talk about that.

Did Kathryn drink? With so many versions of "Catherine" in the family, Kathryn was pronounced the way it looks—but Catherine Nash's name was pronounced Cath*reen* by her sisters and cousins to distinguish between them.

Kathryn wrote of her sisters, Nellie and Antoinette, the other "devils":

> Nellie Brown Nutt is a typical Nutt
> Of whose musical prowess we're proud
> With her bass viol tones and detachable back
> She'll never be lost in a crowd.

Another cousin of Lena's generation, twenty-three-year-old Nellie Brown, a musician, carried her bass viola on her back. Nellie's namesake mother had accompanied her violinist brother, Judge. In 1942 (about the time that Lena was signing her MGM contract), Nellie Brown began singing and playing the piano in Atlanta clubs. There are photos of Nellie at the piano in the 1940s.

Antoinette Nutt's a real smart Nutt
Tho' stubborn as Rock Gibraltar
She cuts up dresses and stumps up shoes
She loves new clothes and Walter.

Antoinette Brown was eighteen years old in 1941. She eventually married her beloved Walter Ricks Jr. There is a picture of Antoinette as an attractive young postwar matron with her children, Cynthia, Patricia, and Walter III.

Kathryn then focused on her Nash cousins:

Catherine Nash Nutt is a charming child
As charming children go—
She sleeps by night and eats all day
And never mentions Joe.

Twenty-one-year-old Catherine Nash's "Joe" was Joseph Frye, her childhood sweetheart. Two months earlier, Catherine had graduated from Spelman College. It was a summer of many graduations—including one for Catherine's fifty-two-year-old mother, Marie Nash, who earned her master's degree in social work from Atlanta University. There is a picture of Marie Nash receiving her diploma, posed with her husband, Dr. Homer Nash; her mother, Catherine "Katie" Webb Graves; and her brother Judge's ex-wife, the famously beautiful Pinkie Chaires Graves. Catherine Nash received a bachelor of library science degree in 1943 from Western Reserve University in Cleveland.

Next in line comes Helen Nash Nutt
A Lady trim and elegant.
If breadth of forehead shows breadth of brain
She's really most intelligent.

Twenty-year-old Helen Nash would graduate from Spelman in 1942 and from all-black Meharry Medical College (her father's alma mater) in 1945. When she told her father that she wanted to go to medical school, he said, "Don't." He did not believe that women should be doctors; one of his many reasons was that he did not believe they could take the sight of battlefield wounds such as he saw in France. But Helen was stubborn—and a man with four daughters is generally programmed to give in. It was wartime, doctors were needed, but the few women who managed to enter medical school were basically forced to choose between families and medical careers. Helen eventually left Atlanta for St. Louis to have a long and successful practice near her pediatrician brother, who shared his own St. Louis practice with one of his five daughters. Helen would have a very happy marriage late in life.

> Of Harriet Nash Nutt we can only say
> Her characteristic is—
> She has gobs of friends and gobs of clothes
> Eczema in summer and Chiz.

Eighteen-year-old Harriet, also pretty and dimpled, was probably as popular and as free a spirit as Atlanta could handle. Her fiancé, Charles Sumner Chisholm (named for the great Massachusetts abolitionist), known as "Chiz," had attended Morehouse College and the Pennsylvania College of Optometry. Harriet would graduate from Spelman. Much later, partly because she smoked, drank, and had a passion for gambling, Harriet became Lena's favorite cousin. As a very attractive widow and sometime high roller, she always had the royal suite gratis when she went to Vegas. Lena was impressed because Harriet went down the Nile, saw the Pyramids, rode on a camel, and sent back witty postcards. Harriet went everywhere, like a nineteenth-century British lady traveler.

Dorothy Nash Nutt is the youngest Nutt
And an ambitious Nutt is she
Wherever the other Nutts are found
Is where Dorothy is bound to be.

Dorothy, aged seventeen in 1941, was the youngest Nash sister. She would attend Talladega College, New York University, and the Teachers College at Columbia University, becoming a college instructor and a school psychologist. On September 1, 1960, Dorothy married William Shack in Atlanta. With a PhD in anthropology from the London School of Economics, Bill Shack was a professor of anthropology at the University of California at Berkeley at retirement. When Dorothy retired, she became a calligrapher. Dorothy and Bill had one son.

In 1941 Homer Nash Jr. was sixteen. He would graduate from Morehouse and Meharry Medical College and have a long private pediatric practice in St. Louis with his daughter Alison and near his sister Helen. One might say, in order for Graves-Nash men to be happy, they had to allow themselves to be surrounded by *women*—like Homer and his *five* daughters.

Now tho' the Nutts do vary all
as does inclement weather
There are some traits—Graves-Brown-Nash traits
which all possess together.

They all are vain and very proud
And, what's been said before
When in talk they do engage
Their voices shriek and roar.

They wave their arms and stamp their feet
which makes them look quite frantic
They chatter like monkeys in a zoo
And mimic every antic.

So when you have an argument
Or a caper you'd like to cut
Refer yourself with the greatest speed
To the family of Nash-Brown Nutt.

And, just as in the movies, the cousins of 1941 became the war brides of 1942. They were all beautiful brides. In August, Kathryn Brown, the pretty amateur poet, became the first Brown-Nash bride. She married handsome Sergeant Neal Kelly of the U.S. Army. A classic war bride, she had no veil and no long white dress. Kathryn wore a becoming day dress, a flirty hat, a big corsage, and a shyly serene smile. Wearing starched summer tans, Sergeant Kelly looked incredibly happy. They were a very appealing young couple.

Swift on the heels of Kathryn and Neal, on September 2, 1942, nineteen-year-old Harriet Nash married Chiz Chisholm, then a twenty-three-year-old Tuskegee Airman. Harriet was a student at Spelman. Harriet, a jolly nonconformist, surprisingly chose a traditional wedding with a long white dress, her mother's Brussels lace veil, and elaborate festivities. Harriet's daughter, Cheryl, described her mother's dress and her father's uniform:

The dress was long and looks like silk charmeuse, flowing and pooling on the floor . . . Daddy is in his Air Force uniform. They loved to tell the story of how they met. Catherine . . . the oldest, was in college and had a party at the house. Mama was given special permission to attend though she was considered too young for college boys. Daddy was one of the Morehouse boys who came . . .

Chiz later became another doctor in the family, with a long practice as an Atlanta optometrist.

The marriage license between Kathryn and Neal Kelly was dated August 4, 1942. In June 1943 baby Elinor Kelly arrived, Nellie Graves Brown's first grandchild. Elinor's birthday was June 30 (the same as that of her distant cousin Lena Horne). There is a pretty picture of Kathryn cradling her newborn. But suddenly, on July 20, 1943, there was a certificate of death for twenty-year-old Kathryn. The cause was "bronchial asthma." It was an enormous tragedy for the family—for her sisters and cousins as well as her husband. Kathryn was buried in Oakland cemetery in the Graves mausoleum. When her father went to war, little Elinor was raised by her grandmother and aunts. There is a photograph of now Lieutenant Neal Kelly and baby Elinor, possibly aged six to nine months old. He wears a strained smile for the sake of the oblivious, adorable baby girl. Senator Harry Byrd of Virginia, the great "patriot," said he would rather "lose the war" than fight side by side with a Negro. Byrd did not fight at all in World War II. Neal Kelly, unlike Byrd, was the real patriot.

As far as many white Southerners were concerned, World War II seemed mostly to be fought between themselves and the black GIs who had been ordered to the Deep South for military training. Negro soldiers training in the South were subjected to discriminatory treatment throughout the war by military as well as civilian racists. All over the South, it seemed that black GIs could be killed with impunity by white GIs, white officers, and white civilians; racism colored everything in World War II, even scientific breakthroughs. Consider the case of Dr. Charles Drew, professor of surgery at Howard University. He invented the blood plasma bank just in time for the war—but could not donate his own blood because he was a Negro. Blacks could receive "white" blood, but whites could not receive "black" blood because of the Southern rule that one drop of "black" blood made a person black. Despite War Department efforts, the military remained intransigently racist.

As far as blacks were concerned, the U.S. military was the most insistently racist public entity in America—worse than the police because the military was almost entirely Southern. In the Southern tradition, rich whites went into politics and poor whites went into the army. Of course, the Southern war against black civilians continued apace. And the state of Georgia still spent three times as much educating white children as black.

In a victory for blacks, on January 6, 1942, the War Department announced the formation of the first U.S. Army Air Corps squadron for Negroes at Tuskegee, Alabama. It was a victory—although many believed that training black pilots in Alabama meant the army wished them to fail. The following January 1943, William H. Hastie, Negro civilian aide to Secretary of War Henry Stimson, resigned in protest over the continued segregation of training facilities in the air force and army. As the youngest military service, the air force was actually the least prejudiced, and it soon announced a program for the expansion of Negro pilot training. Negroes were now accepted throughout the entire technical training command, as well as the Air Force Officer Candidate School in Miami. In 1944, among the pilot officers training in Miami were one Negro and one movie star. The Negro officer candidate was Percy Sutton, a former Eagle Scout from San Antonio, the youngest of fifteen children, all of whom were college graduates. Their father was an educator and an entrepreneur. One brother became the first black elected official in San Antonio; another became a judge on the New York supreme court; and another spent the 1920s in the Soviet Union. Sutton himself attended Prairie View A&M University, Tuskegee Institute, Hampton Institute, and Columbia and Brooklyn College law schools. But he was "silenced" by the entire Air Force Officer Candidate School from the moment of his arrival—the only communication was in the line of duty or, more usually, in the line of insults. The lone movie star was Clark Gable, who had pulled strings to get into the air force at his relatively advanced age when his wife, Carole

Lombard, died in a plane crash during a war bond tour. Gable, who clearly did not give a damn about peer pressure, was the *only* officer-in-training in the whole school to speak a kind word to Sutton—telling him to keep his chin up and not let the others get to him. (How nice that Gable's good-guy image was the real thing.) Much later, Sutton became a New York political powerhouse and Manhattan's longest-serving borough president. Like the black Calhouns of Atlanta, New York, and Chicago, the Suttons of Texas, with their accomplishments and multiple degrees, are a classic Talented Tenth family.

Between 1940 and 1943 the Negro population of Los Angeles grew 30 percent; of Chicago, 20 percent; of Detroit, 19 percent; of Charleston, South Carolina, 39 percent; and of Norfolk, Virginia, 100 percent. Blacks were leaving the lower South in droves looking for war work—and so were Southern whites. Several Northern cities had an extremely Southern mentality—Detroit, for example, had a strong KKK element. During the war, Detroit had the largest NAACP branch in the country. It also had an acute housing shortage because of all those defense workers and a population that had grown by 350,000 since the war began. It is possible that a few persons of either race appreciated the irony of white racists rioting to get into houses named for Sojourner Truth, the heroic black female abolitionist. In February 1942 a mob of some 1,200 men armed with clubs, knives, and shotguns gathered to prevent three Negro families from moving into the two-hundred-unit Sojourner Truth Housing Project, designated by the U.S. Housing Authority, of which Frank Horne was an official, as Negro housing. The three families' occupancy was delayed for two months, until twelve families finally moved in with the help of eight hundred state troopers. The federal government was the only protection blacks had against Southern whites, in the North or South, and this may explain why Southern whites so hated the federal government.

Life magazine had predicted as early as 1942 that Detroit was a racial time bomb. In June 1943 twenty-five thousand white workers went on strike at the Packard Motor Car Company, now producing engines for bombers and PT boats, because three black men were promoted to the assembly line. There was a sort of racist line in the sand. Government laws might force whites to work in the same factory with blacks, but not on the same assembly line. The fervent cry into the loudspeaker of one striker reverberated around the world: "I'd rather see Hitler and Hirohito win than work next to a nigger."

The Detroit explosion was three weeks later, on June 20. It was sparked at an integrated amusement park called Belle Isle by two typically egregious racial rumors concerning the Belle Isle Bridge: one, that a black mother and baby had been thrown off it by a gang of whites; and two, that a white woman had been raped and murdered on it by a gang of blacks. Whites went on a rampage, pulling Negroes out of cars, buses, and movie theaters to attack them. Blacks retaliated by smashing white-owned shops in Detroit's notorious black ghetto, "Paradise Valley" (what a name), where two hundred thousand people lived in an area of sixty square blocks, and where most of the inhabitants had no indoor plumbing. On the second day of the riot, at the request of Walter White, as well as the mayor of Detroit and the governor of Michigan, FDR declared a state of emergency and sent in six thousand federal troops. The NAACP set up relief headquarters. The riot lasted three days. Thirty-four people were killed—of whom twenty-five were black, including seventeen killed by police. Negroes did not have to live in the South to feel like Southerners. And Axis propagandists had a field day about American hypocrisy—shouting freedom for foreigners but not for their own Negroes.

In 1944 the War Department announced the end of racial segregation in recreation and transportation facilities at *all* army posts. The order was widely protested and openly disobeyed in the South as well as in both theaters of war. Racism was worse in the Pacific than elsewhere because of the heavy presence of the U.S. Navy and U.S. Marine Corps, the most Southern (and racist) of the services—West

Point graduated its first Negro cadet in 1877 and Annapolis graduated its first black in 1953.

Everyone was proud and excited when the Tuskegee Airmen, now
the Ninety-Ninth Pursuit Squadron, flew its first combat mission over
the island of Pantelleria in the Mediterranean theater. Cousin Harriet
Nash had married a Tuskegee Airman, Chiz Chisholm, and Lena was
officially "Queen" of the Ninety-Ninth, a title bestowed by members
of the squadron. In June 1944 the squadron became part of the 332nd
Fighter Group under Colonel Benjamin O. Davis Jr., the first black
graduate of West Point in the twentieth century. There were no black
bomber pilots, but the single fighter pilots of the Ninety-Ninth were
the attack and guard dogs of the air in the European theater. They were
recognized as America's best fighter escorts—officially never losing a
bomber. The B-25 bomber crew members had the highest respect for
the pilots of the Ninety-Ninth, who always seemed to swoop in from
out of nowhere to drive off the enemy. "If you didn't know who they
were—you *knew* who they were," said one admiring white tail gunner,
granting a racial compliment. He meant that they flew "black"—
insouciant but dangerous.

As part of the 332nd Fighter Group, in March 1945 the Ninety-
Ninth won the Distinguished Unit Citation (highest unit citation)
for the 1,600-mile round-trip air attack on Berlin. By this time, they
had flown 1,578 combat missions and won 95 Distinguished Flying
Crosses, 1 Silver Star, 1 Legion of Merit, 14 Bronze Stars, 744 Air
Medals and Clusters, and 8 Purple Hearts and were the first U.S. pilots
to shoot down a German jet. Because they were officers, the handful
of black pilots captured by the Germans received better treatment as
prisoners of war than they did as American citizens in Tuskegee, Alabama. When the unit came home, not one member could get a job as
a pilot anywhere in the United States.

Meanwhile, in Atlanta, Dr. Homer Nash, the father-in-law of a
Tuskegee Airman, was honored for his civilian service:

THE PRESIDENT OF THE UNITED STATES OF AMERICA has awarded this Certificate of Appreciation to H. E. Nash, M.D. in grateful recognition of uncompensated services patriotically rendered his country in the administration of the Selective Service System for the period of two years.

The only decipherable signatures belonged to President Franklin D. Roosevelt and Lewis B. Hershey, head of the Selective Service.

More important, Aunt Kate Graves got married at last. Kate Graves, who had accompanied Cousin Catherine on her 1928 trip to Fort Valley to meet Lena Horne, had always seemed the perfect maiden aunt. No one ever expected Kate, an independent career woman and fashion plate, to marry. According to her niece Kathryn Brown's 1941 doggerel, Aunt Kate was "Efficiency Expert No. 1 / She knows just what there is to do / And how it should be done." Kate Graves married an old friend, a tall, attractive widower named William Arnold Sr., who came with a grown physician son, an adorable grandson, and a nice daughter-in-law. Kate came with sisters, brothers-in-law, and adult nieces and nephews. Their marriage license from the state of Georgia, Fulton County, read:

To any minister of the Gospel, Judge of the Superior Court, Justice of the Peace, or any other person authorized to solemnize: You are hereby authorized to join in the Honorable State of Matrimony William J. Arnold, Sr. (COL) and Catherine F. Graves (COL).

"COL," of course, meant colored. They were married on October 7, 1944. Kate, very elegant all of her life, was a lovely bride in a long-sleeved, floor-length dinner dress. Her posture and figure were perfect. Kate was a very *good* fifty-five. She had a very happy marriage.

Kate kept a sort of wedding week diary on her new stationery—as *Mrs. Catherine Graves Arnold, 522 Auburn Ave. NE, Atlanta, Georgia*:

After the wedding, Sat. nite supper with Dr. and Mrs. Hackney 10:30 in honor of Dr. and Mrs. W. G. Arnold, Jr. of Detroit.

Sunday morn 8:30 at the Union Station to see Dr. and Mrs. W.G. Arnold, Jr. off to Detroit.

After breakfast Dr. and Mrs. H.E. Nash called.

Later we went to the cemetery to take the wedding flowers.

Monday nite 10-9-'44

A stag was given for the groom by Mr. Johnnie James.

Tuesday nite 10-10-'44

a dinner for the groom at the home of Mr. Jenkins, Hunter Street.

Tuesday nite 10-10-'44

Mr. and Mrs. W. J. Arnold, Sr. were invited to a bridge party at the home of Prof and Mrs. C.L. Harper in honor of Dr. and Mrs. Raiford of Detroit, Michigan.

Friday 10-13-'44

The bride and groom spent together.
The bride was invited to a bridge party given by Dr. H. Ward Warner.
The bride was unable to attend.

Sat. 10-14-'44

The groom attended the first football game of the season at Ponce de Leon park. After the game, supper with the bride, groom, and mother of the bride. The rest of the evening the bride and groom spent together.

Sunday 10-15-'44

After breakfast, the bride and groom attended the groom's church.

The brief wedding "diary" is a good portrait of Southern black middle-class life: parties, bridge, football, family, and church.

In 1944, an election year, Walter White called the Democratic platform a "splinter":

We believe that racial and religious minorities have the right to live, develop, and vote equally with all citizens and share the rights that are guaranteed by our Constitution. Congress shall exert its full constitutional powers to protect these rights.

The Democrats were always a schizophrenic party—ranging from left-wing Northern liberals to right-wing Southern racists. The statement referring to the Constitution and Congress belongs to the *North*. What was not mentioned was decided by the *South*: the Fair Employment Practices Committee, the poll tax, antilynching legislation, and military discrimination. Meanwhile, Northern Democrats quarreled among themselves over replacing the brilliant (if eccentric) scientist-agronomist Henry Wallace as vice president with Harry Truman, the Missouri haberdasher. Blacks especially favored the Midwestern Wallace over the quasi-Southerner Truman. (Missouri was a slave state that stayed in the Union.) Several Negro newspapers, including the *Pittsburgh Courier* and *New York Amsterdam News*, endorsed Republican Thomas E. Dewey—although later Truman proved to be a friend of blacks when he desegregated the military, causing white Southerners to bolt from the party and become the Dixiecrats.

The Republican platform was less of a "splinter" than the Democratic platform:

We unreservedly condemn the injection into American life of appeals to racial and religious prejudice . . . We pledge the establishment by Federal legislation of a permanent Fair Employment Practices Commission. The payment of any poll tax should not be a condition of voting in Federal elections and we favor immediate submission of a Constitutional amendment for its abolition . . . We favor legislation against lynching and pledge our sincere efforts in behalf of its early enactment.

The Republican platform should have appealed to more blacks. The problem was FDR, the magical man whose voice and personality were made for radio. The other problem was political. Local Democratic machines in the ghettos of the North took care of the poor all year round—all they asked in return was a party line vote every few years. Reformers wailed; the voters could not understand the fuss. Why would they bite the hand that fed them?

The Socialist platform echoed the Republicans:

> We condemn anti-Semitism, Jim-Crowism, and every form of race discrimination and segregation in the armed forces as well as civil life. We urge the passage of anti-lynching and anti-poll tax laws and the prompt enactment of legislation to set up a permanent Fair Employment Practices Committee . . . An America disgraced by racial tensions which occasionally find expression in lynching and race riots cannot lead the way to a peace which depends upon worldwide reconciliation of races on the basis of equality of right.

In 1944 the United Negro College Fund was chartered to support historically black Missionary colleges—by then all falling on hard times thanks to constantly diminishing Southern state support. The Missionary colleges clearly meant everything to Southern blacks—not only because they brought light where there had been strictly imposed darkness, but because they were centers of community pride and civil rights activism as well as learning. By 1964 the fund had raised $34 million. So many wonderful minds were, indeed, not wasted thanks to Missionary schools and colleges and the devoted teachers and benefactors who supported them, black and white. Certainly Cora Horne and all the black Calhouns who had been educated in Missionary colleges and to whom education was so very important would have been pleased.

CHAPTER ELEVEN

North/1950s

BLACKS AND BLACKLISTING

L ENA WAS a victim of the blacklist—but she was not an entirely innocent victim. She knew exactly what she was doing—*sort of*. Between 1946 and 1948 she made a sharp turn to the left. What we know as the red-baiting 1950s actually began toward the end of 1947, when ten screenwriters and directors, known as the "Hollywood Ten," were given prison terms for refusing to testify before a congressional committee. All were former or current members of the then legal Communist Party. And all were members of the Screen Writers Guild, which the producers above all wanted to break. The Hollywood Ten opened the floodgates of blacklisting—which was also an excuse for anti-Semitism, racism, and guilt by association.

All of Lena's political mentors were men of the Left: Uncle Frank Horne, the black New Dealer; poet-professor Sterling Brown, who liked Lena's "clarinet" voice and said "the first African off the boat turned left"; Walter White of the NAACP, the organization in which her grandmother enrolled her at the age of two as a lifetime member, who suddenly popped up to "guide" her career in Hollywood; Barney Josephson of Café Society, a white, jazz-loving, Jewish Communist whose brother died in Spain; W. E. B. Du Bois, the great black radical, who had been in love with Cora Horne's sister, Lena Smith; and, finally, Paul Robeson, her grandmother's protégé. Robeson was clearly the most unforgettable teacher. He always spoke very simply and clearly. No matter how far she rose, he said, she was "never, never to forget the people down the line—the Pullman porters."

For a long time, especially in Hollywood, Lena suffered both inwardly and outwardly under the dual curse of not being "black enough" to be a "real" Negro, but on the other hand being "too black" to be a "real" movie star. I believe that her leftward turn was partly a search for authenticity, as well as a response to a greater disappointment than she ever revealed when she understood that she was never going to have a movie career. It was at Café Society that Robeson told her that she had not yet become "Lena Horne, Negro." Now Lena, aware of her "privileges," was trying very hard to become a Negro. She began to see politics through the prism of color. No one was happier to exploit this than the CPUSA, which at that point was seeking to become more American and less Soviet. Until the Scottsboro Boys became an issue, the CPUSA couldn't figure out what to do about Southern Negroes. The whole dialectic depended on an educated, self-confident proletariat—hardly descriptive of the illiterate, fear-ridden serfs and peasants of the American South. Black Communists in America tended to be educated members of the middle class. The black Southern masses would be impossible to organize. Lena's entire political philosophy could be summed up for a four-year-old: *most Communists seemed to want to help Negroes and most anticommunists seemed to want to hurt them.* Lena believed that her enemies were not Communists, but only the fierce anticommunists who were just as fiercely anti-Negro. She never joined the Communist Party—Paul Robeson told her not to. She believed the party line on race because it was not dissimilar from the philosophy of her grandparents and favorite uncle. Lena had zero interest in Soviet ideology or philosophy. She would have been a terrible Communist— all emotion, no discipline. In the words of writer-editor Paul Berman, reviewing a book in the *New York Times* about Czech writers under Nazi and Communist regimes: "A Communist, one could almost say, is a good-hearted person who knows nothing about Communism."

Besides the fact that Lena was no "innocent" victim of the blacklist, she was a *lucky* victim. People suspected of lesser "crimes" than hers saw their lives and careers in ruins. Larry Parks, whose life and livelihood the House Un-American Activities Committee (HUAC) destroyed mostly because he was Jewish, lived right across the road from us in Hollywood with his wife, Betty Garrett. And wonderful Marsha Hunt, whose liberal ideals included membership in the Hollywood Anti-Nazi League, made more than fifty films between 1935 and 1949 and *three* between 1949 and 1957. Lena was banned from network TV for ten years and from movies for six years, but her earning power in nightclubs was never diminished. She made $60,000 a week at the Copacabana in 1948 and the money only increased through the blacklist years. Lena's career and livelihood were basically saved because the Jewish Mafia, which controlled America's biggest nightclubs in places like New York City, Chicago, Los Angeles, and Miami, could not afford to have her blacklisted. She was, in fact, its *consistently* biggest draw, guaranteeing sold-out crowds. She brought in exactly the right crowd of rich sophisticates, VIPs, and high rollers. She had first encountered the Jewish mob in 1945 at the Flamingo Hotel, in Las Vegas, when she complained to Benjamin "Bugsy" Siegel about the crude introductions she had been receiving from Xavier Cugat, the racist leader of a rhumba band, who was supposed to announce her entrance. "I am so sorry, Miss Horne," said Bugsy Siegel. "Don't worry—I will take care of this personally." By the next show, the rhumba king was groveling. That same year, Louis B. Mayer had asked Lena as a favor to sing at Chicago's Chez Paree, one of the biggest of the Jewish mob-controlled nightclubs, where, playing for less than her normal salary, she broke house records and the management gave her a star sapphire ring. The owner of Miami's Clover Club lent her his own house when she could not find a decent place to stay. Nightclubs truly seemed to be the only place where a performer's talent was more important than her race. There was nothing the men who ran the nightclubs for the mob would not do for Lena—from giving her expensive jewelry to helping get her name off the blacklist. And this turned out to be very important.

Lena had not made it easy for them, and the immediate postwar period had not made it easy for her. Seven Negroes were lynched between 1940 and 1945; six were lynched in 1946 alone. Lena had decided to fight the postwar battles. On June 6, 1946, she appeared at a Madison Square Garden rally for "Big Three Unity for Colonial Freedom" with Robeson, Mary McLeod Bethune, writer Norman Corwin (the king of radio drama), Judy Holliday, and others. Lena probably did almost anything Robeson asked her to do—after all, he was family. According to Martin Duberman's *Paul Robeson*, there were rumors that my mother and Robeson had a romantic relationship, but she denied the story to several Robeson biographers. I believe my mother. First, there was the age difference: the year that she was born he was having his knuckles crushed playing football for Rutgers and making Walter Camp's all-American list. Despite Robeson's undeniably extraordinary warmth, charm, charisma, and gentle-giant appeal to women, Lena was never attracted to alpha males (Joe Louis was the exception that proved the rule). Lena hero-worshipped Robeson for sure, but that was all. She really liked "softer" men—Leslie Howard as Ashley Wilkes, for example, not Clark Gable as Rhett Butler.

Within a year Lena was deeply involved in politics, both accidentally and on purpose. She had no idea, of course, that she would become a *Daily Worker* front-page heroine. August 21, 1947, was Lena Horne Day in Brooklyn. The *Daily Worker* covered the story on its front page:

Brooklyn Welcomes Lena Horne Home

The warmth and humanity that is Brooklyn was extended yesterday to actress Lena Horne, for her contribution to the screen and amity between races. The local girl, born at 189 Chauncey St., in the

Bedford-Stuyvesant area, was cheered and paraded through the streets of the borough which celebrated Lena Horne Homecoming Day. Brooklyn, the county with the first Communist Councilman and Negro ball player in the major leagues, in honoring Miss Horne did itself proud.

Lena was upset that no one bothered to invite any of her old school friends.

By August 1947 she had already made one major decision, to marry Lennie Hayton in Paris since they were an illegal couple in California; and one minor decision, to write a monthly column for the *People's Voice*, a left-wing black paper whose other columnists included Robeson and Du Bois. She would not actually write it; she simply had to give the writers a few names, events, and activities. Some of the columns had elements of the truth, but most were pure party line.

From July 26, 1947, to January 10, 1948, five and a half months, "Lena Horne" appeared to have a regular column in the *People's Voice*. I used the word "appeared" because anyone who knew my mother even casually would know that she never wrote the column for October 18, 1947, for example. I laughed out loud when I read:

> I love football . . . I go to as many games as my schedule permits and get my kicks from a well-tossed forward pass or a dazzling end run . . . I love to see a flashy broken-field runner, a great drop-kicker or a hard-tackling end.

Of course, the really important part of the column starts here:

> As a football fan I've been interested in the growth of democracy within the sport, particularly the increasing participation of Negroes in both college and professional football . . . Some of our Southern brethren are also beginning to take note of the trend towards democracy in sports. Last Saturday an historic event took place in Charlottesville, Va., when the

University of Virginia took the field against Harvard University which had a Negro, Chester Pierce, on its squad . . . Southern teams have regularly refused to play colleges with Negroes on their teams, whether in the North or South . . . There was another lesson in democracy given last week-end in Charlottesville. The Harvard team had been billeted in a downtown hotel, and Pierce had been assigned to the annex of the hotel. The Harvard men, however, held a meeting and decided that team-play should exist off the football field as well as on it. They voted unanimously to move in with Pierce, and, that's where they stayed. This happened right in the heart of Virginia. Who said Jim Crow can't be licked?

The Harvard football team included Robert F. Kennedy, who was in Charlottesville for the game.

Many of the party line columns, of course, make Lena sound something like the characters Boris and Natasha from *Rocky and Bullwinkle*—calling herself "a cultural worker," for example. Some columns contained a smidgen of truth. In September 1947 she wrote about a backstage visit (probably at the Capitol Theatre, where she was having a spectacularly successful run) from Howard Fast:

Howard Fast, one of America's greatest people's writers . . . honored me with a visit . . . I have unbounded respect for Howard, not only for his writings which have moved me deeply, but because he represents a good healthy social point of view and is fearless in expressing it . . . I think it's an indictment of our own democracy when a great artist like Howard Fast is persecuted because of his viewpoint. Let me say here and now that I'm for the guy all the way. For I love a fighter.

Lena never called anyone a "guy" unless it was plural and referred to musicians.

Howard Fast was a special figure in the *real* left-wing world. He was a proud and open Communist, and had been since 1943. New

York–born Fast, three years older than Lena and one of America's most celebrated authors, was also, according to Phillip Deery's *Red Apple: Communism and McCarthyism in Cold War New York*, "the single most important literary figure in the Communist Party of the United States of America." Fast published the first of his sixty-five novels in 1933 at the age of eighteen. His most famous and celebrated novel thus far was *Citizen Tom Paine*, published in 1943—the year that he, like many others during the siege of Stalingrad, joined the Communist Party. *Citizen Tom Paine* sold more than a million copies. From 1944 to 1946 it was distributed to U.S. servicemen abroad as well as to citizens of liberated countries by the Office of War Information, and it was on the "approved list" for all New York City public schools. By 1947 Fast's books were out of schools and out of public and government libraries—and the American Legion was burning copies of *Citizen Tom Paine*. By 1950 Fast would be in prison for refusing to disclose to HUAC the names of contributors to a fund for a home for orphans of American veterans of the Spanish Civil War (Eleanor Roosevelt was a contributor). The Spanish Civil War was more than a "red flag" to blacklisters, many of whom were Catholic. Because a small group of Abraham Lincoln Brigade vets had served in the Office of Strategic Services in World War II as experts in guerrilla and urban warfare, some blacklisters had the notion that these survivors represented the vanguard of a future armed revolution. Fast finished his next novel, *Spartacus*, in prison but could find no publisher when he was released. In 1951 he decided to self-publish:

> I had no money with which to publish the book, but I had friends and I knew that over ten million people in America had read my books. I wrote to these friends. I asked them to buy in advance, sight unseen, a novel called *Spartacus*, which I would publish if and when enough of them sent me five dollars for a subscription to it. It was a strange offer on my part, and I got a strange response.

Within three months, forty-eight thousand copies were sold across America, although the book was never reviewed by mainstream critics or papers. Fast and his wife started Blue Heron Press on their *Spartacus* proceeds and republished W. E. B. Du Bois' out-of-print *The Souls of Black Folk*.

In November 1947 Lena made her first trip abroad and, in the *People's Voice*, went after HUAC. Again, Lena did not write this herself:

Aboard the S.S. *Mauretania* en route to England . . . I'm troubled about the state of freedom back there in the country I've just left. I'm troubled about the current attack on progressives in the movie industry that has been launched by the House Un-American Activities Committee . . . I am concerned about this Washington sideshow because it represents an invasion of cultural freedom in my country. As a *cultural worker* [italics mine], I am directly affected. As the national audience of the movies, the great mass of the American people are also affected . . .

Despite the terrible shortages of the postwar austerity program, Lena found ready-made fans and had a wildly successful run when she made her first trip to the British Isles in 1947. Although *Cabin in the Sky* and *Stormy Weather* were never shown to white American troops, they had been shown throughout the British fleet. There was a whole coterie of British jazz lovers who knew Lena's early records. There was all the excitement of a royal wedding. And Lena fell in love with British fans—some of whom (actor James Mason's mother, for one) brought her rationed gifts like eggs and chocolates. She loved touring the British Isles almost as much as she hated touring at home in America, where she never knew when Jim Crow would swoop in to spoil the trip.

Lena did not have to wait to get home to get a sense of political turmoil. She got it in mid-ocean, sailing from Plymouth to New York on the SS *America*. She received a letter on board on December 19, 1947, from a member of the crew:

Miss Lena Horne, Stateroom U-48, S.S. America

Dear Miss Horne, We regretfully inform you that permission to attend our meeting has been refused you on the part of Mr. Alexanderson, Executive officer, and by Captain Anderson, Master of this vessel. We, the crew members are not surprised at this attitude being fully aware of the consistent anti-union attitude constantly and consistently manifested on the part of the authorities on board this ship, representing, as we know, the U.S. Lines policy of hostility toward us, members of the National Maritime Union. Nor is the fact that you are a member of a minority irrelevant to the case. We know that the crew members will be greatly disappointed and will certainly protest this action on the part of the Master in the vigorous manner peculiar to us seamen. For your information, we had also invited the Hon. Rhys J. Davies, Member of Parliament, to attend. He, too, accepted. Permission has also been denied him. Mr. Davies occupies Cabin S-5.

Most regretfully yours,
For the crew, Scipio Collins, Ship's Chairman

Lena politely refused to perform at the captain's gala.

The end of 1947 had been momentous in her life. Far more important than finding a whole new audience when she toured the British Isles was marrying Lennie in Paris. They sailed home from Europe with the happy, if criminal, secret of their French marriage. They called ship-to-shore and told me to keep the secret—which I did. They got back in time for my tenth birthday, four days before Christmas, and I remember finding Lennie the same—not like a bridegroom at all. From the very beginning, he was a wonderful stepfather: loving, kind, supportive, and funny. He could always make me laugh at myself. Any children of divorce who have this sort of stepfather know how special and important he is—especially for adolescent girls. I considered him my father. There was also good news from California. Lena and Lennie were no longer in fear of imminent arrest—the California Supreme Court had found the antimiscegenation law unconstitutional. Happily New York, which became their Eastern base camp, as Lena toured the world of international nightclubs and music halls, had no such laws.

January 1948 saw the beginning of the Henry Wallace campaign for the presidency on the Progressive Party ticket. At Robeson's urging, Lena actively campaigned for Wallace—until August, when Truman sent the first Civil Rights Message to Congress and announced the desegregation of the military. Lena switched her endorsement from Wallace to Truman—and sang at Truman's inauguration. The black vote definitely helped Truman defeat Strom Thurmond and the Dixiecrats on the right and Henry Wallace and the Progressives on the left. The Dixiecrats, Southern Democrats pledging "segregation forever," had formed their own party when Truman desegregated the military. Truman actually had a history of good relations with black voters as part of the Democratic machine of Kansas City, Missouri, where he had a large black constituency. The Truman inauguration, thanks to his show of friendship with blacks, was the most integrated since James A. Garfield's. Garfield, an abolitionist and Union war hero, ran on a pro-Reconstruction platform and won the presidency in 1880 without a single Southern state—but with the black vote. Garfield was assassinated in 1881.

The NAACP was clearly on the wrong track in 1948 when the board of directors refused to renew the contract of W. E. B. Du Bois, who, the year before, had organized and prepared the 155-page petition *An Appeal to the World*. The subtitle said it all: *A Statement of Denial of Human Rights to Minorities in the Case of Citizens of Negro Descent in the United States of America and an Appeal to the United Nations for Redress.* Du Bois had founded and created the NAACP, but now he was kicked out because he "supported certain ideologies that were alien to the Association." Too bad the NAACP went the way of New York University, the first privately endowed school to take disciplinary action against individuals whose political opinions did not comply with HUAC—and not the way of Harvard, where Chancellor James B. Conant upheld the right of dissent and criticized "governmental agencies" that inquired into educational institutions (although he did not approve of individuals who invoked the Fifth Amendment while testifying).

Despite her political activities, for which she had not yet been "named," 1948, like 1943, was a career breakthrough year for Lena. All through the 1940s she made $10,000 a week in nightclubs. Now she was paid $60,000 a week by New York's Copacabana on East Sixtieth Street, where she broke every house record. After the lights went down, I was sometimes allowed to peek at the show. I watched my mother and the audience. I remember crowds—there seemed to be standing room only even in the club. Except for a trio of musicians—bass, piano, and drums—and my mother's voice, there was absolute hushed silence (no waiter service). The audience seemed rapt—the women as well as the men. And the women were smiling. I know I was smiling because I had never seen anyone look so beautiful. She was wearing a white dress—which meant, by superstition, that it was the first show, opening night. The Copa loved Lena and she loved the Copa. That is, she loved Jack Entratter, the man who ran the nightclub. A large, hulking man (a Jewish Tony Soprano) with bad feet, Entratter wore shoes that looked like leather boxes. He was very protective of Lena. She called him "Big Creep" and he called her "Little Creep." In her previous engagement at the Copa, in 1945, Lena had discovered that Negro friends and ordinary Negro members of the audience had their reservations refused. This time an integrated audience was written into her contract.

After the Copacabana group moved to the Sands Hotel in Las Vegas a year or two later, Lena performed there every year for a decade, and Jack Entratter's two daughters became my best Vegas friends. Hollywood choreographer Robert Sidney wrote about Lena in Vegas in a memoir, *With Malice Towards Some*:

Jack Entratta [*sic*], the entertainment director at the Sands Hotel, chose Lena above everyone else as his favorite performer. That was a big order because the Rat Pack—Frank Sinatra, Sammy Davis, Jr., Dean Martin and company—all played there. But in Jack's book Lena was number one . . .

Lena broke all social tradition at the Sands. She was probably the first black performer ever permitted to actually stay, sleep and live at the same hotel where she worked . . . One day at the Sands, this bigoted woman came flying into the office and wanted to see the manager. Jack Entratta happened to be there. He said, "What's the problem madam?" And she said, "There's a black person in the swimming pool." The black person was Lena's daughter Gail. Jack said "And?" She said, "I want her out of that pool or I check out." Jack said, "Ma'am, may I carry your bags now?"

The Sands clearly decided that integrating the pool was a small price to pay for attracting the highest rollers, breaking attendance records, and giving no trouble to the management.

The story of the Sands swimming pool was something of a Vegas legend—sometimes *I* was the swimmer and sometimes it was my brother, Teddy. I think Entratter chose Lena as his favorite because by Vegas standards, unlike the Rat Pack, which wanted to make every night a stag party, Lena and Lennie were practically Victorian—no wild drinking, no brawling, no trashed rooms or trashed chorus girls, no heavy gambling, and no entourage of badly behaved hangers-on. After all, despite no clocks and despite the curtains drawn against the day, the Sands was a spit-and-polish high-end resort. Vegas standards, however, *did* permit every gay male dancer on the Strip to come between shows to offer homage to Lena. Gay men were a very small Vegas subculture, as necessary and as familiar as showgirls—and they were always nice to me. Our family favorite was Jimmy Barron, an agelessly handsome young blond man from an old Virginia family who, to that family's chagrin, first skated with Sonja Henie, then, worse, after an injury became a Vegas chorus boy. One of the clubs—not the Sands—had a famously beautiful showgirl who was really a boy. I met her with my mother and Jimmy Barron, having no idea until many years later that she was anything other than she appeared. She was sitting by herself in the empty chorus dressing room, staring into the mirror. My mother said to me, in a rather loud voice, "Isn't she beautiful." It was not a question; it was a statement of fact. Everything about the person we were visiting was dazzlingly white, from her white, white skin to her platinum hair to the white ostrich plumes of her costume. I have never forgotten her face. She was exquisite, almost too delicately beautiful to be real—an angel crossed with Marilyn Monroe. But I had never seen anyone look so sad. She never smiled—even as my mother showered her with compliments.

Robert Sidney also wrote something about Lena that I have heard so many times—how the movies never *"got* her":

The magic of Lena had to be seen. It was never captured on a recording or on film. When you were in the audience watching her, your emotions were raised to the highest level you had ever known. This woman was magic.

I certainly remember sensing some of the magic sitting in the Empire Room of the Waldorf-Astoria hotel, and getting goose bumps on first hearing my mother sing Rube Bloom and Johnny Mercer's "Day In, Day Out" or Rodgers and Hammerstein's "The Surrey with the Fringe on Top"—both unique renditions with Lennie's brilliant arrangements. I will never forget composer Saul Chaplin, father of my good friend Judy (the future Mrs. Hal Prince), solemnly telling us both, as we watched Lena perform at the Fairmont Hotel in San Francisco, that we were watching "the greatest nightclub act in the world." Lena loved San Francisco because it was not at all like Hollywood. And she loved the Fairmont's owners, the charming and civilized Swig family. The other famous San Francisco hotel across from the Fairmont, the Mark Hopkins, did not admit Negroes, even as entertainers.

As reigning queen of the nightclubs, through sheer talent and professionalism, Lena had made the best of a bad situation. "I hate show business!" she would scream in her dressing room to warm up her vocal cords. She did not pad her act with chatter. She *sang*. She really hated nightclubs, considering them unsanitary and unsavory. Her dresser and best friend, Irene Lane, a motherly white-haired figure who had been a Broadway dresser, draped every corner of the dressing room with clean white sheets. Her nightclub life was about *delegating*. She made her musical preferences known through Lennie—and all others through her manager, Ralph Harris, a former song-plugger friend of Lennie's. Ralph, a handsome tennis-playing ladies' man who looked a bit like Burt Lancaster, protected Lena from the most unpleasant aspects of life on the road. All of my friends had crushes on Ralph. I did not have a crush on him, because he was like another wonderful stepfather. Later, I would talk to him about boys, which I could not do with Mother and Lennie.

Lena was a complete professional and expected the same from everyone she worked with. She was never late for a rehearsal or a performance. She was courteous to everyone. She never berated an underling—that was a job for Lennie or Ralph. Unlike the pals in the Rat Pack, she never drank before or during a show. She would plead the Fifth on drinking after the show—but could not have more than two drinks because alcohol interacted badly with the diet pills (Dexedrine or Benzedrine) she had been hooked on since 1943 at MGM. She usually went to bed at three or four in the morning, after a light supper of something like scrambled eggs. She and Lennie had separate bedrooms. They watched TV together in her room. She usually had breakfast around three in the afternoon—something like a steak or beef stew. She never ever smoked. She also, all her life, ate lots of dark chocolate, which may have been one of the secrets of her basic good health. Stamina was important—she worked hard. Before TV killed nightclubs, this was a highly remunerative line of work.

By now aged eleven, I was enrolled in one of Manhattan's most progressive schools, an integrated school on the edge of Harlem at 110th Street and Fifth Avenue, where I learned no math or English grammar and never had homework. I went to live as a paying guest with what was surely one of the most progressive families on Morningside Drive. My hosts, the Reverend and Mrs. Richard Morford, known and loved as Dick and Aileen, were heroes on the left—not that I knew that at the time. What I did know about the Morfords, who had two daughters—Linda (a bit younger than I) and Susan (a Radcliffe freshman)—was that they seemed to have a wonderful marriage. They were the happiest people I had ever met. I had never seen two people more cheerfully devoted. Whenever they saw each other their faces lit up in the biggest smiles. (Mother and Lennie laughed a lot—they were both fun and funny. But she often complained, mostly about her love-hate relationship with her career. And he, Camel cigarette in one hand and drink in the other, was usually half tuned out, listening to music on the record player.) Aileen was an administrator at my progressive school. Today I would say that she looked like a twentieth-century American nun. Busy and energetic, with a trim figure in a well-cut suit and sensible shoes, Aileen did not bother with makeup. She had the brightest blue eyes, prematurely white hair, and naturally pink cheeks. (Aileen's daughter Susan had salt-and-pepper hair at seventeen.) Like many white Protestant clergymen, Dick, a Presbyterian, was big, shaggy, and amiable. Unbeknownst to me, he had just been released from prison for refusing to give up the membership list of the National Council on American-Soviet Friendship, of which he was director from 1946 to 1980. The government took his passport away.

Michigan-born Dick was a graduate of New York's Union Theological Seminary and a member of the New York City presbytery, the church's local governing body, for more than fifty years. From 1942 to 1945 he was the Washington lobbyist for the United Christian Council for Democracy, a federation of the social action agencies of four Presbyterian denominations. The American-Soviet Friendship Council was founded in 1943, at the height of Soviet-U.S. World War II friendship, at a mass rally in Madison Square Garden. A Hollywood rally soon followed, with a message of support signed by Charlie Chaplin, John Garfield, Katharine Hepburn, James Cagney, Gene Kelly, Edward G. Robinson, Rita Hayworth, and Orson Welles. Every person on that list, except Rita Hayworth, was called a Communist for appearing at the rally. There were Bundles for Britain and *everything* for General and Madame Chiang Kai-shek—why not a salute to valiant Stalingrad? The council believed that the United States and the Soviet Union should join together in their common fight against fascism, and that peaceful cooperation between the two countries should continue in the postwar era. Stressing education and cultural exchange, the council did not take positions on political issues. In 1945, just before Morford became executive director, the organization was served with a subpoena by HUAC and ordered to submit its membership and financial records. Morford refused to turn over the records and served three months in prison for contempt of Congress. In 1963 the Subversive Activities Control Board, which had previously found the council to be a Communist front organization, unanimously struck down that ruling.

Lena was not the only Horne under a political cloud. In 1948 Dr. Frank Horne, a founder of the National Committee Against Discrimination in Housing (NCDH) and still a government employee, was questioned by the Civil Service Loyalty Review Board. He defended himself successfully. If Lena was suspect because of her connections with Café Society, Robeson, and Du Bois, Frank was suspect because he was a New Dealer. The Loyalty Review Board questioned him twice, in 1948 and 1954. In 1949 he became a member of the Civil Service Committee of Expert Examiners for the Housing and Home Finance

Agency (HHFA). Better still, or so it seemed, he married again. The bride, a glamorous divorcée named Mercedes, came from a famous black Washington family. All the family had the same distinctive trait, a natural streak of white in otherwise jet-black hair. Mercedes looked as white as white could be, but, to my eyes, too much like *Snow White's* "wicked queen" to be up to any good. The "wicked" side of her personality came out when she had one or two too many—which was often. Frank was miserable and threw himself into work. Mercedes seemed to have little to do in Washington except shop in stores where Negroes were not allowed and drink in white bars. I suppose she was the "tragic mulatto." In 1949 Frank was one of the anthologized poets included by Langston Hughes and Arna Bontemps in *The Poetry of the Negro, 1746–1949*.

In 1950 Paul Robeson joined Dick Morford, Howard Fast, artist Rockwell Kent, author-philanthropist Corliss Lamont (whose children were at my school), and others on the left in having his passport revoked. Robeson's passport would be restored in 1958 when the Supreme Court ruled that the State Department had no right to deny any passport because of "beliefs and associations." Presumably the others got their passports back also. I once sat on Robeson's knee as a child and he sang a Russian lullaby. In retrospect, a very socialist gesture—but it seemed to come naturally because he was so big and gentle. I certainly felt safe and protected. I remember his rumbling voice was warm and very soothing. Russians said that he sang like Chaliapin. Cora's former protégé was also the favorite star of London dockworkers, Welsh miners, and titled British. I think what drove the right wing mad was how much Paul Robeson was loved around the world—the Old World, the New World, and the Third World. He gave concerts everywhere, so taking away his passport took away his livelihood because his only appearances were abroad. He gave a famous concert on the Canadian border, but in America he could sing only in black churches. (Robeson's brother Ben, World War I chaplain with Edwin Horne's 369th Regiment, was the longtime pastor of Harlem's venerable A.M.E. Mother Zion Church.) Although he refused to tell HUAC whether he was a member of the Communist Party, somehow, unlike others who refused to testify, Robeson was never put in prison. The right wing probably feared that he would become an international political martyr, in the manner of Eugene Debs and Mahatma Gandhi. He was possibly a true believer, and certainly a fellow traveler and a recipient of much Soviet benevolence, but not everyone was sure that Robeson, who told Lena not to join, was actually a party member. Some people felt that he was too much the *free man* to put himself under party discipline. Robeson himself neither confirmed nor denied. He fought racism his whole life. Like Lena and many others, he did not always question the motives of his allies because blacks had so few of them.

Lena, whose passport was never in danger, now spent a great deal of time abroad. She felt at home in London because the British had embraced another elegant black singer: Elisabeth Welch, a favorite of both Cole Porter and Noble Sissle. The British seemed to understand what Lena was about. While Lena's heart was in France, because that was where she married Lennie, she always thought the French secretly wondered why she was not wearing bananas like Josephine Baker. Her fans were not all sophisticated Londoners, however. Lena found "the greatest audiences in the world" in the industrial towns of Birmingham, Bristol, Manchester, and Glasgow. She could barely understand what they said, but they were true fans, and they really let the performer know it. They came every night, showing the kind of mass enthusiasm that Lena had experienced only once before, when she appeared in person with Duke Ellington and his orchestra at the big Broadway movie theater where *Cabin in the Sky* was showing. She found the same stomping, cheering audiences that screamed their appreciation. After the show, hundreds of fans were always waiting, with mounted police to keep order. Lena stood for hours signing autographs. The scenes were repeated all over the Midlands. Were Lena's fans forerunners of soccer hooligans? Or was Lena the forerunner of a rock star? Perhaps it was simply an appreciation of some American musical "magic" in otherwise pretty grim postwar lives. She was presented in Britain by the Grade brothers, Lew and Leslie, who became titans of British entertainment. A decade or so later in London, when I introduced myself to Lord (Lew) Grade as Lena's daughter, his eyes lit up. "Lena was our first American star," he said with a sigh of nostalgia.

For *me*, the 1950s meant school and traveling. School was where I spent most of my time. Hotels were a close second. In 1950, in the eight grade, I went away to a Quaker boarding school, Oakwood Friends School, in Poughkeepsie, New York. While certain boys' schools (Exeter and Andover) had long admitted a few blacks, no girls' boarding school would do so. But Quaker schools were always coed, integrated, and international—like real life. Yoshiro Sanbonmatsu, a Japanese American who taught literature, was the first great teacher I ever had—only the Quakers would hire him. Because of Yosh, I read *Moby-Dick* straight through on a train from New York to California and felt as if I were drunk on words. I was Oakwood's first black cheerleader. The tall, slim Dent brothers from New Orleans, sons of a black educator, were basketball stars. The soccer team was terrific because we had the sons of Hungarian refugees as well as Latin American oligarchs. One of the most beautiful girls in the school was Moroccan, and there were Dutch sisters who spent World War II in a Japanese internment camp. There were other celebrity parents besides Lena: Rex Stout, Pearl S. Buck, Poppy Cannon (Mrs. Walter White), and Sylvia Sidney. Eleanor Roosevelt spoke at my graduation. Oakwood continues to remain coed, integrated, and international.

Despite Quaker pacifism, Oakwood made news during World War II, because an Oakwood graduate was one of the famous Four Chaplains (two Protestants, a Catholic, and a Jew) who gave up their life jackets to sailors and were seen praying, arms around one another, as their troopship went down. While I was an Oakwood student, we were visited by

the Hiroshima Maidens, teenage girls all horribly disfigured by radia-
tion, in America for medical treatment thanks to the Quakers. When
Lennie and Lena (who had become a lifetime member of Hadassah,
a women's Zionist organization, after meeting and liking its president
at a benefit) went to Israel in 1952 for a series of concerts to celebrate
that country's fourth anniversary, Lennie sent a postcard about the
Quaker teacher who was the only person permitted to go back and forth
between Israeli and Arab lands without a permit. I admire the Society
of Friends for everything it has done and continues to do for humanity.

Weekends and short school holidays were spent either with school
friends or with saintly Aida Winters, a friend of Lena's from the Brooklyn Junior Deb days. Aida was a half sister of two great black artists,
Romare Bearden and Charles Alston, and the wife of opera singer
Lawrence Winters. She was an angel to me. But all real holidays were
spent with Lena and Lennie wherever they were, in Europe or America.
Although I did everything in Vegas with the Entratter girls, or my step-
cousin Michele Hart, the daughter of Lennie's sister, I mostly traveled
alone by train across the country, or by ship to Europe, to meet Mother
and Lennie wherever they were. I started with trains at age eleven and
ships at thirteen—traveling first class and carrying succinct lists of
what to do and how much to tip so-and-so. (No one at any juncture in
the 1950s, by the way, seemed to worry about pedophiles or kidnappers.) We traveled only by the French Line; in a pinch we would go by
Cunard—but never by the United States Line after Lena's first trip.
Jim Crow ruled America's waves. But the French Line was really fun
and glamorous—and, at least, the British were nice. In 1950 I went
to Europe by myself on the *De Grasse*, the same ship that took Cora
Horne to her grand tour in 1929. The *De Grasse* had seen better days.
She had been a troopship during the war and was slightly battered. I was
not at all lonely. I enjoyed myself utterly. First of all, I was a fashion
voyeur and the women in first class wore beautiful French gowns for
dinner. I watched them arrive because I ate in the first sitting (children

and old people) at a table by myself, as my mother had requested (to avoid incidents with "bad" Americans), wearing a sort of party dress and happily alone with a book. I dined on soufflés in every possible flavor. I went to the movies every day; they were all in French—but who cared? The actors all had wonderful faces. I fell in love with Gérard Philipe in *Le Grand Meaulnes*. Since I was never lonely with a book, I made a new reading discovery. The only English-language novels in the first-class library were by H. G. Wells. I discovered *Tono-Bungay* and could not have been happier. Only once did I fly. As I was flying alone to Las Vegas, the plane ran into a storm—a scary storm, with lightning and turbulence and flight attendants shooting looks at each other. We finally got in safely, but long overdue. Mother, red-eyed and calming down from hysterics, met me at the airport and did not let me fly again anywhere until I was out of college. I had not been frightened in the plane. I thought it was sort of exciting fun, like a roller coaster. Unlike my mother, I had no concept of mortality. (I was never afraid on a plane until I brought my two-month-old daughter Amy home to New York from London where she was born. It did not take a storm—fear began at takeoff. For years after, I could not fly without a pill and a drink.)

Aged thirteen, I was "Madly for Adlai," but otherwise indifferent to politics. Lena campaigned for Stevenson early on. From Lee Israel's biography of columnist Dorothy Kilgallen:

There was a party once, during the early fifties, at the Greenwich Village apartment of Bob and Jean Bach. Adlai Stevenson was running for president. Lena Horne was standing in front of the piano. To the tune of "I Love to Love," Lena sang: *I love the Guv / The Guvnah of Illinois*. As she was singing, she looked at Dorothy and said, "Hope I'm not offending you." Dorothy raised her glass and replied in a shy, slightly inebriated voice, "That's all right. It's a better song than 'I Like Ike.'"

In 1950 W. E. B. Du Bois, aged eighty-two, ran for U.S. senator from New York on the American Labor Party ticket and got just over two hundred thousand votes. (It is somehow touching that two hundred thousand New Yorkers, all probably very young or very old, would want to put eighty-two-year-old Du Bois in the U.S. Senate.) I met Dr. Du Bois two years before his political run, in my mother's dressing room at the Copacabana. He sat in a chair and held his carved African cane almost as if he were a chieftain holding a spear. I could only stare. I was eleven; he was eighty—I was transfixed. He wore a cream-colored linen suit, perfect with his beige face and little white beard. He looked so *perfect* and so *important*. I remember shaking his hand and feeling utterly tongue-tied with an impulse to curtsy. I remember my mother saying, "Dr. *Du Boyze* has just come back from Africa."

In the summer of 1950 we stayed in the most glamorous hotel I had ever seen, all curving marble staircases and blazing chandeliers. The Hotel Raphael in Paris had been the home of the German high command during the occupation. It was from the Raphael that Lena and Lennie revealed their marriage of three years earlier. It was from there that Lena and Lennie went out to pose at a sidewalk café for *Life* magazine: Lennie in his distinctive yachting cap, and Lena in her Jacques Fath suit and incredibly becoming Parisian hat. Lena got hate mail from both blacks and whites.

Reality at home was very different—and stranger than ever. Hollywood's biggest red-baiter and blacklister, Roy Brewer, from 1945 to 1963 head of the powerful International Alliance of Theatrical Stage Employees and Motion Picture Machine Operators (IATSE, pronounced *I-At-See*), suddenly changed his mind about Lena. In 1950 he had listed her as a subversive in his infamous booklet *Red Channels*. But in 1952 he was suddenly eager to help clear her name. IATSE was heavily rumored to be mobbed up. I believe that it was really to do a favor for his mob friends. Lena may have voiced opinions that powerful people did not like, but the Jewish mob that ran American nightclubs needed her and the movies needed Jewish mob money.

On November 13, 1952, Roy Brewer wrote to a CBS executive "with respect to Lena Horne," saying there "should be no further question about her position." The executive replied that Brewer's letter would be "helpful in removing any cloud that may have restricted the use of Miss Horne's services." As quickly as Brewer had tried to smear her, he had turned around and cleared her. CBS was considered the most liberal network. Lena had powerful CBS-connected friends. (With Robeson's career destroyed, perhaps HUAC felt it did not want to look as if it was going after every important black person in the country, even though it was.) Meanwhile, Lena developed ulcers—but continued to fight for her earning power. She learned how to get off the blacklist with the help of Lennie's agent, who told her to contact Brewer himself, who would steer her to one of the "clearing" people who would get the word out that she might get off the blacklist. Without going before a congressional committee, she could be hired again.

On June 28, 1953, two days before her thirty-sixth birthday, Lena wrote a twelve-page letter on Sands Hotel stationery to Roy Brewer. Here are excerpts:

Dear Mr. Brewer,

If at any time I have said or done anything that might have been construed as being sympathetic toward communism, I hope the following will help to refute this misconception.

To begin with, I am aware that a good deal of my attitudes were motivated by personal prejudices which were conditioned in me from birth. You will probably understand this.

There has been a great deal of curiosity about my friendship with Paul Robeson. My family had known him for many years. My grandmother, who was an ardent social worker, was instrumental in obtaining a scholarship for him when he was very young . . . I have heard it said many times that he influenced me sympathetically toward communism. This I must emphatically deny. However, at the time I met Robeson, in 1940, I was going through a serious personal crisis. I had begun to realize that I was being classified as a "lucky Negro." I heard this from Negro leaders and read it in the press. I realized that there were many Negroes who hadn't received the "breaks" as I presumably had. This became a very heavy burden . . . I explained this problem to Robeson at the time and he suggested that I might help myself by taking an active interest in the problems of other people, generally, and in the Negro people, specifically. As an example, he recommended that I help raise money for a milk fund being sponsored by the Council for African Affairs [W. E. B. Du Bois' organization] for the benefit of African mothers . . . Many similar benefit appearances followed thereafter . . .

She spoke about HICCASP (the bogeyman of the right wing), which supported the Fair Employment Practices Bill and helped her when Hollywood neighbors tried to have her evicted. She revealed that she had been invited to join the party in 1941 by "a man named Pettis Perry." Perry, a Negro, was the Communist Party candidate for lieutenant governor of California in 1934. He was indicted for conspiracy under the Smith Act in 1951 (he would be convicted in February 1953 and sentenced to three years in prison). Lena realized that Communists had "played upon my racial insecurities, and made me overly sensitive to each slight and injustice to Negroes to the point where I was quite willing to appear for any cause that might aid them." She understood that it was "in the classic pattern which the communists design for minority people." She ended the letter:

I have always known that America offers the greatest chance to all people, to achieve human dignity—and since this terrible experience I am more determined than ever to do what I can to impress these principles on the thinking of all people I come in contact with.

She signed her letter "Most sincerely." I find the tone of the letter to be utterly sincere and very slightly defiant. When she talks about "personal prejudices" that Brewer would "probably understand," she is talking about white racism. She is truthful about Robeson—he advised her in no uncertain terms *not* to join the party. She admitted helping Du Bois' organization, the Council on African Affairs, but did not say that he was a friend of her grandparents'. And by saying she was "more determined than ever" to impress the principles of "human dignity" on everyone she met, Lena made it clear to Brewer that while she intended to be quiet, she would not entirely shut up.

Brewer did not reply to the letter, but with a phone call passed her on to a New York blacklist "clearinghouse" in the person of George Sokolsky, a right-wing political columnist, whose first remark to Lena was "I understand your difficulties completely—I once had a Chinese wife." It was a pro forma visit; Brewer had effectively cleared her. Taking a paternalistic tone, in effect Sokolsky absolved Lena of the political sins of her wayward youth.

In October 1953, after the Eisenhower administration made concentrated efforts to dismiss him, Frank Horne was named assistant to the administrator of the Housing and Home Finance Agency (HHFA). Frank considered the reassignment a "demotion"—being "kicked upstairs." His new position had only vague powers. In 1954 he was investigated once again for "leftist" activities; this time for participating and aiding in the defense of racial relations adviser Edward Rutledge, a colleague accused of being a Communist sympathizer. Eventually, with the help of Frank and others, Rutledge was cleared. In 1955, because of the hostility of the Republican National Committee toward his New Deal policies and achievements, Frank was finally terminated from HHFA. The following year he and Mercedes moved to New York City, where everything was fine as long as Mercedes was sober—although she denied having a problem. Frank, as usual, threw himself into work. In 1956 Mayor Robert Wagner appointed him executive director of the

New York City Commission on Intergroup Relations under Chairman Herbert Bayard Swope. In 1957 Frank developed the nation's first laws against discrimination in public housing and introduced the Open City Housing Project to promote racially integrated neighborhoods. Frank never stopped being heroic; he had rescued little Lena when her mother abandoned her in Georgia, and he probably thought he could rescue poor Mercedes, with her white streak and her white skin and her inability to face life sober.

I was sixteen in 1954. I think *Brown v. Board of Education* was the first time I actually *read* the front page of the *New York Times*. The following year I went to Radcliffe—chosen because the only college girls I knew, Susan Morford and Judith Grummon (from Oakwood), were both Cliffies. There were no more than a handful of Negro "girls," as we were called. But Harvard as an entity was far more openly sexist than racist or anti-Semitic. There were classrooms, whole buildings, and physical areas where "girls" were forbidden entry. Harvard discriminated against women and probably would have boasted about it if there was anyone who cared enough to complain. My favorite story comes from one of my early dorm mates, a member of the Radcliffe basketball team (as were her mother and grandmother). They were in the middle of a varsity championship game with Tufts when the Harvard basketball team suddenly appeared on the court, yelling, "Get off!" It was Harvard's practice hour.

I was lucky enough to attach myself to the relatively nonsexist, sophisticated camaraderie of the Harvard Dramatic Club. The members were wonderful, quirky, talented people. I was a terrible actress with a small gift for comedy, but I won a prize at the 1959 Yale Drama Festival for playing the lead in Molière's *School for Wives*. I have no idea what I did, but I convulsed the audience and even broke up my partner in the scene. As a student, I was not what was known as a "grind." I worked only in small spurts—and I now regret this very much. I did manage to write a thesis on Colette (the French department disapproved because she had only just died) and graduate cum laude. I was determined to have a busy, fun college social life, and I did; but my student life reflected my dreadful progressive education. I had no idea how to study. If I was interested, if I *cared*, I got high marks—such as my A in Professor Arthur M. Schlesinger Jr.'s "American Intellectual History" course. On the other hand, I am ashamed to say that I got my natural science grade changed from F to D by crying to the section man (the person who actually dealt with the students of august professors). In my senior year, two events had repercussions: my roommate's fiancé (white) was picketing Woolworth's in Cambridge because of its Southern racial policies, and I worked for Massachusetts senator John F. Kennedy's reelection campaign—mostly stuffing envelopes.

I was also part of the *Eloise* gang. Kay Thompson's greatest revenge on Hollywood was to write the brilliant children's book *Eloise* with the magical and essential illustrations by Hilary Knight, another friend. Lena and Lennie, in fact, appear in *Eloise in Paris*, seated outdoors at Fouquet's café with their small dogs, Jadie the pug and Lila the alpha dog Pekingese.

From Kay Thompson's biography:

> Subliminally or otherwise, Kay drew inspiration from the many precocious young girls she'd known over the years, including Liza Minnelli, . . . Gail Jones (daughter of Lena Horne), Lucie Arnaz (daughter of Lucille Ball and Desi Arnaz), . . . Portland Mason (daughter of James), . . . Margaret O'Brien . . . and many others.

By 1957 Lena considered herself removed from politics. Lena's semi-pal Howard Fast dropped a political bombshell on February 1, 1957. According to the front page of the *New York Times*, "Howard Fast said yesterday that he had dissociated himself from the American Communist party and no longer considered himself a Communist." By 1957 the *Daily Worker* had closed, and the Communist Party, which in 1947 had seventy-four thousand members, now counted three thousand. The downfall was not entirely because of the success of American red-baiting and blacklisting—the disaffection came from something the Russian Communist Party brought on itself. In 1956 Nikita Khrushchev delivered a four-hour "secret speech" denouncing the crimes of Stalin. By the time the secret became known, the effect on American Communists was devastating. "This was not why I joined the Party," said Steve Nelson, proletarian hero and former commissar of the Abraham Lincoln Brigade. That particular "god" had failed, to the heartbreak and dismay of many true believers.

With politics essentially behind them, and Lena's 1957 album *Lena Horne at the Waldorf Astoria* the top-selling album by a female performer in the history of RCA Victor, Lena and Lennie returned to Europe and Arthur Laurents, the author of *West Side Story*, came back into Lena's life in Paris:

> Paris adored Lena. In return, she sang "Que Restes-ils?" and the city was totally hers. One more reason to feel more at home in Paris than back home was the belief Paris was color-blind. She would never have walked down Fifth Avenue as easily as we walked down the Champs-Elysées one day, looking for a drugstore that sold makeup. The base she used was much darker than her own skin and covered her sprinkle of freckles. That day, her skin against her light lavender cashmere sweater and skirt made her more beautiful than any of her lighter sisters. The laconic Parisian saleswoman in the store gaped adoringly: "I know! You're Doris Day!" "No, I'm Doris Night," Lena answered. She would not have made that joke back home.

The first time I met Arthur, I was a Radcliffe sophomore and he had written *West Side Story*. Suddenly, he was always there. He talked to me; he listened to what I had to say. He was funny. Meanwhile Lena was appearing in a show that she knew to be infinitely inferior to *West Side Story*.

Jamaica, starring Lena Horne, was once a project called *Pigeon Island*, starring Harry Belafonte. When Lena announced her upcoming role in *Jamaica* during a guest appearance on *The Ed Sullivan Show*, advance ticket sales soared to nearly a million dollars. But outside New York it had been a disaster. In Boston they said, "Thank God for Josephine Premice," who was brilliant and got all her laughs. Lena was frozen in fear and on the verge of a breakdown. I witnessed it. The fights between the producer and the writers were nonstop. Script changes were constant. It was very close to the opening—possibly in Philadelphia or New Haven, in a hotel room. She simply broke down in sobs, saying, "I can't do it. I can't do it." Despite her mini-breakdown, despite the vicious battles between the writers and the producer, there was a typically happy Broadway ending—as in a Busby Berkeley movie. It was all about *star power*.

On October 31, 1957, a dressed-to-the-nines audience of celebrities attended Lena's Broadway opening in *Jamaica*. "When you make your entrance tonight, make it like you belong there and stand still" were the last words that director Bobby Lewis said to Lena before he left her dressing room. Lena did as she was told. The standing ovation, before she said a word, was deafening. She gave an opening night party at the Waldorf for the cast and crew. David Merrick, the dreaded producer who never smiled, arrived with the first telephoned report of the rave reviews. "Well, I always said you were a money runner," he said, kissing her cheek. Lena wished he had told her sooner.

In 1958 Lena was so happy to be back in New York and in a Broadway hit, despite the fact that she and Lennie bought a ten-room apartment in the same building where George Sokolsky, the blacklister, had "cleared" her name five years earlier. I loved our new home base, where, although I was away in college, I had my own room instead of using the library/guest room. Lena went on a decorating spree and Lennie installed a sound system. And they had parties. I was away for most of them, but my birthday and Christmas were special. They had wonderful Christmas parties at 300 West End Avenue. Parties meant Broadway friends like Gwen Verdon, Noël Coward, Richard Burton, and Laurence Olivier and family like Uncle Frank and Uncle Burke and wives, with lots of singing around the piano, tons of food and drink, and dancing in the foyer—Arthur Mitchell of the New York City Ballet taught us the boogaloo, a line dance of fleeting popularity. Or maybe it was the mashed potato. Lena's theatrical friends were her peers in the Broadway "classes" of 1957 to 1959, which was how long *Jamaica* ran. Richard Burton's wife, Sybil, was a special friend. While Richard and Lena were onstage in their respective shows, she would pop over to Lena's dressing room to have a civilized drink with Lennie. This was the same dressing room where Lennie called me in one evening before the show for a *serious* talk, while Lena, listening to every word, furiously concentrated on doing her makeup. I sat, he stood. It was ominous. "I have something to tell you," he said, looking at me with a grave face. *Oh God*, I thought, *what could it be?* Taking a very grim tone, he then said, "There is a rumor going around that your mother and I are gay." Since I thought it was the funniest thing I had ever heard (and no one was ill or dying), I burst out laughing in amusement and relief—causing Lennie to bend over and kiss me on the forehead and Lena to pause, wide-eyed, in mid-powder puff.

I had been brought up with gay people. Not that I really knew what "gay" was. I think I sort of discovered something like "gay" when I was eleven or twelve and there was one boy in my ballet class. He was a slight object of fun to us girls behind his back. The word "gay" was never used—it was the other F-word ("fairy")—but the ballet teacher was great, treating him very seriously. I began taking gays seriously in college: Walt Whitman, Amy Lowell, Willa Cather, Gertrude Stein, Oscar Wilde, Jean Cocteau, and so forth. I loved the novels of Mary Renault. When I was young there seemed to be a natural affinity between gays and blacks. I came to perceive that so many of mother's friends were gay—and those who were white were often Southern. I suppose they identified with each other as outcasts or victims of a region or both. I often got crushes on my mother's handsome and charming male friends. Many of the gay men and women I knew in the 1950s were in long-standing, seemingly happy monogamous relationships and were always invited to parties as couples. It was these friends whom I thought of when Lennie said there were rumors about Mother and him—but the whole concept of Mother and Lennie being gay struck me as funny.

Gay rumors aside, I know that this was a very happy period in my mother's life. She had fulfilled a dream. She was in a hit show and had a wonderful caricature on Sardi's wall, in which she looked gorgeous, not grotesque, wearing a white turban and a black Chanel suit. Kitty D'Alessio, a pioneer in fashion advertising, and a beloved family friend through the generations, was vice president of a Madison Avenue agency and account executive for Chanel—so Lena had a lovely collection of Chanel suits. She was finally at home, and working in her beloved New York; it was almost like being back in Café Society. The only missing element in that happy time for Lena was the fact that my brother, Teddy, was rarely permitted by our father to come and visit. When he did come, whether for Christmas or summer, Lennie was happy because he and Teddy listened to jazz and stared at the chessboard together for hours.

When *Jamaica* closed after two years, Lena had a big letdown. The producers of the musical version of *Destry Rides Again* asked her to costar with Andy Griffith—but Griffith refused to appear opposite a Negro. So Lena and Lennie took a slow boat to Rio to forget their troubles. As musicians, they naturally adored Brazil. They brought back incredible bossa nova records that they played for friends. They also brought back a middle-aged white American priest who had befriended them on the boat coming home. I can't remember his name, but he was a Jesuit missionary on home leave after many years. After the second or third week of his visit, despite the fact that he was charming and fun, we began to wonder when he would begin the next stage of his voyage. A week or two later he finally packed up, with feelings of goodwill on both sides. I remember having a distinctly positive attitude about priests, though this one seemed to spend much of his time lying on the couch in Lennie's music room listening to bossa nova and drinking Heineken beer. He was on vacation, after all.

In the summer of 1959, the year I graduated from Radcliffe, Teddy finally rejoined the family and we were all in Europe together. Teddy and I bonded on that trip—where suddenly everything that was bothersome in younger brothers no longer mattered. He had grown from a hopelessly ill-groomed, annoying young boy to a Brooks Brothers–clad young man who towered over me and was found to be quite irresistible by females of all ages and nationalities. He wore horn-rimmed glasses, behind which he had his grandmother Edna's beautiful green eyes. He was a debater and a Young Republican—that was our father Louis' influence (the machine Democrat had become a machine California Republican and publisher of a civil service magazine). All past squabbles disappeared in the face of our new need to cover for each other. In the summer of 1959 he could safely go to hashish-smoking Parisian jazz joints with African poets and beautiful women—and I could continue my sub-rosa late-night friendship with Burt Bacharach, who, even though he was already a noted composer, was Marlene Dietrich's accompanist in her one-woman show. Marlene and Lena were theoretically great friends, but somehow I thought it best that neither be too aware of my friendship with Burt (as nice as he was handsome). I would go to dinner with friends and then meet Burt after the show. I was "working" (*interning* really) at *Marie Claire*, a sister publication of *Paris Match*. I helped to arrange pillows for photographs. The moment the summer was over, I realized that I hated Paris. The autumn leaves only made me long for a bright October day in New York. I now passionately hated a city I once had loved, but had seen only in spring and summer. Naturally I felt too embarrassed and ashamed to tell anyone, having found an apartment to share and a fancy "job." So I managed to hold out until the wettest, dreariest Christmas ever. There we were, Lennie, Mother, and I, all three of us really missing New York. Senator Kennedy had been right at Harvard's commencement when he predicted that I would not stay in Paris, but would come home. Now I came home to try to help him win the White House.

I did indeed campaign for Senator Kennedy, bouncing around in a small plane with some slightly older luminaries like Mrs. Willie Mays, in her thirties, and Mrs. Chester Bowles, a delightful white-haired woman in her sixties, who was my roommate on the road. Kennedy was considered a friend of the Negro as well as youth. Mrs. Mays and Mrs. Bowles represented their husbands. And I was "youth." In my very short set speech, I said that a vote for Nixon was a vote for a man who had "never been young." Senator Kennedy lost every state we visited—Kentucky, Ohio, Tennessee, and New Jersey.

When he got back from Europe, wanting, correctly, to get away from our father, who lived in Los Angeles, Teddy transferred from UCLA to Berkeley. Unsurprisingly, his life was turned upside down. He abandoned the Young Republicans. He had never been a red diaper baby. Now he made up for lost time, but the diaper was metaphorically black, not red. The next time I saw him, when he came to visit me in New York, he had discarded his horn-rims for small round wires, his Brooks Brothers suit for a well-worn safari jacket with buttons about Angela Davis and Huey P. Newton. He was reading Hermann Hesse. And he had a marijuana habit. He was a true *sixties* person and I was a late *fifties* hopeless square. His new incarnation was actually the height of fashion. Because he was bearded and very thin, having developed a kidney ailment resulting from poor medical care in Paris, he looked like an ascetic revolutionary. It was the look that all the New York and Hollywood "with-it" people were trying to emulate. Teddy was funny and sad. He knew he was sick, but he hated the dialysis machine with every fiber of his being. Even though he returned to L.A., I was frankly pleased that his radical conversion seemed to repudiate our father's conservative Republican politics.

Chapter Twelve

South/1950s

POSTWAR

COUSIN CATHERINE Nash was the first black Calhoun *post*war bride. Unlike her cousin Kathryn, who married an army man—and unlike her sister Harriet, whose husband, Chiz, became a Tuskegee Airman—Catherine had been in no hurry to marry. So she did not rush into marriage with Morehouse graduate Joseph Page Frye. "The charming child . . . she sleeps by night and eats all day and never mentions 'Joe'" was how Kathryn described the only cousin who did not marry her prewar love. Instead of being a war bride, Catherine got her master's degree in library science, began her career, and waited until the war was over before marrying a veteran who never saw combat. John S. Harris was a former second lieutenant in the 617th Bomb Squadron of the 477th composite group of the Tuskegee Airmen. John's date of entry for active duty was August 4, 1945—two days before the atomic bomb was dropped on Hiroshima. The Japanese surrendered ten days later.

According to his honorable discharge paper, John Harris was born in Richmond, Kentucky, in 1924. He had brown hair and eyes, was five feet eleven inches tall, and weighed 168 pounds. His civilian occupation was student and his military occupation was pilot. Under "campaigns and battles" the entry was: none. Under "service schools attended": pilot training. Under "decorations and citations": the American Campaign

Medal and the World War II Victory Medal. John completed his pilot training in the last Tuskegee class. By 1945, the air force had begun to desegregate itself. John Harris trained as a bomber pilot, not a fighter pilot; this meant that future bomber crews would be integrated. But there were still no civilian jobs for black pilots.

John Harris and Catherine Nash met at Kentucky State, where she was a librarian and he was a freshman on the GI Bill. They were married in 1948. Their state of Georgia, Fulton County, marriage certificate, read: "I hereby certify that John S. Harris (COL) and Catherine Graves Nash (COL) were joined together in the Holy Bonds of Matrimony on the 5th day of September 1948 by me Homer G. McEwen, Pastor First Congregational Church, Atlanta, Georgia." First Congregational had been the spiritual home of so many Graveses, Nashes, and Calhouns over the years. The twenty-eight-year-old bride was beautiful in a white satin gown, with a veiled headdress framing her radiant face. The large wedding party included Harriet's three-year-old daughter, Cheryl Chisholm, as flower girl. Catherine and John's daughter, Karen, would be born in 1953.

Karen Harris remembered her parents:

> I think Daddy majored in history because his first job here in Atlanta after they married was as a history teacher at David T. Howard High School [the school that Walter White won the funds for during World War I]. After I was born he got a job with the old Schlitz beer company . . . He handled the black distributors. He was gone a lot, but all that changed when Schlitz promoted him and we moved to Milwaukee.

After World War II, certain industries, especially beer, whisky, and cigarettes, realizing that black buying potential was significant, began aggressively wooing postwar Negro families with advertisements in black magazines and newspapers. They also sought out talented black candidates, especially veterans, for mid-level executive jobs. Schlitz called itself "the beer that made Milwaukee famous." Working for Schlitz in Milwaukee was a very good job indeed for a black veteran. Corporate America was inching itself to the forefront of postwar desegregation.

Catherine was three years younger than her third cousin Lena Horne, whom she did not really know—though they met in Fort Valley, Georgia, in 1928 when Lena was nearly twelve and Catherine was almost nine. Catherine would no more have had Lena's political problems in the 1950s than fly to the moon. She might very well have had Lena's *opinions*, but she never would have voiced them outside her home. Unlike Catherine, Lena had been raised in the North, and her grandparents there, having come from the South where politics were forbidden to Negroes, had a passionate faith in political action. Lena had been formed by the politics of Cora the Republican/suffragist/uplift activist and Edwin, the lapsed Republican Tammany man. Catherine, a Southern Negro woman who came of age in World War II, would have had less than zero opportunity for political expression. So Catherine, like many Southern women white and black over the decades, became a domestic goddess. In the words of her daughter:

> She made ALL my clothes until I went to college! . . . Singlehanded she crocheted tams (about 50) for the drill team at our high school where she was the Librarian. No one ever suspected my clothes weren't from [a store] . . .

Was 1945–1946, the moment of victory against the Axis and the moment when the world was still idealistic about the United Nations, the point when America could have become more liberal about race? *Not* in the South. Black soldiers were hated—especially black soldiers who came home wanting to vote. Killing black voters was still encouraged and condoned by white Southern officials, including U.S. senator Theodore Bilbo of Mississippi (cited in Richard M. Dalfiume's

Desegregation of the U.S. Armed Forces), who called on "red-blooded Anglo Saxon" Southerners to use "any means" necessary to stop blacks from voting. "If you don't know what that means," Bilbo added, "you are just not up on your persuasive measures."

In the North, oppression took the form of blacklists and red-baiting. In the South, everything was more visceral. "The first nigger to vote will never vote again" read a sign on a black church during the 1946 Georgia primary. Maceo Snipes, a black veteran, the only black to vote in Taylor County, Georgia, was taken from his house and shot to death the day after the election. Two days later, on July 25, 1946, in Walton County, Georgia, George Dorsey, a twenty-eight-year-old black veteran of the war in the Pacific; his twenty-three-year-old wife, Mae Murray Dorsey; and Roger Malcolm, aged twenty-four, and his wife, Dorothy Dorsey Malcolm, who was seven months pregnant, were all killed—taken from a car driven by a white man, J. Loy Harrison, who employed both couples as sharecroppers. The mob stopped the car and sixty bullets were pumped at close range into the bodies of the two black couples. Harrison, the only eyewitness, was brave enough to be quoted in the August 5, 1946, issue of *Time* magazine:

> A big man who was dressed mighty proud in a double-breasted brown suit was giving the orders. He pointed to Roger and said, "We want that nigger." Then he pointed to George Dorsey, *my* nigger [italics mine], and said, "We want you too, Charlie." I said, "His name ain't Charlie, he's George." Someone said "Keep your damned big mouth shut. This ain't your party."

The Dorsey-Malcolm lynching "party," known as the Moore's Ford lynching, was said to be "the last mass lynching in America." But no charges were ever brought against any of the twenty men rumored to be part of the lynch mob. For all practical purposes, lynching in the South, which white Southern senators would not permit to become a federal crime, was a state-sanctioned institution—and victims were always murdered with impunity. But most decent people everywhere were appalled by Moore's Ford, including President Harry Truman, already angered by assaults on Negro vets in uniform. "My God! I had no idea it was as terrible as that! We've got to do something!" said Truman when Walter White, the influential NAACP leader, informed him of the Georgia murders. So he set about desegregating the U.S. military and creating the Presidential Committee on Civil Rights.

One young black Atlanta lawyer and World War II veteran was also ready to act. Donald L. Hollowell, a former army second lieutenant, was made so bitter by his treatment and the treatment of black GIs in the war that he determined to make a difference. Hollowell is quoted in *Saving the Soul of Georgia: Donald L. Hollowell and the Struggle for Civil Rights,* by Maurice C. Daniels:

> I grew up considerably in the military . . . I learned how to work with men and to guide them; to administer an office; to be disciplined in conduct and habits. At the same time there were many bitter experiences that were sufficient to cause a man to hate. And I am confident but for the fact that I found Jesus along the way back when I was about 15 and had practiced a relationship with Him, I would have entered civilian society with a heart full of hate . . . but I also knew that hate consumes one and that one has to use that energy constructively . . . That's what I chose to do.

In 1940, for example, there were only seven black lawyers in Georgia: three in Atlanta, two in Savannah, and one each in Macon and Augusta. But by 1945 black Atlanta lawyers were winning blacks the right to vote in the Democratic primary. Hollowell, in partnership with the NAACP Legal Defense Fund and the great Constance Baker Motley and Thurgood Marshall, became the foremost civil rights lawyer in Georgia. Unfortunately for Hollowell, in 1948 he also came to the attention of J. Edgar Hoover.

In a January 1948 memo Hoover wrote: "You are requested to conduct a thorough and discreet investigation to determine the loyalty and patriotism of the above-named individual Donald Lee Hollowell . . ."

Two years earlier, in October 1946, when Hollowell was a student at Lane College in Tennessee, he was elected to represent the Lane student body at the Southern Negro Youth Congress convention. Paul Robeson was a guest speaker at the convention—reason enough in 1947 for the attorney general to deem the whole convention "subversive." For Hollowell, however, meeting Robeson was inspiring:

> He was a big man. A big, dark-brown-skinned, heavy-voiced, beautiful-voiced man who loved what he did. Who was smart—when at Rutgers was an honor roll man. He was smarter than the average man. Therefore, he saw no reason for himself to be subjugated because of his color . . . When he sang "Climbing Up," it just made your soul feel the need, and your mind to understand that this is a man who believed that you have to work at eliminating those things which stand in your way.

Hollowell's life was now thoroughly investigated, and it was determined on February 8, 1948, that there was nothing "derogatory" or pro-Communist in his background. But in March Hoover asked the FBI's Washington field office to see if HUAC had anything on Hollowell. The field office reported that "inquiries failed to indicate any lack of patriotism or loyalty for US Government." In September 1949 the U.S. assistant attorney general wrote a rather cryptic memo to Hoover on the subject of Hollowell that basically stated that there was no evidence to warrant "prosecution" at this time. Should "additional proof" be received, or should "confidential informants become available to testify," the division would, of course, "re-examine the case." The only explanation for Hoover's obsession with Hollowell was, of course, that he hated blacks almost more than he hated Communists. He especially hated blacks who were working for civil rights.

In August 1948 Harry Truman's Executive Order 9981 desegregated the U.S. military and created both a Fair Employment Practices Committee and a Civil Rights Commission. Truman came from the border state of Missouri, which had stayed in the Union but remained a slave state. As a young Democratic politician working for the Kansas City Pendergast machine, he inherited a black ward and knew blacks as individuals. As a World War I officer, he had sympathy for black troops. But there was nothing new in the 1948 Georgia elections. In Montgomery, Georgia, the local NAACP president was beaten for escorting blacks to the polls. In Vidalia, Georgia, a man named Robert Mallard was lynched because he voted.

It was an election year. The Republican platform, which favored a federal antilynching law, was also in favor of military desegregation:

Lynching or any other form of mob violence anywhere is a disgrace to any civilized state, and we favor the prompt enactment of legislation to end this infamy . . . We are opposed to the idea of racial segregation in the armed services of the United States.

The Democratic platform said:

We again state our belief that racial and religious minorities must have the right to live, the right to work, the right to vote, the full and equal protection of the laws on a basis of equality with all citizens as guaranteed by the Constitution.

The Democratic Party called on Congress to support the president in guaranteeing Negroes the right of full and equal political participation, equal opportunity in employment, the right of security of person, and equal treatment in the service and defense of the nation. But white Southerners did not want blacks to vote, or to have decent jobs or a sense of personal safety. They especially did not want blacks to defend their country—so thirty-five Southern delegates walked out of the Democratic convention and formed the Dixiecrat Party, whose candidate was Strom Thurmond:

> We stand for the segregation of the races . . . We oppose and condemn the action of the Democratic Convention in sponsoring a civil rights program calling for the elimination of segregation . . .

Southern Democrats continued to reject all efforts to make lynching a federal crime.

The Progressive Party's platform stated:

> The Progressive Party condemns segregation and discrimination in all its forms and in all places . . . [It supports] Federal anti-lynch, anti-discrimination, and fair-employment practices legislation, and legislation abolishing segregation in interstate travel . . . and full use of Federal enforcement powers to assure free exercise of the right to franchise . . . a Civil Rights Act for the District of Columbia to eliminate racial segregation and discrimination in the nation's capital . . . the ending of segregation and discrimination in the Panama Canal Zone and all territories, possessions and trusteeships.

Henry Wallace's Progressives were about twenty years ahead of their time. Blacks were torn during that election year, choosing between a racial revolutionary and the man who desegregated the army. At first Lena supported Wallace. The good thing about the racial revolutionaries: they were the most idealistically inclusive party since the abolitionists. Progressives were the only party of all races, creeds, colors, ages, and social and economic conditions in America, running the narrow political gamut from pink to very red. The trouble with the racial revolution was not the open Communists—it was the many background figures who were in what Lena's friend Howard "Stretch" Johnson (the

Cotton Club dancer who became a very important Harlem Communist) called "Deep Freeze." Johnson, the brother of Cotton Club chorus girl Winnie Johnson, described the underground organization:

> We divided our top leadership, of which I was a part, into three segments: One segment we called the Availables, who continued to function in the open; the second segment consisted of the Unavailables, who were linked to the Availables through a courier system; and then a third segment we called the "Deep Freeze," whose members were not active at all but were just holed up somewhere in case FBI surveillance and reconnaissance exposed those who were in the Unavailable category. We also had a fourth group whose members were sent out of the country to eastern Europe or the Soviet Union. We said they were "On Ice" . . . I was so well known, having been in show business and everything, that it was decided I should join the ranks of the Unavailables.

The Communist platform read:

> The most shameful aspect of American life is the Jim Crowism, the terror and violence imposed upon the Negro people, especially in the South . . . [it called for] a national FEPC law . . . the outlawing of the Ku Klux Klan . . . Federal enforcement of the 13th, 14th, and 15th amendments.

Black voters bypassed the pink and the red, even Paul Robeson, and gave their votes to the man who desegregated the military—which says a lot about how blacks felt about being in the military, despite the shameful treatment they received from their government and the Jim Crow army in both world wars. The Atlanta Negro Voters League was founded in 1949 to concentrate the Negro vote on candidates most favorable to blacks in local elections. Atlanta had the first Negro-owned radio station that year: WERD.

In 1949 Dr. Helen Nash, aged twenty-eight, third of six children born to Homer and Marie, became the first black woman to join the attending staff of St. Louis Children's Hospital. Described by her cousin Kathryn as "A Lady trim and elegant / If breadth of forehead shows breadth of brain / She's really most intelligent," Helen had received her bachelor's degree from Spelman College in Atlanta in 1941—and, against her father's wishes, in 1945 she received her medical degree from Meharry Medical College in Nashville, America's only black medical school. She completed her internship and pediatric residency, including chief residency, at Homer G. Phillips Hospital in St. Louis. Opened in 1937 as a segregated hospital to serve the black community, Homer G. Phillips was the only place in St. Louis where nonwhite doctors could get internships and residencies. (Helen was named president of the Homer G. Phillips medical staff in 1977.)

Homer Nash Jr., the lone Nash brother, actually had the first postwar wedding. "Homer Nash Nutt's a mighty fine Nutt / of which there is no doubt / His vocal tones range from do to so / while in height he seems to sprout." A graduate of Morehouse and Meharry Medical College, twenty-two-year-old Homer Nash Jr. married Ellene Terrell Bentley in Columbus, Ohio, on August 25, 1947. Ellene had attended both Fisk and Atlanta University. Homer and Ellene moved to St. Louis to be near Helen, who was already a hospital resident. Homer soon began a successful private pediatric practice.

In 1950 the Nash children lost their grandmother Katie Webb Graves, aged eighty-eight. Her husband, Antoine, had died ten years earlier. She and Antoine were an example of a long, devoted marriage—an inspiration to their children. Katie had been the family matriarch, the redoubtable yardstick of rectitude. Katie, who called herself "Catherine" after she married Antoine Graves, was always a child of Reconstruction. One of the Talented Tenth, Katie took uplift and good works seriously—like her cousin Cora. Katie's life was the Southern version of Cora's. They were both clubwomen—but belonging to very different clubs. Much of Katie's Southern philanthropy was church-oriented, while Cora's Northern philanthropy counted on lay benefactors. Southern clubs were mostly mini-Chautauquas—gatherings for self-improvement on every possible subject save anything controversial. That went double for politics. Cora on the other hand, was fighting real social and political ills—not discussing horticulture. Both women were important leaders in their communities. Katie's importance came from her husband. As Mrs. Antoine Graves Sr., she was the wife of one of the most successful black men in Atlanta. Cora won her importance on her own. Yes, she was married to Edwin F. Horne, a key figure in New York's Black Tammany, but she was also a member of the National Republican Women's Auxiliary. Cora was her own woman. Katie, who had everything except political and social freedom, was a prisoner of her time and place in the segregated South. Katie had a long, happy, loving marriage—Cora did not. But fate had brought them together in other ways. Each of them lost her eldest son. It was to Katie that Cora wrote in 1918 when her newlywed son, Second Lieutenant Errol Horne, died in the influenza pandemic. Writing on black-bordered stationery, Cora said that Errol's young wife, Lottie, was "a wreck," that Errol had a military funeral with full honors, and that his commanding officer had been very complimentary—but "O, it is a deep, deep sorrow."

In the summer of 1950 the national convention of the NAACP decided on a full-scale attack on educational segregation. In response to blacklisters, the organization ordered its own investigation of Communist infiltration. This was a year of many firsts: the American Medical Association announced its first Negro member; Althea Gibson became the first Negro to play in the National Tennis Championship games at Forest Hills, New York; and the first black player in the National Basketball Association, Charles "Chuck" Cooper from Pittsburgh, who played at West Virginia State and Duquesne, was drafted by the Boston Celtics. But there were still Northern cities with Southern mind-sets. Chicago was one of the worst because Southern blacks and whites migrated at the same time. Statistics show that between 1940 and 1950, a total of 1,597,000 Negroes moved out of the South. The Chicago race riot of July 12, 1951, erupted when a veteran, a bus driver, tried to move into an apartment in Cicero, Illinois—reputed to be home to the Chicago Mafia. A white mob smashed the apartment windows and set fire to the furniture. Governor Adlai E. Stevenson called out the National Guard. On July 15 the NAACP announced that the apartment building was now black-owned and would be rented to black and white veterans.

In 1952, for the first time in seventy-one years, there were no recorded lynchings in America. But it was no wonder that only 21 percent of blacks voted for Eisenhower. He was remembered and disliked by blacks for testifying against the desegregation of the military. Now he told the NAACP that he opposed federal aid to segregated school systems, but would not dictate to Southerners how to run their schools. In 1953 the NAACP began its ten-year Fight for Freedom to end all racial discrimination by 1963. And the Supreme Court agreed to hear five school desegregation cases—culminating in *Brown v. Board of Education* in May 1954. White Citizens' Councils, the "respectable" face of racism, now sprang up all over the South. White Citizens' Councils, known as the "Country Club KKK," sought to obstruct the 1954 decision in any way possible—through racist "education" as well as covert violence.

Atlanta's own Walter White, the hometown boy who was so brave during the race riot of 1906 when he pondered the idea that he might have to kill a man, died in New York City in March 1955 at the age of sixty-one. The Atlanta University graduate had been executive secretary of the NAACP since 1931. According to the *New York Times* obit:

Mr. White, the nearest approach to a national leader of American Negroes since Booker T. Washington, was a Negro by choice. Only five-thirty-seconds of his ancestry was Negro. His skin was fair, his hair blond, his eyes blue and his features Caucasian. He could easily have joined the 12,000 Negroes who pass the color-line and disappear into the white majority every year in this country. But he deliberately sacrificed his comfort to publicize himself as a Negro and to devote his entire adult life to completing the emancipation of his people.

In 1930, while not yet executive secretary, White led the defeat of President Hoover's appointment of Judge John J. Parker of North Carolina to the Supreme Court because Parker openly espoused racial segregation. In 1938 White came closer than anyone else to getting a federal antilynching bill passed, but it was defeated by seven weeks of Southern filibuster. Despite his personal feelings and the persuasions of his wife, FDR never publicly fought for the bill, which the NAACP had been officially pursuing since the 1920s. Roosevelt needed white Southern support in Congress more than he needed black votes, which he had anyway. But White was the author of FDR's FEPC executive order on discriminatory practices in war industry employment. And in 1948 he was responsible for Truman's stand on civil rights that caused Dixiecrats to leave the Democratic Party. In 1949 White divorced his first wife to marry popular South African–born journalist Poppy Cannon, food editor of *House Beautiful* magazine. (Poppy and Walter White became social friends of Lena and Lennie.) But White's second marriage was a scandal because Poppy was white. Oddly enough, his first wife was just as "white" in appearance as Poppy Cannon, but no one had been scandalized then.

In 1955 Atlanta desegregated the municipal golf course, but not the schools. The Georgia Board of Education passed a resolution revoking the license of any teacher who taught mixed classes or belonged to the NAACP. This was great for the NAACP, which had a surge in membership, and bad for the Georgia Board of Education, which was seen as a joke, even by many whites. Atlanta was fortunate in its mayor, William B. Hartsfield, who believed that the business of Atlanta was business—and good business required racial peace. Hartsfield, considered one of Atlanta's greatest mayors, would serve six terms (1937–1941, 1942–1961), build biracial coalitions, and, in August 1961, oversee the peaceful integration of Atlanta schools. After he left office to become "mayor emeritus" and a consultant for the Coca-Cola Company, Hartsfield would call Atlanta the city that was "too busy to hate."

And Georgia was not Mississippi. Lynching returned to the South in 1955, with three in Mississippi, including that of Emmett Till. A black minister was lynched for voter registration action. As a result of white terror tactics, the number of registered black voters in Mississippi dropped from twenty-two thousand to eight thousand in less than a year. And a state official sought to create an "Authority for the Maintenance of Racial Segregation," with the power to punish people for "interfering with individual rights under the auspices of the Federal Government like FBI officers investigating Constitutional violations."

In 1956 Senator Harry Byrd of Virginia called for "massive resistance" against school desegregation. The only Southern senators who refused to sign the manifesto were Lyndon Johnson of Texas and Estes Kefauver and Albert Gore Sr. of Tennessee. That year attorney Don Hollowell successfully defended the NAACP against the state of Georgia, which had demanded membership records and inflicted a fine of $25,000 against the Georgia branch of the organization. Hollowell also sued the University of Georgia Law School, in Athens, to admit Horace Ward, a black student. The NAACP had already won a major victory in the 1936 case against the University of Maryland Law School. Since the state did not have a black law school, it had to admit a black student to the white school. Now Hollowell, joined by an NAACP team, sought the same sort of ruling for Horace Ward in Georgia—but Ward was suddenly drafted into the Korean War. Governor Eugene Talmadge claimed to have had no hand in the action—but he had told an aide, "Keep that damn nigger out of the University of Georgia while I'm governor."

In 1946 Nellie Brown, the musical Brown sister, had received a bachelor of arts degree from Clark College, part of the Atlanta University Center (Asa Ware's famous dream). While still in high school, then throughout the 1940s and 1950s, she had played the piano in various Atlanta clubs and restaurants. According to Catherine Nash's daughter, Karen, "she played at everybody's wedding in Atlanta Black Society." A rare Southern "child of divorce," Nellie was a divorcée herself. When she received her BA from Clark College in 1946, she was Nellie Brown Flanagan. In 1950, when she received her master of arts degree from Teachers College at Columbia University, she was Nellie Patricia Brown Mosley. As a pianist and composer she won prizes and even had a song recorded. On October 15, 1956, she signed a standard songwriter's contract with Dootsie Williams, Inc. The contract produced a 45-rpm record on the Dootone label called "Crazy Over You," sung by the Calvanes. Dootsie Williams, Inc., seems to have paid Nellie one hundred dollars for the rights to four songs.

Outside Atlanta life remained difficult and dangerous for Southern blacks—and their white friends. In April 1957 in Americus, Georgia, snipers shot at Dorothy Day, the white Catholic peace activist, who was visiting the courageous interracial Baptist Koinonia community. Fortunately the drive-by snipers missed. In her *Catholic Worker* column of May 1957 she described the incident: "Last night I was shot at for the first time in my life . . . It is strange how the fear always comes afterward, your bones turn to water, and your whole body seems to melt with fear."

The Koinonia community continued to be threatened by terrorist attacks for its defiant stand against segregation.

In 1957 Atlanta, displaying the old mind-set, created a reading test for voter registration that the *Atlanta Constitution* said probably no one could pass. But changes were coming to Atlanta. That year Ella Baker, a fifty-four-year-old former NAACP field secretary, became executive director of the new Atlanta-based Southern Christian Leadership Conference (SCLC), led by the Reverend Martin Luther King Jr. of Atlanta's Ebenezer Baptist Church. The SCLC was founded, in the words of James Weldon Johnson, to redeem "the soul of America." As Dr. King wrote in January 1957:

> This conference is called because we have no moral choice, before God, but to delve deeper into the struggle—and to do so with greater reliance on non-violence and with greater unity, coordination, sharing and Christian understanding.

The conference released a manifesto, encouraging black Americans to "to seek justice and reject all injustice" and to dedicate themselves to the principles of nonviolence "no matter how great the provocation." It also called on whites to realize "that the treatment of Negroes is a basic spiritual problem." The goal was to create an organization that would coordinate and support direct nonviolent action across the South. A small office was established on Auburn Avenue, with Ella Baker as SCLC's first and, for a long time, only staff member. Baker would prove to be one of the most charismatic and important leaders in the movement, believing in "group-centered" rather than "leader-centered" action.

Another future leader of the new nonviolent civil rights movement arrived in Atlanta in 1957 to attend college. As cited in *The Saving Soul of Georgia*, Julian Bond wrote:

> Even though Atlanta was a modern segregated city and the burden of segregation didn't fall as heavily on black people in Atlanta as it did, say, in rural Mississippi, nonetheless, the Atlanta I found in 1957 was a completely apartheid society. There were some chinks in that apartheid armor. The Atlanta University Center . . . had white teachers teaching black people, probably against the law in Georgia [shades of Asa Ware], and there were the occasional white exchange students at Spelman, Morris Brown, Clark, Morehouse, or Atlanta University . . . but in all

public places—restaurants, lunch counters, movie theaters, every place in life—there was a rigid divide enforced by law between black and white.

Unlike the rest of the city, Asa Ware's thriving educational and social center for Atlanta blacks, Atlanta University, was still as essentially "color-blind" as when Moses Calhoun entrusted his daughters to its care. Asa Ware's nineteenth-century dream had become a twentieth-century reality. The first major campaign, the Crusade for Citizenship, began in late 1957 to educate and register thousands of disenfranchised prospective voters for the 1958 and 1960 elections. In 1958, twenty-eight Southern counties in various states with Negro populations up to 82 percent of the total population did not have *one* Negro voter. That year, to fight desegregation, the Georgia legislature suspended the compulsory school attendance law in the case of a child forced to attend school with children of another race. And credit was given on the state income tax for contributions to segregated private schools.

By the end of 1959 Alabama, Georgia, Louisiana, Mississippi, and South Carolina had not even begun token desegregation. The state of Georgia authorized the governor to close any school that ordered desegregation. And the state university refused to educate blacks even though their taxes supported the institution. Atlanta's blacks were tired of waiting. From *Saving the Soul of Georgia*: "In the grand tradition of Atlanta's black middle class, the community activists selected two candidates with impeccable and wholesome backgrounds."

Charlayne Hunter, the daughter of an army chaplain, and premed student Hamilton Holmes, son of a middle-class family long active in the civil rights movement, had applied for admission to the segregated University of Georgia in July 1959. (She became the celebrated journalist Charlayne Hunter-Gault.)

And Siny Calhoun's great-granddaughter Cheryl Chisholm, daughter of Harriet and Chiz, was selected by community activists to desegregate an Atlanta high school. The year 1960 promised to be memorable.

Chapter Thirteen

North/1960s
"NOW"

THE FIRST time I heard "We Shall Overcome" the singers were members of the Student Nonviolent Coordinating Committee (SNCC, pronounced *snick*), the offshoot of Ella Baker's Atlanta-based Southern Christian Leadership Conference (SCLC, pronounced *slick*). Like the 1930s, the 1960s were an era of acronyms. The students in SNCC came from the same Missionary institutions that educated the Talented Tenth. The place was the 1961 National Student Association congress at the University of Wisconsin at Madison. I was at the NSA congress as an observer for the New York–based National Scholarship Service and Fund for Negro Students (NSSFNS, pronounced *nessfeness*), where I was a counselor advising black college applicants on available scholarships. I worked at NSSFNS because I belonged to the Kennedy generation. "Give something back" was the generation's mantra. Among my Harvard and Radcliffe classmates there seemed to be only two career paths: the Justice Department and the Peace Corps. I opted for a different route but followed the pattern by choosing a nonprofit organization.

Madison, Wisconsin, one of the great college towns in America, was a revelation. The Wisconsin campus made Harvard seem puny. I had never seen middle America before. I knew both coasts, but nothing in between. Now here was Madison, as beautiful as any European tourist attraction, under an endlessly vast sky. The landscape, so *clean*, dotted with barns, silos, lakes, and cows, was certainly exotic in its way to a city-dwelling New Yorker. The beauty of Wisconsin in the summer was in the flatness, the spaciousness—flat, yet lush and green. I had the same feeling of American spaciousness earlier that summer when I first saw Detroit, only my sense was vertical, not horizontal. I thought the smokestacks were thrilling—soaring into the stratosphere. (Since I was then polluting my body with cigarettes, air pollution was of no import.) I was newly in awe of the beauty of America. As an undergraduate, I was a typical Harvard elitist-Francophile-Anglophile, but as a child I had read and reread Stephen Vincent Benét's "I Have Fallen in Love with American Names." As a World War II child, I had also been patriotic. Now, in the summer of 1961, thanks to JFK and "giving back," I suddenly felt patriotic again.

The Southern civil rights battles of the early 1960s were between the *haves* and the *have-nots*—between the *armed* and the *defenseless*. Because of a plethora of martyrs, and the egregiously despicable actions of the armed, the have-nots won the moral high ground early. For the first time there were unbiased eyewitnesses: news photographers and television cameramen who went South in combat mode. The battle of black children and teens against dogs, fire hoses, and rabidly racist police was indelibly captured, on double-page spreads, in *Life* magazine, *the* news photographer's magazine. *Life* turned the craft of news photography into an art form. *Life* was not alone. A front-page *New York Times* photograph of a brave little black girl going to school in New Orleans with her very big U.S. Marshal escorts suddenly became an iconic Norman Rockwell painting on the cover of the *Saturday Evening Post*. In certain circles it was an earthshaking event: a clear editorial statement on the side of integration by the conservative magazine. The moral battle was won. Middle America above the Mason-Dixon Line was on the side of the angels—or at least sympathetic to them.

At this point, the politics of black nationalism and "not in my backyard" white liberalism had not yet intruded on the sympathy of white Northerners, who enjoyed feeling superior to their Southern counterparts. Politics were not the point. The civil rights movement was about blacks having the same constitutional rights as every other taxpaying citizen: equality under the law, no taxation without representation, and voting rights. Official political victory came with the Civil Rights Act of 1964—but it took the assassination of another president who was a so-called friend of the Negro for it to happen. Northern sympathy toward the South had evaporated. The South had no moral persuasion, no equivalent of the small girl and the students; it had only snarling haters, some of whom later regretted their actions. Congressman John Lewis told of the man who came to his office in tears to confess that he had been the one to beat him so terribly on the bridge in Selma, Alabama. In Little Rock, a young black girl, Elizabeth Eckford, isolated from the other "Nine" seeking to integrate Little Rock Central High School, received an abject public apology some twenty years later from the most hate-contorted white teenager of all, an otherwise pretty young woman with a hideous hate-twisted face. The civil rights battles of 1960–1964 were clearly about moral persuasion. Although the civil rights movement was an unarmed revolution, it did have two powerful weapons: *images* in newspapers, in magazines, and on the evening news; and *songs*—above all, Pete Seeger's version of an old hymn, "We Shall Overcome."

Charismatic student leader Tom Hayden of the University of Michigan, editor of the Michigan student daily and a founder of Students for a Democratic Society (SDS), was NSA's president in 1961. It was later revealed that several NSA members were working for the CIA. I'm sure that Hayden was not. He was the real radical deal—author of the SDS manifesto, the Port Huron Statement, and a freedom rider. In 1961, however, a burning issue of the conference was whether the NSA would formalize its relationship with SNCC. It seemed a fait accompli, but the radical right Young Americans for Freedom (YAF) successfully campaigned against it. The Spanish proverb applies: "If you are not left when you are young, you have no heart. If you are not right when you are old, you have no head." YAF, protégés of William F. Buckley Jr., were far too young to be so heartless.

I sat in on SNCC strategy meetings. The participants were students and mostly Christian believers. They were revolutionaries only in the sense that they were integrated Southerners. The born-again Christians were especially fervent in their belief in integration. Besides born-again Christians, there was a solid corps from Loyola in New Orleans, a Jesuit institution, with another charismatic student leader named Bill Cauldwell, who became a friend. When all of us, black and white together, joined hands in a circle at the end of the first meeting and sang "We Shall Overcome," it was a profound experience. Unable to wipe my eyes, I hung my head as I sang and swayed, and tears streamed down my cheeks. I was embarrassed—how dare I cry if SNCC people did not?

It was the same summer that I first came to know young progressive white Southerners. I actually knew many progressive white Southerners, but they were mostly old and gay—or they were writers who drank and had a love-hate relationship with the region. I was interested in white Southerners who were more or less my age and who had come of age in a segregated society with all that it entailed. How did they deal with peer pressure? How did they come to believe in integration? I met two young white women in SNCC, Casey Cason and Connie Curry, who told their stories in *Deep in Our Hearts: Nine White Women in the Freedom Movement.* First of all, not enough attention has been paid to the fact that all over the South, the YMCA and YWCA were unsung heroes of the civil rights movement. No matter the local laws, the right of the Y to have integrated meetings was sacrosanct—as long as no food or drink was served. (In the South food or drink made it a party.) Despite this idiotic Southern law, Y's all over the region at least allowed blacks and whites to have contact with each other.

Casey Cason, a beautiful blond Texan with her own star quality as Tom Hayden's fiancée, talked about her life in the "Southern Freedom Movement" at the University of Texas in Austin, which she entered as a junior in 1957:

> I found the Y early on . . . Here I met black students and entered campus politics, becoming a regional and national Y officer . . . Here I learned the term "Student Christian Movement," sometimes shortened to "student movement," long before there was one . . . Through the Y, I was grounded in a democratic manner of work, exposed to and educated about race, and a participant in direct action—though not in civil disobedience . . .

At the NSA congress, Casey was immediately scooped up by the left student caucus, called the Liberal Study Group—forerunners of SDS. This was the early 1960s, but both Casey and Connie were very 1950s women—always keeping an eye open for "Mr. Right." Casey wrote:

> I loved the excitement and edginess and detailed political thinking in the Liberal Study Group, and the guys were sexier, sharper, and more verbose than the Y fellows had been. I met Tom Hayden here, the man I would later marry. When he interviewed me for his campus newspaper he told me how he'd been to California and demonstrated against the execution of Caryl Chessman. He started crying, because he was so angry remembering that he could not stop the legal murder. I was captivated by his intensity and his funny face with its very sad eyes.

I met Casey Cason only once, but twenty-six-year-old Connie Curry, a warm, wonderful woman and a natural leader, became a good friend. Connie, a North Carolina native whose parents were not political liberals and had never talked about racial injustice, first spoke out about race herself in fourth grade when a boy in the cafeteria line referred to one of the servers as a "nigger." Connie rebuked him, and for her action he later knocked her into a puddle. It made her a liberal. She also described her life in the movement in the book *Deep in Our Hearts*:

> Probably the most enlightening and broadening experience of my teen-age life was attending the United States National Student Association (USNSA) congress in Bloomington, Indiana. It was the summer of 1952, and I had just finished my freshman year at Agnes Scott College, a small Presbyterian women's college in Decatur, Georgia. I must admit that my entry into this NSA world was not entirely from noble motives . . . "Great way to meet interesting men," I thought.

NSA lost some members, including Emory and Georgia Tech, after the 1954 Supreme Court decision declaring the "separate but equal" concept unconstitutional. In 1957, after Columbia graduate school, twenty-four-year-old Connie was recruited by beloved New Left political activist Allard K. Lowenstein, who had been president of NSA in 1950, to be an organizer of the Southern Student Human Relations Seminar and field secretary of the Collegiate Council for the United Nations, supported by the Marshall Field Foundation:

> The sit-in movement spread like wildfire during the spring of 1960, and my office, supported by the Southern Regional Council's network, began to report on what was happening. By March 1, we had put out a newsletter listing the places where demonstrations were occurring, how many arrests were being made, and what help was needed . . .
>
> By Easter, more than seventy thousand mostly black southern college students were involved in demonstrations.

These young people, disciplined and heroic, were the most inspirational people of basically my own age whom I had ever met. I left the conference with the distinct feeling of spiritual malaise. I was most impressed by their open spirituality. I had been a religious child, sleeping under the gentle eyes of Our Lady, whose picture faced my bed; reading and rereading *A Child's Lives of the Saints*; praying every night on my knees; preparing for my First Communion in the Catholic church down the hill from our house in Hollywood; and longing to wear the beautiful white dress that I could look at but not touch. In the pivotal year of 1943, surely influenced by her Hollywood friends, my mother suddenly snatched me, as they probably saw it, from the clutches of Rome. No more First Communion, no more beautiful white dress. I gave up all religious observances except nightly prayers, which my mother often prayed with me. (Like many other lapsed Catholics, she sometimes went to church on Palm Sunday or Easter.) I put religion away, until a Quaker boarding school taught me to appreciate silent meeting. Quakers sang Negro spirituals, almost my favorite music, every Sunday might. I agreed with Mark Twain that spirituals ought to be America's national music.

Except for the fact that I read some unforgettable books, college was a spiritual wasteland. It would never have entered my mind to seek out the YWCA. I was trying to be sophisticated. Religion was the opiate of the masses or fanatics or both—Francis Cardinal Spellman was one of our favorite villains. When I came back to New York from Wisconsin, however, and realized that I envied the SNCC people their faith without fear, I began going to Grace Episcopal Church, where a friend from Harvard was a priest. It marked the beginning of an evolving religious conversion—from Catholic childhood to Quaker teens to an Episcopalian interlude to a flirtation with Buddhism and back to Catholicism. My great-grandmother Cora Horne went from Congregationalism to Catholicism to Ethical Culture to Bahá'í. Spiritual seeking was clearly part of my DNA. I eventually returned to my childhood home in the Catholic Church—but the journey began with discovering America and singing "We Shall Overcome" with integrated Southern Christians.

✻   ✻   ✻

Lena began the new decade worrying about authenticity, too. She felt alienated from the black community. She did not live like a Negro, and she did not think like a Negro. But her skin was still black and she still faced the discrimination that all blacks felt—except on a different scale. She felt she had been *a good little symbol*, but nothing had changed; in the South, blacks still could not vote and their children could not get a decent education. Lena had a lot of anger at the end of 1959. She had a right to be angry. Andy Griffith's bigotry kept her from playing a part that she really wanted (and helped contribute to the fact that she would be twenty-four years between Broadway shows). Now she was back in her old life, shuttling from club to club. She hated it. It must have felt great for Lena, early in 1960, to unleash her anger on a drunken white bigot at the Luau restaurant in Beverly Hills. She and Lennie were meeting Kay Thompson for a drink. Kay was late and Lennie went to phone her, at which point Lena, at a table on the balcony, looked down upon hearing a drunk demand service of a waiter, who said he was in the process of serving "Miss Horne." "So what?" the drunk shouted. "She's just another nigger. Where is she?" Lena jumped up from the table, shouting, "Here I am, you bastard, I'm the nigger you couldn't see!" and started throwing things. The man was hit by an ashtray and the waiters led him away bleeding from his forehead. The story made all the papers and Lena got a bundle of fan mail, mostly from Negroes. Sammy Davis Jr. used the incident in a later movie—with himself as Lena throwing things at a drunken bigot.

Lena was ready to take the next steps. By now, she was angry with herself for consenting for so long to be a symbol. Her search for a constructive path to protest now led her to join the Delta Sigma Thetas, a national black nonprofit public service sorority with political clout, founded in January 1913 by twenty-two Howard University women who wanted to use their collective strength to promote academic excellence and aid for the needy. The first public act of the Deltas was to participate in the Woman's Suffrage Procession in Washington, D.C., in March 1913; they were asked to march at the end of the parade so as not to offend Southerners. The twenty-two original members soon became many thousands. Working on Delta projects, touring, and making speeches seemed appropriate to my mother's age and the sort of life she lived. There were benefits, very clearly for the Deltas and also for Lena. Delta activities helped bring her out of the deep depression she had suffered with the closing of *Jamaica*.

Back in New York, the first year of the new decade ended with another party for Noël Coward, on his sixty-first birthday that December. Kay Thompson gave the party and forgot to order food. Kay's personal motto was "Food is the enemy of man." But the guests sent out to Reuben's for sandwiches and the champagne flowed. Kay and Lennie played two pianos. Noël sang, Lena sang, Richard Burton sang, and Larry Olivier did a tap dance in his bare feet and boxer shorts on top of one of the pianos. It was probably good to forget politics for a while.

I liked my job at NSSFNS, where I matched up black high school seniors with college scholarships. I liked the job, but I hated the traveling. In 1962 I got a new job—on the clip desk at *Life*. It felt like the best job of my young life. It was the first job I ever had that was *never* boring—not for a nanosecond. At $125 a week, the clip desk job meant guarding the AP and UP wires, and reading and clipping multiple copies of dozens of daily newspapers from around the country. In the cheerful, bustling Time-Life Building on Avenue of the Americas, the *Life* clip desk was central and open to anyone who wanted to check the wires. One of my favorite visitors never spoke, because he was always in a hurry—the helmeted and goggled motorcycle daredevil who raced back and forth from the airport to pick up film and take it to *Life*. The clip desk was the lowest editorial position on the magazine, and was always manned by a "girl"—usually a graduate of a Seven Sisters college. While I had the requisite Seven Sisters degree, and, like all clip desk girls, became incredibly well-informed on current events, I was still an anomaly. I was the first Negro clip desk girl at *Life*. In 1962 we were still called Negroes; and not yet having discovered Africa, we were deeply offended if anyone called us "black."

Racism and anti-Semitism, overt or casual, were not the norm at Time Inc. because Henry Luce, who grew up in China, the child of missionaries, was neither a practicing racist nor a bigot. Time Inc. was proudly liberal—liberal Republican, that is, which, where race was concerned, generally meant good manners and a sense of fair play. In the early 1960s there were still many Americans without either when it came to Jews and Negroes. I could never have gotten a job with the conservative Hearst, for example, and neither could great Jewish, black, or female *Life* photographers like Alfred Eisenstaedt, Robert Capa, Gordon Parks, and Margaret Bourke-White (whom Hearst would have rejected for being a liberal Democrat). *Life* was the wildly successful *first picture* news magazine, the illiterate younger sibling of *Time* and *Fortune,* both of which people had to read, instead of just turning pages to look at pictures. Luce had clearly learned from movies that people liked to see faces. So *Life* had full-page faces, and whole stories told in photographs that were printed in small panel strips, like comics. Luce wanted to shape his times. And his times saw the rise of fascism, which he saw as the great enemy of democracy. Both Japanese and German fascism, which Luce fought in his magazines, extolled the idea of a master race. *Life* was born in 1936, the year that Jesse Owens debunked Hitler's racial theories. In World War II, both *Life* and *Time* famously championed the Tuskegee Airmen. In 1943, *Time* and *Life* both did picture essays on twenty-six-year-old Lena Horne, whose success was supposed to be proof to the Allies that America, unlike Germany and Japan, was not a racist country. Perhaps not as socially redeeming as NSSFNS, Time, Inc., nevertheless passed the race and religion tests with flying colors. Casual misogyny, however, was totally overt.

Except for photographers, women at *Life* were second-class citizens and were *all* paid less than men. Except for photographers, women could not cover danger zone stories, like the bloody desegregation battle of the University of Mississippi, where a French journalist was killed. Most of the editors at *Life*, Olympian figures in shirtsleeves who stood around a huge table planning the weekly magazine as if they were strategizing a battle, seemed to be World War II veterans. They also seemed to be Protestant, Republican, Ivy League types who nonetheless enjoyed the fact that an Ivy League Irish Catholic Democrat, John F. Kennedy, a verified war hero, was in the White House. In 1962 and '63 there were only three and a half *big* stories: the Kennedys, the astronauts, and civil rights—the half-story was Vietnam. We saw Madame Nhu up close when she came to visit a fellow Catholic, Clare Boothe Luce, Mrs. Henry Luce, to explain why Buddhist monks were immolating themselves to protest the Luce-supported Nhu family's injustices. It was the last idealistic phase of both civil rights and Vietnam. The two struggles were closely connected. Before the 1960s turned ugly, civil rights and Vietnam created a generation of slightly left-of-center and slightly right-of-center idealists who both believed that JFK, the first president born in the twentieth century, was on their side.

Political idealism, however, did not preclude sometimes giving the clip desk girl a friendly pat on the bottom if these men passed her in the hall. The pats were avuncular rather than lustful—as if given absent-mindedly to a good animal, or a child. They were, above all, gestures from on high. Protestant Ivy Leaguers who had won the war had an enormous sense of entitlement—but they never would have patted Margaret Bourke-White, whose camera made her an honorary man. The patting gesture seemed to be reserved for the clip desk girl simply because she was a "girl," or possibly to acknowledge her existence without having to remember her name. Since my feminist consciousness was in the cellar, I did not speak out. Strong women were not generally admired by either men or women. In reality the pats did not bother me—they seemed to go with the clip desk job. After six months on the clip desk I was promoted to reporter. The title had no gender, and no pats, but women reporters still got less pay than men in the same job. I did a story with W. Eugene Smith, a photographer of great humanism, known for his compassionate photo essays ("A Country Doctor" was one of his most famous). As the reporter, I made notes for the picture captions and carried Smith's equipment.

One of the secrets of my success at *Life* was a small pill from a doctor known to many sophisticated New Yorkers as "Dr. Max," or "Dr. Feelgood." He never bothered to examine patients, but he handed pills to people who came to him via word of mouth. Young New York career girls, then as now, were constantly dieting. With Dr. Max's pill, you were never hungry. You took one half in the morning and concentrated like a demon all day. With one half in the evening, you could "twist" like a demented person all night. The "secret" of the pill was unknown to me. I had never heard the word "speed" used in a medical context. I was lucky that I had learned very quickly in college that I could not drink—so I never mixed speed and alcohol. I traveled in a crowd that was called "international" (in an unkinder era its members would be known as "Eurotrash"). There was lots of French spoken, especially by people who were not French. Between working and dancing, and the pill, I had little time for food or sleep. I lived on cigarettes, coffee, candy bars, Coca-Cola, and the occasional enormous meal on weekends when I had not taken the pill. When I eventually stopped taking Dr. Max's pills for good, I wondered why I was so tired all the time.

In the spring of 1963 Lena and Lennie were at their house in Palm Springs glued to the television as Birmingham, Alabama, under Sheriff Bull Connor and his dogs, horses, and fire hoses, exploded in a war against black children and teenagers. The Deltas had actually asked Lena to go to Birmingham to sing on the steps of the Sixteenth Street Baptist Church on Mother's Day. But Lena was afraid to fly. She had not flown since the war, having been frightened on too many army tours. The request had come too late for her to take the train. She was sorry and asked them to give her more notice next time. She immediately felt guilty. Of course, she would fly the next time. What was going on in Birmingham was warfare against unarmed black youth. That same evening she got a call from James Baldwin, saying that Attorney General Robert Kennedy wanted to meet with some prominent Negroes to discuss the civil rights situation. It was Lennie who helped her make the decision to fly to the attorney general's meeting. Apparently the clincher to his argument was "If you don't go, maybe you won't love *me* anymore."

The meeting, in a private apartment, appeared to have been tense from the beginning—all the white people were on one side of the room, and all the Negro people on the other. The exception was the actor Rip Torn, a white Texan and friend of Baldwin's, who sat on an ottoman on the Negro side and admitted that he had once been a racist from a family of racists until one day he just basically decided that it was stupid. The attorney general and his aide Burke Marshall sat together. The Negroes were Lena, Baldwin, Lorraine Hansberry, Harry Belafonte, Dr. Kenneth Clark (the sociologist, who came armed with statistics), one or two others, and Jerome Smith, a young man from SNCC.

The meeting was a disaster. While the Negroes praised the attorney general's stand against the University of Mississippi and support for the admission of James Meredith, and while they agreed that the Kennedy administration had done more for civil rights than any other administration in history, they also argued that it was not enough. They expected and needed more—quickly. The South was not budging on school desegregation and voting rights. The attorney general felt for them and understood their pain; he spoke about his own family and the kinds of discrimination it had to fight. Unfortunately, this did not establish rapport with the New York Negroes, whose minds could wander to the Draft Riots and Irish cops. His off-the-cuff prediction that there would be a black president in forty years was openly jeered. (Nevertheless, it was the perfect timetable for Barack Obama.)

Lena believed that the Negro group would have appreciated Robert Kennedy's efforts more if young Jerome Smith of SNCC had not been there. Smith had been in the South, working for voter registration. His wife and children had been sent away for their safety. He had been jailed and beaten and was still physically injured from what had been done to him. He communicated the basic suffering of Southern Negroes and the shredding of their constitutional rights. The attorney general was taken aback by the naked fury of the young man. James Baldwin asked Smith if, feeling the way he did, he would fight for his country. Smith said he would not. He said he would risk his life in Mississippi but would not risk it in Vietnam so long as the United States tolerated Mississippi.

I was working on the *Life* clip desk when Lena went to Jackson, Mississippi, for the NAACP. Billy Strayhorn and Jeanne Noble of the Delta Sigma Thetas went with her. They were met at the airport by NAACP Mississippi field secretary Medgar Evers, a war veteran. He expressed his regrets that they could not stay with him and his family, but his house had just been bombed and was not yet repaired. Dick Gregory was also part of the rally—one of a group who wanted to take to the streets for a more militant protest. But the NAACP had decided that there could be no street protest in connection with the rally, and Evers, whatever his real feelings, had to go along with that. Gregory was angry and claimed that the reason for the ban on a street demonstration was that the NAACP was trying to "protect" Lena. Even after he used her as a scapegoat for his anger, Lena always spoke well of Dick Gregory. She actually had great respect for his courage. He was not afraid of being arrested or beaten—Lena, however, was terrified.

Life covered the rally—Evers was a *Life* stringer and Lena was the mother of a staff member. It printed a beautiful full-page close-up of Evers and Lena, who sang "This Little Light of Mine" at the rally. She was completely in awe of the children and young people who were not afraid to go to jail. In fact she was in awe of all the civil rights workers and, typically, felt inadequate. She thought that Medgar Evers was the bravest man she had ever met. She remembered the words of a Jackson teacher: "Medgar is our courage."

Two days later, on the night of June 12, 1963, Evers was assassinated outside his home by a KKK sniper. On the morning of July 13, Lena got the news that Medgar Evers had been killed during the night just as she was about to appear on the *Today* show to talk about the Jackson rally with Hugh Downs. Although she had been up since 5:30 A.M. for coffee and makeup, she had not turned on the radio or the television. She was so shocked and incoherent that she thought she could not do the show. She managed to pull herself together, but had no idea later what she actually said.

A week later, *Life*, which arranged for Evers' burial in Arlington, published a haunting full-page portrait of Myrlie Evers at her husband's funeral. On June 19 the D.C. bureau of the NAACP led the congressional fight for a comprehensive civil rights bill. President Kennedy introduced the bill. Once again it was moral persuasion. It took the murder of a very good man.

W. E. B. Du Bois died in Ghana on August 27, 1963, the day before the March on Washington. It is a pity that he did not see the march. Lena was there in Washington, wearing her NAACP cap, for what has been rightly called a "great human moment." I followed the march from the *Life* clip desk, where I now had an "assistant." She and I agreed that the best March on Washington story by far came from the great Harriet Van Horne, a columnist and writer on the *World Telegram*. She made us both cry. Newspapermen used to call writers like Van Horne "sob sisters." She certainly made me sob. The march itself was really a day of peace and joy led by all religious denominations. It was the first spiritual love-in. America had never seen anything like it.

Eighteen days after the March on Washington, Birmingham exploded. September 15 was Youth Day; many of the young people and children had marched with Dr. King and were veterans of Bull Connor's water hoses and attack dogs. Thanks to television news stories of previous violence, the Birmingham business community and city officials had recently opened lunch counters and schools to blacks. But haters are sore losers. Addie Mae Collins, Carol Denise McNair, Carole Robertson, and Cynthia Wesley, aged eleven to fourteen, were killed by a bomb placed a few feet from the basement ladies' lounge of the Sixteenth Street Baptist Church. It was timed to go off during Sunday school.

According to *Free at Last: A History of the Civil Rights Movement and Those Who Died in the Struggle*, a project of the Southern Poverty Law Center, the FBI investigation found that the bomb was planned by the Klan in response to the new school desegregation order. An eyewitness saw four white men plant the bomb—but no one was charged with the crime. The day after the bombing, a white lawyer named Charles Morgan gave a speech in Birmingham:

> He asked his audience: "Who did it?" and gave his own anguished answer: "We all did it . . . every person in this community who has in any way contributed . . . to the popularity of hatred is at least as guilty . . . as the demented fool who threw that bomb."

After his statement, Morgan was ostracized by the white community of Birmingham. Fourteen years later, in 1977, the Alabama attorney general reopened the case. A seventy-three-year-old Klansman named Robert Chambliss was charged with first-degree murder and a jury found him guilty. He died in prison.

Frank Horne had suffered a stroke in 1960. The right side of his body was slightly paralyzed. In 1962 he was investigated once again for his activities in so-called leftist organizations—again he was able to defend himself and was cleared. He founded the National Committee against Discrimination in Housing (NCDH) and went back to work (from 1962 to 1973) as a consultant on human relations with the New York City Housing and Redevelopment Board to see that there were no discriminatory hiring practices among private contractors and subcontractors working for the city—and to see that all city-owned or -funded housing was integrated. His marriage to Mercedes was over. He lived in Brooklyn's St. George Hotel and, like his father, dined out and went to the theater in Manhattan. And he kept busy. In October 1964 he helped write the NCDH ten-year-plan to end discrimination in housing. In February 1966 he attended the Notre Dame Conference on Federal Civil Rights Legislation and Administration. The following year he was awarded the plaque of the Housing and Urban Renewal Conference for "dauntless courage . . . in the battle for open housing." Later he wrote a collection of poetry called *Haverstraw*. In "He Won't Stay Put: A Carol for All Seasons," he wrote:

> . . . and mighty Martin Luther King
> he ain't got no Santy this year
> Nor blazing Malcolm X
> Nor gallant Bobby Kennedy
> Nor fearless Medgar Evers
> Nor brothers Goodman, Schwerner and Chaney
> Nor a million pot-bellied Biafran kids
> Nor a million red-necked Mississippians . . .

Frank's work appeared in *The Crisis, Opportunity, Phylon, Carolina* magazine, the *Interracial Review,* and other publications. According to Sterling Brown, a musical version of "Letters Found Near a Suicide" was still performed. Sixties students loved Frank's "Suicide" poem—about the death of a young college athlete with absolutely no mention of race.

The November 1963 issue of *Show* magazine was famous for its cover. Lena, wearing a long white dress, was posed standing halfway through a torn white paper curtain. Was she caught between two worlds, or was she the crossover breakthrough? I helped her write the piece, since I was a "journalist." It was about civil rights and was very good for Lena in a special way:

> I don't want to sing the same old songs or act in the same stereotypical musicals. There is a great problem for me as a performer in all this. I am not about to get a guitar and start doing protest songs . . . And I'd look pretty silly at the Waldorf in a Balmain dress describing the feelings of small children attacked by dogs and hoses . . . But there has to be some way for a sophisticated urban adult to express the movement . . .
>
> The greatest protest songs are coming from the Southern students. I can't sing *these* songs, but I think that songs can be written and plays and musicals produced which simply put the Negro in the context of the world—not necessarily as youth in protest . . . just as people who are around and alive . . . I think it is the great chance of my generation to try and express this.

A few days after the *Show* piece came out Lena got a call from Harold Arlen. He had a song, he said, that he originally wrote with Ira Gershwin. Yip Harburg would give it new lyrics. It was called "Silent Spring" and was dedicated to the four young girls who were killed in the Birmingham church bombing. Almost at the same time Jule Styne came over to play the score of *Funny Girl.* Lena told Styne that she was sick of hearing songs he had written for other singers. So Styne and Lena's longtime pals Betty Comden and Adolph Green created new lyrics to "Hava Nagila" and called it "Now." It was naturally infectious and the lyrics were rousing. "Now is the hour!" It became a cause célèbre when some radio stations banned it from being played. The song, a product of Tin Pan Alley and Broadway, actually came from the hearts of people who understood the struggles of formerly enslaved people. Lena was thrilled with "Now"—she finally had a protest song that she could sing in a way that was true to her and to the movement.

"Now" was the perfect song for her to sing at Carnegie Hall on the second night of the two-night Frank Sinatra–Lena Horne two-benefit concerts in the fall of 1963. Sinatra's charity was an international children's fund, and Lena's charity was SNCC. The first evening, for Sinatra's charity, sold out instantly. It was a very glamorous New York event—everyone was there. Lena had a great success with the Harold Arlen medley—but Lena and Sinatra, basically the same age, had a complicated relationship. Lennie knew him from the Dorsey days. Lena thought he was a great singer and a musician's singer. And she certainly agreed with his outspoken liberal politics and his message of interracial unity and harmony. Sinatra had come under scrutiny from HUAC earlier than Lena, and he had basically been under surveillance by the FBI since 1945. Sinatra was "fingered" as a Communist by the well-known American fascist Gerald L. K. Smith, who founded the America First Party and lobbied for the release of all Nazi war criminals convicted at the Nuremberg trials. Smith petitioned HUAC:

> I petition this committee of Congress to investigate the activities of FRANK SINATRA who, on the surface seems to be just a highly paid emaciated crooner, but who recently gave support to a meeting of the American Youth for Democracy which held an elaborate banquet at the Hotel Ambassador in Los Angeles and which organization was recently branded by J. EDGAR HOOVER as the successor to the Young Communist League and one of the most dangerous outfits in the nation.

But Lena's problem with Sinatra was that in her eyes he was less than gentlemanly. Sometime in the late 1940s, Lena was deeply insulted when she and Lennie were invited to Palm Springs for a weekend with Sinatra to find no sign of his wife and that all the other women guests were starlets and party girls. Insulted not only for herself but for her friend Nancy Sinatra, instead of staying for the weekend, she and

Lennie left after dinner the night they arrived. Now Frank arrived too late to rehearse the duets they had planned to sing for both evenings. This was not an insult, but Lena hated "winging it" and was happy only when she was overprepared.

The second evening, for SNCC, the cheap seats sold quickly but the expensive tickets did not. Lena wrote letters and made phone calls to everyone she knew, and did not know. Carnegie Hall finally sold out the expensive seats. The result was an amazing spirit on the SNCC night—everyone in the audience felt part of something special. Lena was so thrilled that she had to say something. "I don't make speeches," she said, "but tonight I have this overwhelming feeling of gratitude and pride that I am a New Yorker." The audience yelled and clapped and clapped. Lena thought the ovation was because the audience members were participating in something bigger than themselves. It was a great moment in her life. When she sang "Now" she finally felt "authentic." For once she felt the symbol had been useful.

Lena went from the SNCC concert to Washington to pose for pictures with President Kennedy as a member of the celebrity committee for the president's reelection campaign. Frank Sinatra was not involved. Richard Adler of Broadway organized the performers.

Working at *Life*, I met Sidney Lumet. We were introduced by James Lipton, later the host of television's *Inside the Actors Studio*, then a TV writer and friend of Lena and Lennie's. When I met Sidney, one of the great directors of live TV, he had just finished his second movie, *Long Day's Journey into Night*, with Katharine Hepburn, Ralph Richardson, and Jason Robards Jr. Sidney's first movie, *12 Angry Men*, was critically acclaimed. But when Sidney and I decided to marry, Lena and Lennie were not happy. First there was the sixteen-year age difference—I was twenty-six and he was forty-two. And they did not like the idea that I would be his third wife. The actress Rita Gam, who had a brief movie career, was his first wife. His second wife was Gloria Vanderbilt; some of her friends who also knew Lena rushed to express their rather snobbish disapproval.

Sidney was the successful child actor son of Yiddish-speaking actors. He spent World War II in the China-Burma-India theater in the Signal Corps (where all the actors went), and caught dengue fever. When he got out of the army, he went to see his agent, who said, in typical agent fashion, "Too bad you didn't get taller." So Sidney, on the short side, like so many ex–child actors, gave up acting to become a great director.

JFK was assassinated on November 22. It was utterly heartbreaking and unbelievable. Sidney and I and another couple had dinner that night at the Russian Tea Room. The restaurant was absolutely packed, but utterly silent. No one even looked up when I slapped Sidney's face when he questioned whether Kennedy had been a great president. The next day Sidney and I were married by a judge. We canceled the musicians; half the guests did not come—the "Room" provided by the Waldorf suddenly looked too big. The Reverend Stephen Chinlund, my Episcopalian priest friend from Harvard, said a sad blessing. And Sidney and I spent our honeymoon glazed in front of the TV.

We had two daughters: Amy, born in 1964; and Jenny, born in 1967. Amy was born in London while Sidney was filming *The Hill*. She was born more or less at the same time as Lord Mountbatten's twin grandsons. The queen came to the hospital to see the twins, but according to the nurses, when she toured the nursery she stopped in front of Amy's cot and said, "That's the one *I* want." Jenny was born in New York, but went to nursery school in London when we all went back for Sidney to shoot *Murder on the Orient Express*, produced by Lord Brabourne, the father of Mountbatten's twin grandsons.

In 1965 Lena was "investigated" by the Johnson White House and "Now" was remembered in an FBI letter to Bill Moyers, President Johnson's assistant:

Dear Mr. Moyers:

Reference is made to the memorandum dated November 16, 1964 . . . requesting name checks concerning Carol Channing and ten other individuals who were described as entertainers. The FBI has not investigated the following individuals and our files contain no derogatory information identifiable with them.

Carol Channing	Peter Gennaro
Debby Reynolds	Mike Nichols
Carol Burnett	Elaine May

When it came to Lena, the FBI stated that she had already been investigated under the Kennedy White House and that a summary of information concerning her had been sent to Kennedy's assistant Kenneth O'Donnell on January 5, 1962. In addition to the information contained in that summary, FBI files reported that the *Los Angeles Times* for November 1, 1963, stated that some Los Angeles radio stations banned the playing of Lena's recording of "Now," describing it as a "biting, angry integration message." The article further described the record as voicing a "strong racial freedom message," and the lyrics calling for action *now* "strengthened the racial unrest in the United States."

Although the earlier information sent to the Kennedy administration did not keep Lena (or me) from being invited to the White House, Lena was never invited to anything by the Johnson administration.

CHAPTER FOURTEEN

South/1960s
OVERCOMING

THE 1960–1964 civil rights movement, simply called "the movement," was an old-fashioned grassroots movement of all ages, races, regions, and religions—although it was predominantly young, black, Southern, and Protestant. The movement was born in the same historically black Missionary colleges and universities that educated the Talented Tenth. The new civil rights movement, in fact, spoke the language of Reconstruction, making almost the same demands. Everything that was wanted had already been guaranteed by the Constitution: freedom, equality under the law, and voting rights—none of which was actually practiced, especially in rural areas. The legacy of Reconstruction remained undeniable. All large-scale humanitarian efforts in America owed an inspirational debt to Reconstruction, which encouraged an outpouring of dedication on the part of white teachers from the North who went to the dangerous, war-torn South. It happened again one hundred years later, when courageous young white Northerners descended on the South to face terror and murder in projects like the Freedom Rides and voter registration.

With the organization of SNCC, the youth branch of Dr. King and Ella Baker's Southern Christian Leadership Conference, in April 1960, the movement became a young persons' crusade. The SNCC organizational meeting took place during Easter weekend in Raleigh, North Carolina, at Shaw University (named for Colonel Robert Gould Shaw of the Civil War Fifty-Fourth Massachusetts Infantry). Marion Barry from Nashville (future mayor of Washington, D.C.) was elected the first chair. But Atlanta won the prize as the location of SNCC's headquarters. In April 1960 the young people of Atlanta took center stage. They announced themselves that spring with a full-page ad in the *Constitution* paid for by the white Southern writer Lillian Smith, author of *Strange Fruit*, the antilynching novel. It read:

> We the students of the six affiliated institutions forming the Atlanta University Center . . . have joined our hearts, minds, and bodies in the cause of gaining those rights which are inherently ours as members of the human race and as citizens of these United States . . . We must say in all candor that we plan to use every legal and non-violent means at our disposal to secure full citizenship rights as members of this great Democracy of ours.

The ad did not say, "We the students *and professors.*" It was an announcement that the young people not only were in the front lines, but were planning the strategy. Asa Ware would have been proud. And he would have been proud of Katie Webb's great-granddaughter, who was among the younger, but certainly not the youngest, members of the movement. The NAACP leadership of Atlanta picked fifteen-year-old Cheryl Chisholm, daughter of Harriet Nash and Chiz Chisholm, to be one of the high school "integrators." The heart of *almost* every black Calhoun had swelled with pride when Cheryl was named an "integrator." Her mother, Harriet, however, was not thrilled, doubtless thinking of fifteen-year-old Elizabeth Eckford, traumatized behind her dark glasses, facing the pack of yowling whites in Little Rock. Harriet decided that Cheryl would not go through that particular ordeal. Instead she would face a much milder ordeal. Cheryl went north in the fall of 1960 to essentially desegregate a white girls' boarding school, Northfield, in Massachusetts. "Alone in her blackness," she had great success. Bursting with confidence typical of the Southern branch of the black Calhoun women, Cheryl was an excellent student and a talented modern dancer.

Before leaving for Massachusetts, Cheryl appeared on television on NBC's news program *White Paper* with several other Atlanta teens to discuss school integration. Cheryl remembered:

[My mother] wanted me to go to Northfield where one of her peers had gone, so off I went in the fall of 1960 to the cold (on so many levels!) wilds of New England. In order to take those secondary school tests that were required, my mother and I, in hats and gloves, had to go to the Westminster School where I was segregated in a separate room by myself with my own private monitor. My rage made me swear to blow them all off the map, which I did, and the same followed at Northfield where they gave me a single room usually reserved for seniors, and assumed that I couldn't possibly be a first rate student, being Black and from the South. I kicked ass in the advance placement courses, won the French prize, speaking like a Parisian academician and writing a scholarly thesis in French, was a featured dancer in many productions then was the only one to get into Radcliffe. While there, I taught a freedom school in Dorchester during the Boston school mess and traveled in the summers to Hawaii and Brazil as a concentrator in anthropology doing field work and experiencing the confusion and enlightenment of how differently race was constructed in other places . . .

That fall, just before the presidential election, Dr. King was arrested in Atlanta for taking part in a sit-in. Senator Kennedy called Coretta Scott King to express his concern. Dr. King was released the next day. Kennedy's phone call guaranteed that he would win the black vote wholeheartedly, despite old prejudices against Catholicism.

Between 1947 and 1962, twelve blacks were lynched—a far cry from the 1930s when there was a lynching every three weeks. Still, Southern states did all they could to destroy or hinder the NAACP. Roy Wilkins suspended Robert Williams as president of the Monroe, North Carolina, NAACP branch when Williams urged meeting "violence with violence" and "lynching with lynching." Blacks had to take the moral high ground—it was all they had. All over the South, they were denied voting rights, especially in rural areas. City officials in Tuskegee, Alabama, redrew city lines to exclude all but ten of the four hundred black registered voters. There was a reign of terror against blacks who tried to vote; they were driven in fear of their lives from the polls—beaten, fired, homes destroyed, finally murdered. In large urban areas, like Atlanta, middle-class property-owning blacks could vote—supporting the almost entirely black Georgia Republican Party.

In 1962 the black population of Atlanta was largely responsible for the election of a progressive mayor, Ivan Allen Jr., the businessman son of a prominent family. Middle-class black men had voted in Atlanta since 1870, keeping the Republican Party alive in the South. The difference between Atlanta and the rest of Georgia cannot be exaggerated. There is a vast difference between night rider/KKK racism and Jim Crow racism. Allen's opponent was arch-segregationist restaurant owner Lester Maddox, who used ax handles to drive away black customers. In the solid tradition of Atlanta's business community, Allen was not a practicing racist. In fact, he was already known as "progressive." In 1947 he was the first white head of the Community Chest to attend a fund-raising dinner for the Negro Community Chest. In 1960, as vice president of the Atlanta Chamber of Commerce, he publicly announced that segregation was bad for business. On the day he took office as mayor of Atlanta, he proved himself a radical by integrating the cafeteria and having all the "white" and "colored" signs removed from city hall. After Allen's conversations with Dr. King and young people from SNCC, his pragmatic business conviction became a moral conviction.

Allen now advocated and led the desegregation of public Atlanta. In a key speech, he asked Atlantans to inspire "the world":

I wasn't so all-fired liberal when I first moved into City Hall, but when I saw what the race-baiters were doing or could do to hold back the orderly growth of Atlanta, it infuriated me and eventually swung me to the extreme end opposite them.

Allen was so impressive that in July 1963 President Kennedy personally asked him to come to Washington to testify in support of what became the Civil Rights Act of 1964. Allen was the only Southern white elected politician to speak in the bill's favor. He called segregation "slavery's stepchild":

I have to be honest with myself and admit that up until the time I had to make the decision whether to go to Washington or not go, my liberalism on the race issue had been based to a large degree on pragmatism: it was simply good business for Atlanta to be an open city, a fair city, a "City Too Busy to Hate," a city trying to raise the level of its poorest citizens and get them off the relief rolls . . . I am certain that at this point I had finally crossed over and made my commitment on a very personal basis. And I think I took some of my friends with me.

After his Washington testimony, many white Atlantans refused to speak to him, and Allen and his family were under police protection for a year, having received death threats.

Death threats were a serious matter in the South in 1963. The centennial of the Emancipation Proclamation saw the Southern practice of assassination run amok. In April, William Moore, a white ex-marine, now a Baltimore mail carrier, who planned to walk from Chattanooga, Tennessee, to Jackson, Mississippi, to protest segregation, was killed by a sniper while resting on the side of an Alabama highway; in June,

Medgar Evers was shot dead by a Mississippi sniper; in September, Addie Mae Collins, Carol Denise McNair, Cynthia Wesley, and Carole Robertson were killed by the Birmingham church bombers; and in November, President John F. Kennedy was killed by an assassin's bullet in Texas.

W. E. B. Du Bois, an iconic adopted son of Atlanta University, had died, aged ninety-five, in West Africa the day before the August 1963 March on Washington. It seems sad that Du Bois, in his despair, could not have waited a little longer before giving up on America. In 1961, at the age of ninety-three, he had joined the Communist Party and moved to Ghana, where he died. If he had only seen the March on Washington before becoming a Communist and moving to Africa, he would have seen a movement that was both integrated and moral—led by students of all ages and clergy of all faiths. The civil rights movement recognized Du Bois as its founding father. At the same time, because of his age and African life, he was seen as somewhat detached. He had been born a free Yankee in western Massachusetts, in the beautiful Berkshires—a boy whom color did not touch until he went south. Because he went south, he *chose* to be a *Negro* instead of the *American* he had always felt himself to be in Massachusetts. Then in old age, he chose to become an African and a Communist. What does it say about Du Bois? It says he never found a home in America, although his family had lived in the same place since colonial days. It looked as if Du Bois rejected America—but maybe America rejected *him* because he was black and wrote the truth about racism. Indeed, maybe America broke his heart because, after all those generations, it looked in 1961 as if systemic racial injustice would never go away. Despite his titanic accomplishments, Du Bois may well have died in great sadness. The black left, whose leadership came from the middle class, was born in despair.

In 1964, forty-three-year-old Dr. Helen Nash, a black Calhoun and the first black woman to join the attending staff at St. Louis Children's

Hospital, married James Abernathy, with whom she shared a love of travel, boating, and dogs. Helen was another late but happy bride.

That year newspapers reported that the Atlanta Housing Authority had honored her grandfather by naming a senior citizen high-rise after him:

> Atlanta honored a long deceased Colored citizen in this vein Monday morning by naming the latest housing project after him. The Antoine Graves project for senior citizens will bear the name of the man who apparently was first to conceive the need and possibility for planned residential neighborhoods for his race in this city, and did so much toward achieving that end that his memory will be preserved in a land mark that will stand for generations to come.
>
> Antoine Graves died in March 23 years ago, at the age of 79, and has many grandchildren and great-grandchildren to toast his memory.
>
> But more than this he apparently won the respect of powerful white leaders and businessmen in the earlier days of Atlanta while gaining just as great a reputation as a man proud of his race, and willing to struggle for the betterment of the people . . . Two of his daughters, Mrs. H.E. Nash, wife of a pioneer Atlanta physician, and Mrs. W.J. Arnold, whose husband is in real estate, live in the city.

Other black communities in America were not as peaceful as Atlanta. It was a summer of race riots: in Jacksonville, Florida; Dixmoor, Illinois; Philadelphia, Pennsylvania; Jersey City, Keansburg, and Paterson, New Jersey; and Rochester and Harlem, New York. There was a split in the NAACP after the summer rioting, when Roy Wilkins spoke of "criminal elements" in the riots. It is uncertain whether Wilkins was speaking of the real thing or just a "criminal"-style "homeboy" wardrobe. There was never any "criminal element" in the Southern protests, by the way—the "criminals" all came from Northern gangs.

Approximately 38 percent of Negroes of voting age in the South were registered to vote compared with 60 or 70 percent in the North. Some one thousand volunteers, white and black, were involved in the "Mississippi Summer" voter registration project. Young people poured into the South like nineteenth-century Missionary teachers—essentially to teach civics by establishing "Freedom Schools." Mississippi's civics lesson began with multiple murders: Charles Eddie Moore and Henry Hezekiah Dee in May; and James Chaney, Andrew Goodman, and Michael Schwerner in June. (Moore, Dee, and Chaney were black and Goodman and Schwerner were white.) Elsewhere, in July, Lieutenant Colonel Lemuel Penn, a black army officer driving home to Washington, D.C., after army reserve training at Fort Benning, was shot and killed by a sniper on a Georgia highway. The South was a war zone.

Curiously enough, while the streets of the South were erupting, the racial atmosphere between black and white men in the real war zone of Southeast Asia was described in this period as "sweetness and light." The Vietnam War was the first war since the Revolution in which blacks and whites served together from the outset as equals under the American flag. There were really two Vietnams. Those who were there in the early 1960s, products of Eisenhower social moderation and Kennedy social justice, were mostly volunteers and full of patriotic idealism. Those who arrived in 1968 or later, after all the assassinations, were draftees whose thoughts on patriotism and the military were probably nihilistic.

On February 21, 1965, Malcolm X was assassinated in Harlem. A few days later, attention turned again to the South. On February 26 Jimmie Lee Jackson of Marion, Alabama, just outside Selma, was shot and killed by a policeman whom Jackson had attacked when the policeman struck Jackson's mother. Jackson's death triggered the biggest civil rights demonstration since the March on Washington. It was also, sadly, one of the bloodiest. Dr. King and John Lewis of SNCC had decided at once that a march from Selma to Montgomery, the state capital, to protest Jackson's murder and support voting rights would be a good outlet for community anger and grief. On March 7, before the unarmed marchers had even left Selma, the violent police assault on them at Pettus Bridge was captured by television cameras. The marchers were beaten back. But thousands more volunteers, black and white, recruited by TV images of horrendous police brutality, poured into Selma for the second march—which produced one of the most iconic civil rights images of all. Matt Herron's great picture for *Look* magazine, shot from below, looking up to three young people in white shirts, two boys and a girl, leading the parade under a John Ford sky, followed by billowing Stars and Stripes, seems to be a meeting of the spirit of the civil rights movement and the Spirit of '76. But the brutality continued. By the time the Selma-to-Montgomery march was over, two more civil rights workers, both white, were dead. James Reeb, a Unitarian minister, was beaten to death on a Selma street, and Viola Liuzzo, a Catholic Michigan housewife, was shot by a sniper on the road outside Montgomery as she drove marchers from Selma to Montgomery.

"Don't Tread on Me" read the posters of the National States Rights Party, three of whose members were indicted for the night rider assassination of Willie Brewster, a black worker in a pipe foundry in Anniston, Alabama, after a States Rights Party rally in July 1965. After thirteen hours of deliberation and twenty ballots, an all-white jury returned a second-degree murder conviction against one of the men, who was sentenced to ten years in prison. It was the first time in the civil rights era that a white person was convicted of killing a black person in Alabama. The verdict was a shock to black and white alike.

Elsewhere, Oneal Moore, a black deputy sheriff, was killed in June in Louisiana; August saw the Watts riot in Los Angeles. Also in August, in Lowndes County, Alabama, Richard Morrisroe, a Roman Catholic priest from Chicago, and Jonathan Daniels, an Episcopal seminarian studying in Cambridge, Massachusetts, were both shot. Morrisroe was wounded, but Daniels was killed at point-blank range by a deputy sheriff who claimed Daniels had pulled a knife on him. Morrisroe and Daniels had both responded to Dr. King's call to clergy of all denomination to support the voting rights marchers. Daniels had decided to stay on after the march. When he arrived in Alabama, Daniels wrote: "I lost my fear in the black belt when I began to know in my bones and sinews that . . . in the only sense that really mattered I am already dead, and my life is hid with Christ in God."

That same August Congress passed the Voting Rights Act of 1965, eliminating all qualifying tests for voter registration that abridged the right to vote on the basis of race or color. Calling on Congress to pass the bill, President Johnson had used evocative words: "[We] must overcome the crippling legacy of bigotry and injustice. And we shall overcome."

According to Tuskegee University data, between 1882 and 1968, the number of racially motivated murders of black men and women in Georgia was second only to the number in Mississippi. Overall, in that same period 4,743 black persons were hanged, shot, or burned alive in the South. Those who "disappeared" were not counted.

This is not the end of the story, however. In 1981 Casey Cason returned to Atlanta and wrote a kind of epilogue of her experience:

> Connie Curry and Julian Bond recommended me for a job in Atlanta, with the Southern Regional Council . . . The day I arrived to interview, John Lewis and Julian came by and we sat on Connie's front porch to have a drink. I found myself breathing shallowly, feeling panicked. When I left the South we could not have appeared together publicly in a white neighborhood in this way. The next day Connie and I went to City Hall.
>
> When I left Atlanta, the only nonwhites in City Hall would have been a janitor, kitchen help. Now almost everyone, both elected officials and employees, was black. These two events showed me that we had in fact defeated segregation . . . Then I went to work as administrative aide for the Department of Parks, Recreation and Cultural Affairs. I was with black folks again, in Mayor Andy Young's Administration . . .

The Reverend Andrew Young, a New Orleans–born ordained minister and Howard graduate, was a pastor in Atlanta, where he worked with the Southern Christian Leadership Conference. In 1964, aged thirty-two, he became SCLC's executive director. In 1970 he became the first African American to represent Georgia in the House of Representatives. President Jimmy Carter later named him U.S. ambassador to the United Nations, but Young had to resign in 1979 because he had met in secret with the Palestine Liberation Organization's UN observer. The resignation did not stop him from being elected the second black mayor of Atlanta in 1981. As Casey Cason noticed in her mildly ironic way, the entire city government of Atlanta now seemed to be in the hands of 1960s freedom fighters. Following in the footsteps of other business-minded Atlanta mayors, however, Andy Young brought in $70 billion of new private investment.

Coda/1980s
Honors/North
LENA

T HE 1970S took a terrible toll on Lena. They were a time of mourning. All the men in her life died almost at the same time. Big Teddy's death came first, early in 1970. It was not entirely a surprise—a matter of age and a bad heart. Little Teddy's death, in September of that year of kidney failure, was not entirely a surprise, either—she knew it might be sooner rather than later. Her beautiful boy had become a gaunt, wasted figure. For Lena, it was a tragedy almost beyond repair. Little Teddy had the cards stacked against him from the beginning. He was under two when his mother suddenly disappeared from his life because of our father's sexism—"you take the girl, I'll take the boy." Consequently, he never had a mother or a sister; Lena never had a son, and I never had a brother. I saw my little brother intermittently—the longest period was in 1943 and 1944, when he played cowboys and Indians and I played with dolls. And his Hollywood kindergarten teacher got into trouble with Lena for reading *Little Black Sambo* to the class. In the mid-1950s he liked country music and Ike, while I was "Madly for Adlai" and preferred Piaf to Presley. He became a polished, well-dressed Young Republican sophisticate at UCLA, where he starred on the debating team and found himself pursued by all manner and ages of women. In 1959 Teddy transferred from UCLA to Berkeley. The darling little boy who talked about "Snow White and the Seven *Drawers*" had become a tall, bearded, beautiful, ill man, kept alive by dialysis, who spoke about Hermann Hesse and Frantz Fanon and certainly admired Brother Huey Newton. He lived in Los Angeles, was married twice, and had four children. He felt he was a prisoner of dialysis—and essentially chose to go off it. Teddy's death was a deep, deep blow to my mother, even though she knew it would probably come at some early point.

The final blow—Lennie died seven months later, in April 1971. Just as Teddy's death was not really unexpected, neither was Lennie's— mainly because he enjoyed bad health habits. He was the ultimate gourmet, with a diet of butter, eggs, red meat, and copious amounts of spirits, wine, and nicotine. Like his first wife, Lennie was a ticking time bomb for a stroke. Because he came of age in the 1920s, he drank all day long (midmorning beer, wine for lunch, midafternoon beer, two or three martinis, wine for dinner, and brandy later). He was never drunk, only smiling and mellow. He also, starting before breakfast, consumed five or six packs of Camel cigarettes every day. Like his first wife, he suddenly sat up with a headache and was gone. Frank Sinatra's private plane flew Mother, Sidney and me, and Amy and Jenny over extremely bumpy mountains from Los Angeles to Palm Springs for Lennie's funeral. Bighearted Arthur Freed, whose unit produced the great MGM musical movies of the 1940s and early 1950s, was there to weep over all his "boys" who were dead or dying.

Lena, who said that the near-simultaneous losses "cracked her open," basically retired to Santa Barbara to live with her grief. Eventually, she was coaxed out of retirement by Alan King, one of her favorite people, as good-hearted and wise as he was funny—and a distant cousin of Lennie's. No one ever had an unkind word to say about Alan or his wife, Jeanette. Alan opened for Lena all over the country when she used to tour the nightclubs—he was her favorite comedian because he was a raconteur. So she slowly went back to work. She fell in love with

Sesame Street and sang my Harvard classmate and friend Joe Raposo's great song "Bein' Green" with Kermit the Frog. She performed in the musical *Pal Joey* on the road. She toured in concert with Tony Bennett, singing Harold Arlen medleys. And in 1978 she played Glinda the Good in the movie version of the Broadway musical *The Wiz*, directed by her son-in-law, Sidney Lumet. Everyone agreed that Lena singing "Believe in Yourself" was the best moment in the picture, whose stars were Diana Ross and Michael Jackson. A sweet, shy, almost fragile young man, Michael Jackson came to dinner and spent all of his time with our children. But Sidney and I were divorced soon after *The Wiz*—and this did not help Lena's doldrums. She hated the idea of my divorce even more than she had hated the idea of my marriage. I loved Sidney; we were friends. We had wonderful daughters—but after fourteen years, the marriage was over. I was a different person. It was the height of women's lib, which I basically ignored—although I admired Gloria Steinem and Betty Freidan. I was much too frivolous to be liberated. I was seriously into fashion and parties and movie stars. I did not read books; I read magazines. I was a sad case. Sidney was a workaholic and, like all directors, very controlling. He was really happy only when preparing, shooting, and cutting a film—or spending Sunday afternoons lying on the bed watching football while I took the girls to the playground. But I know the moment I knew I had to have a divorce. It had nothing to do with Sidney's bad or good qualities, and everything to do with me. This may sound idiotic, but it is true; I saw *A Doll's House* on television and I knew it was the story of my life. I had allowed myself to be infantilized and now this marriage was my prison. I had to get out of prison and save my life. Sidney, a very sensible person, said I should try a shrink, not a divorce. My wonderful "shrink" was Mildred Newman, coauthor with her husband, Bernard Berkowitz, of *How to Be Awake and Alive*, the best-selling mid-1970s popular psychology book. I saw Mildred for a year, but I still wanted a divorce. I had indeed been sleepwalking through my life.

If the 1970s were a time of mourning, the 1980s were a time of celebration on several fronts. My mother was happy to celebrate my marriage to Kevin Buckley, a journalist and foreign correspondent. Kevin had spent 1968–1972 in Saigon during the Vietnam War. Kevin, Yale class of 1962, a man whom Sybil Burton called "beautiful inside and out," was a saintly stepfather. His patience and amusement with my teenaged daughters reminded me of Lennie. Amy and Jenny adored him and often called him "Kev." Amy figured him out: "Dad is hopelessly late *thirties*—Mom is hopelessly late *fifties*—at least Kev is early *seventies.*" She said this in the eighties.

In March 1981 Lena made her famous reappearance on Broadway after twenty-four years. Her one-woman show, *The Lady and Her Music*, was not just great but phenomenal. The reviews were unanimously extraordinary, and the awards were too numerous to count. On her opening night, I personally saw Leo Lerman, Al Hirschfeld, and Swifty Lazar, separately, wiping away tears. Normally unsentimental, these men had known Lena for forty years and clearly something had been triggered. Lena had become a legend in her lifetime—awarded the Kennedy Center honors. To her surprise, she also became an icon for young women. They lined up outside the stage door amazed by her age, her voice, her beauty, her stamina, her humor, and her cheerful, unapologetic worldliness. When the *Daily News* asked her, sometime in the 1980s, if she thought President Reagan was sexy, she only replied, "For heaven's sake!" She became Glinda the Good Witch, the wise woman elder, for all the young Dorothys far from home. Lena admired strong, confident women, but never considered herself a "feminist" because she always needed a male spokesman to feel "protected." There are many nuances to feminism; "Believe in Yourself" covered them all. By the first quarter of the 2000s there was suddenly a whole new theatrical generation of young women named "Lena." Not a coincidence, I believe, since "Lena" had never before been a popular name. The real Lena was, of course, unique. Her musicality, like her courage and discipline, was hers alone. But her beauty and stamina came from the black Calhouns and all their admixtures.

After the opening, the theater staff kept a list of VIP backstage visitors—it was like a roll call of mid-twentieth-century arts and entertainment. Most of these people were her friends, certainly with air-kissing rights. There were musicians and composers: Eubie Blake, Harold Arlen, Cab Calloway, Benny Goodman, Lionel Hampton, Charles Aznavour, and Quincy Jones. There were singers: Bing Crosby, Mabel Mercer, Aretha Franklin, Michael Jackson, Barbra Streisand, Johnny Mathis, Sammy Davis Jr., Harry Belafonte, Diana Ross, Sarah Vaughan, Eartha Kitt, Rosemary Clooney, Carmen McRae, Liza Minnelli, Bobby Short, Nancy Sinatra, Dionne Warwick, Marilyn Horne, Birgit Nilsson, and Beverly Sills. There were comedians: George Burns, Milton Berle, Red Buttons, and Phyllis Diller. There were dancers and choreographers: Martha Graham, Agnes de Mille, Jerome Robbins, Dame Margot Fonteyn, Mikhail Baryshnikov, Natalia Makarova, Zizi Jeanmaire, Arthur Mitchell, Erik Bruhn, Gelsey Kirkland, Sir Robert Helpmann, and Carmen de Lavallade and Geoffrey Holder. There were Hollywood names: Lillian Gish, Katharine Hepburn, Myrna Loy, Sylvia Sidney, Jane Withers, Claudette Colbert, Jennifer Jones, Angela Lansbury, Ginger Rogers, Claire Trevor, Jane Russell, Lucille Ball, Burgess Meredith, Alexis Smith, Kathryn Grayson, Gregory Peck, James Mason, José Ferrer, Kirk Douglas, Rex Harrison, Gina Lollobrigida, Sam Spiegel, Yul Brynner, Jack Lemmon, Elizabeth Taylor, Roddy McDowall, Debbie Reynolds, Janet Leigh, Joan Collins, Julie Andrews, Shirley MacLaine, Anthony Quinn, Sidney Poitier, James Coburn, Jack Nicholson, Jean-Pierre Aumont, Tony Randall, Lily Tomlin, Meryl Streep, Dudley Moore, Robert De Niro, Donald Sutherland, Albert Finney, Anne Jackson and Eli Wallach, Ruby Dee, Sir John Gielgud, Paul Newman and Joanne Woodward, Rock Hudson, Mike Nichols, Elia Kazan, Lena's ex-son-in-law, Sidney Lumet, and Lena's two good girlfriends of the 1950s and '60s, Suzy

Parker and Jinx Falkenburg. There were Broadway luminaries: Helen Hayes, Ethel Merman, Mary Martin, Hal and Judy Prince, Neil Simon, Adolph Green and Phyllis Newman, Joel Grey, Nancy Walker, Carol Burnett, Tommy Tune, Molly Picon, Stella Adler, and Vincent Sardi. There were media names: Ed Bradley, Harry Reasoner, Johnny Carson, Gordon Parks, Arthur Godfrey, and William S. Paley. There were activist names: James Baldwin, Paul Robeson Jr., Bayard Rustin, Andrew Young, Dr. Kenneth Clark, and Ernest Green of the Little Rock Nine. There were resonant political names: Jacqueline Kennedy Onassis, Coretta Scott King, Lady Bird Johnson, Nancy Reagan, former mayor Robert Wagner, Governor Hugh Carey, Vernon Jordan, future mayor David Dinkins, and Mayor Ed Koch. There were foreign dignitaries: the president of Vanuatu; Michael Manley, former prime minister of Jamaica; Kurt Waldheim, UN secretary-general; Count and Countess Bernadotte (Swedish friends); and the Nigerian tribal kings. Surprisingly, there were sports stars: "Jersey Joe" Walcott, Roy Campanella, Dave Winfield, Tom Seaver, Bucky Dent, Earl "the Pearl" Monroe, Don Newcombe, Arthur Ashe, Billie Jean King, Muhammad Ali, and Mrs. Jackie Robinson.

My favorite tributes came from Bing Crosby, Marilyn Horne, and Lillian Gish:

"I've seen them all—you are the greatest! What you do is artistry of the highest order—dignity—style-class-warmth, and musicianship in rare degree. I always knew you sang like a bird, but seeing you in person is something again. It's a memory I'll always treasure."

—Bing Crosby

"Lena is the Queen! I love her! She is the song recitalist of one's dreams! And how **fresh** that voice sounds after years and years of using it to its fullest—a tribute to a superior technician."

—Marilyn Horne

"To sit in a capacity filled theatre and discover that the artist on the stage is singing to you alone and no one else is a unique experience, but then that is Lena Horne, a lady who makes me humble to be in her profession and **very** proud to be an American."

—Lillian Gish

After a year on Broadway, Lena took her show on the road. In San Francisco, the vice president and coach of the 49ers football team came to the opening. In Los Angeles, Mayor Tom Bradley came. And Robert Osborne wrote a review for the *Hollywood Reporter*:

It is the ultimate one-woman exhibition. Not only are the lady and her vocal cords at the absolute peak of their sorcery but both are gorgeously presented in a package that makes for one sweet, sassy and deviously disciplined evening in the theatre . . . Probably the greatest compliment one can pay to the professional side of Lena Horne is that her show . . . is still a *growing* recital, sharp as a tack after several hundred performances and still as fresh as if spontaneously devised during a mid-day rehearsal . . . She's warm, funny and in total control . . . Healthy, disciplined and talented as Lena Horne is at age 65, the lady is some inspiration.

In April 1983 she returned to Atlanta for the first time since childhood—to be greeted somewhat in the manner of a prodigal daughter. From the *Atlanta Journal-Constitution* of Sunday, April 17:

LENA STORMS INTO ATLANTA
MS. HORNE SEEKS CHILDHOOD TIES
DURING 5-NIGHT ENGAGEMENT . . .

In a manner considerably less formal than Alex Haley's published search for his ancestry, Ms. Horne is hunting for . . . her family members . . . By virtue of her personal mission, Atlanta may very well be the most important stop on her U.S. tour, which began shortly after Ms. Horne closed her popular Broadway show June 30th last year—her 65th birthday . . .

Asked about her childhood recollections of the city, she said, "I went to Booker T. Washington Junior High (seventh grade) and to Summer Hill Grade School (sixth grade). I remember a school teacher named Mrs. Thelma Rivers. She was a great teacher . . . I lived on West Hunter Street . . . I'm sure I have schoolmates there. Some, I hope, still remember me."

Cousin Catherine was in Milwaukee, but Cousin Harriet was in Atlanta to greet Lena. The *Journal-Constitution* recorded their first meeting:

OCCASION FOR JOY—Lena Horne and a previously unknown cousin, Harriet Chisholm of Atlanta, meet each other for the first time backstage at the Fox Theatre . . . a "joyous occasion."

And she met her beloved teacher, Miss Helena (not Thelma) Rivers—a meeting also recorded by news photos:

A teacher and her "star" student—Miss Lena [*sic*] Rivers, a retired Atlanta Public School Teacher who taught at the world famous Washington High School, is warmly revisited by her world famous "star" student, Miss Lena Horne.

Lena met not only Miss Rivers, but a much-loved playmate, Mildred White. She and Lena and Miss Rivers were also photographed together:

Ms. Helena Rivers and Mildred White Smith visit with Lena Horne in her dressing room during her appearance at the Fox Theatre. Mildred was a playmate of Lena Horne . . . This picture depicts the three reviewing pictures of her childhood days with several playmates.

It was a busy five days. Accompanied by her new best friend and black Calhoun cousin, fun-loving Harriet, Lena toured Atlanta. She was photographed happily pointing out the attractive brick house on West Hunter Street, renamed Martin Luther King Jr. Drive. The house was now the office of the black newspaper the *Atlanta Inquirer*, whose "computer room" had been Lena's bedroom. She also made flying visits to Booker T. Washington High School, Morehouse College, and the Atlanta University Library, where she toured the W. E. B. Du Bois Collection and looked up Cora's graduation date. Her visitors backstage at the Fox included delegations of students from Spelman and Clark colleges—part of Asa Ware's dreamed-of Atlanta University complex. And with great pleasure, she dined after a performance with Mayor Andrew Young and his wife, Jean.

The honors continued to be reported in Atlanta even after she left. In May the *Constitution* noted: "Nancy Reagan, Lena Horne and Connie Chung were voted among the 10 most influential women of the year by sorority members of the University of Southern California . . ."

The *Inquirer* wrote that Lena, Richard Burton, and Jack Lemmon would host the 1983 Tony Awards and that Lena would receive the 1983 NAACP Spingarn Medal. Cora Horne and Walter White would definitely have been pleased.

When Lena left Atlanta, Cousin Harriet put together a photo album with a sweet message:

Welcome back, Lena. Welcome to Atlanta. Hoping your "trip back home" added pleasant and meaningful moments to your life. It added much to mine in a very real sense. Perhaps, in another time and place Cora, Lena and Kate are happy too.

When Lena died on Mother's Day 2010 at the age of ninety-two, she was remembered and eulogized around the world and close to home. An editorial in the *Tablet*, a Brooklyn Catholic newspaper, remembered her as a child singer at St. Peter Claver Church, whose pastor, Father Bernard J. Quinn, a pioneer in black Catholic ministry, is being considered for sainthood. The piece, by Ed Wilkinson for the column, "The Editor's Space," went on to say that Father Quinn built the parish center where Lena first performed in public:

> Not only was Lena Horne born in Brooklyn, but she was also baptized a Catholic in Brooklyn and educated in a Catholic school in Brooklyn. Father Paul Jervis, pastor of St. Martin of Tours parish in Bedford Stuyvesant, explains that Horne was baptized in Holy Rosary Church on Chauncey Street . . . Horne remained true to the faith, with burial from St. Ignatius Loyola Church on the upper East Side of Manhattan . . . Jesuit Father Walter Modrys, the retired pastor of St. Ignatius Loyola, celebrated the funeral Mass. In his eulogy, he recounted a time when, upon first meeting Horne, she admitted to "feelings of shyness." She referred to her "persona" that she shared with others. It was her performance mode, she said. Father Modrys recalled that, years later, at Horne's 80th birthday party at Avery Fisher Hall in New York, someone asked her to sing. "She started slowly, clearly struggling," he said, but "here comes that 'persona' clicking in." And "sure enough," the priest added, "we watched the transformation of an elegant 80-year-old woman into the 25-year-old-starlet that no one could ever forget."

I love and miss my mother, but I do not mourn her. Her life should be celebrated—not mourned. She had a beautiful funeral Mass at the church she had attended every Easter that she could. She was not really a Mass-goer, but she liked priests—especially slightly elderly music-loving Jesuits who liked martinis. Audra McDonald sang "This Little Light of Mine," the spiritual Lena sang in 1963 at Medgar Evers' last voting rights rally in Mississippi. A delegation of former Tuskegee Airmen were also in the church to salute their World War II "sweetheart"—they were applauded by the congregation.

A family truth was revealed in Richard Corliss' *Time* magazine obituary, "A Great Lady Makes Her Exit":

[Lena Horne] fashioned one of the 20th century's most exemplary and poignant show-business careers . . . Performing into her 80s, she remained a beacon for black performers, a divinity to audiences of all colors and a lingering, stinging reproach to the attitudes that had robbed her of her Hollywood prime . . . Horne had the fine features, soprano stylings and genteel comic touch of, say, an Irene Dunne. Except Horne wasn't Caucasian. Like other black performers who might have been top stars—like Paul Robeson and Nina Mae McKinney and Josephine Baker . . . she was part of a great generation lost to a crippling national prejudice . . . [W]hen stars her age were moldering in retirement . . . Horne, still impossibly radiant, continued to flourish, tacking on to the end of her career the renown that should have been hers at the beginning . . . The anger she had repressed in her youth came out forcefully but smoothly, in anecdotes and epigrams, and was carefully modulated into irony or nostalgia.

That was the voice of Horne the entertainer. She wanted to instruct her '80s audiences, not indict them. As a child, she had wanted to be a schoolteacher, and onstage or in the talk-show-guest chair, that's what she so superbly was: the professor and the lesson, an inspiring example of outliving prejudice, turning stormy weather into blue skies and beauty into truth.

Richard Corliss made it clear that the battle for Lena's heart and mind was won by Cora, thank goodness, and not poor Edna. Yes, my mother was a teacher. I sat on her lap, and she taught me to read. She taught me "Now I Lay Me Down to Sleep." She taught me to sing "The Owl and the Pussycat." And she gave me my first civics lesson when I was six or seven, when she sat me down to say that she had just been with an American soldier whose mother and father were Japanese, who had lost both his legs and come home to find his house burned down. She told me that she sang "America the Beautiful," and the soldier cried, and she cried.

Like her grandmother, Lena did not believe in age-inappropriate activities. My mother always entered *my* world—she never brought me into hers. Like her grandmother, my mother never really approved of show business. I did not enter her world, except under controlled circumstances, until I was probably fourteen or fifteen, when I could hang around the dressing room, see celebrities, and stay up for late supper. That's when I saw the world of Lena Horne. I realize now that through most of my life, I never knew "Lena Horne." I knew someone called "Mom," but I never really knew "Lena." I caught a glimpse of her perhaps, watching her in the mirror when she put her makeup on—a fascinating exercise. She covered her light beige face, sprinkled with freckles, with dark brown pancake makeup (under the lights it was not so dark) the way she had been taught at MGM—where she was given modified Joan Crawford lips. She liked glamour. She liked haute couture fashion, Paris, and breakfast at 3 P.M. She read until dawn.

Despite doing the *New York Times* crosswords daily, and reading volume after volume of French history, my mother was always pleading her "dumbness"—mostly because she left school at sixteen, and also because most of her friends were very smart people. I was surprised at how articulate and psychologically astute she was. Edna can be forgiven much for giving Lena books instead of toys and dolls (where she could not compete with Ted Horne). Cora was also a great book-giver. Books saved Lena's spirit as well as her mind.

My mother and I discussed everything under the sun, except politics and sex. I knew we were Democrats. As far as my mother was concerned Eleanor Roosevelt walked on water—as for FDR, she had romantic dreams about him. We never discussed the facts of life. She left a book on my bed called *The Stork Didn't Bring You*. Books, in fact, were one of our great bonds. She talked about books she loved as a child (they were usually about orphans) and gave me volume after volume of Dr. Dolittle and Nancy Drew. Mom and I loved to read while traveling. We exchanged Penguin mysteries on trains and ships. Such was our quest for wonderful books that when I arrived at our London hotel, traveling alone, at age sixteen, from school in upstate New York, I had barely walked in the door before she said, "You've *got* to read this," and thrust into my hand the first James Bond book.

I was fascinated to discover that the song "Now" was not only remembered, but also not just an American phenomenon. In 1964 the Cuban Santiago Álvarez made a five-minute political film, also called "Now." It was a montage of civil rights pictures with Lena's voice the only sound track. It was rediscovered some fifty years later by the young left. I was touched by comments on the Web. This was from a young woman named "Jane":

> Some folks think that Lena Horne's signature song is "Stormy Weather" but her real signature is "NOW." For her politics, Lena Horne was blacklisted; she was dedicated to justice, and "Now" is probably the song she cared for most. The great filmmaker, Cuba's Santiago Alvarez, captured the essence of Lena Horne's "NOW" . . . as a virtual anthem. If anyone questions why so many people at the time became revolutionaries, here is the answer.

A young man named "Adam" remembered it as "a call to arms for those who would stand against injustice":

> I first saw "Now" in college and it's stuck with me ever since, to the point that I keep a copy of it on my phone at all times. Horne

made plenty of other contributions in entertainment's long history, but this is my personal memory of her . . . R.I.P. Lena . . . you will be missed.

I am pretty sure that Lena never ever heard of Santiago Álvarez or his film. She certainly never mentioned it to me. Despite her long-ago detested stepfather, Cuba was not really on her radar. But she would have been very pleased.

CODA/1980s

Honors/South

DR. HOMER E. NASH

IN MARCH 1981, the same month that saw Lena's triumphant return to Broadway, Atlanta greatly mourned the death of black Calhoun Dr. Homer Nash Sr., aged ninety-four, the patriarch of the Nash family and the father of cousins Catherine, Harriet, Helen, and Homer. In contrast to Lena's sadness, the 1970s had been all about honors for Dr. Nash. The tall, elegant old man, white-haired and brown-skinned, was truly beloved in the black community of Atlanta. He had become an Atlanta icon, like his father-in-law, Antoine Graves Sr., who had been so adamant about Dr. Nash not marrying his daughter Marie until he had established himself. The father of two more doctors, and the grandfather of one, Dr. Nash practiced medicine in Atlanta for seventy years. He was honored as the oldest practicing black doctor in Georgia, as well as the longest-practicing doctor of any race in Atlanta. The black Calhouns, North and South, never stopped bringing honor to the family.

A 1972 newspaper interview, published when Dr. Nash was eighty-six and had been practicing in Atlanta for sixty-three years, was titled "Meet Dr. Homer Nash":

> He was the son of a common laborer and a maid; he worked his way through Meharry Medical College (class of 1910); he manned a

World War I field hospital with 41 ambulances, and, for 33 years has persuaded mothers to immunize their children at a Fulton County clinic, while at the same time being available to his own patients at 239 Auburn Ave. NE.

In 1973 a special Father's Day recognition was reported—Marie and Homer Nash, with daughter Harriet and her husband, Dr. Charles "Chiz" Chisholm, and their daughter, Cheryl, with her husband, Charles Hobson, were all photographed:

Dr. Homer E. Nash, a pioneer citizen of Atlanta, was honored by the First Congregational Church . . . as the Father of the Year and an eminent senior citizen who has rendered outstanding services to both his church and community . . .

The honors continued. In December 1976 Dr. Nash, aged eighty-nine, became the first recipient of the W. E. B. Du Bois Award of the Du Bois Institute of Atlanta University. And in February 1978 the *Atlanta Daily World* observed Dr. and Mrs. Nash's sixtieth wedding anniversary with an interview with Marie Graves Nash:

Despite inclinations to believe that their story is one of the classic "love at first sight" romances, Mrs. Nash says that actually the opposite is true. She had known and dated Dr. Nash five years before they were finally married. "We used to go to a lot of different parties together. I think that was around 1914 and 1915," she said, meticulously care- ful to keep the years straight. "Yes, it had to be around then because I remember I had just graduated from Atlanta University."

Theirs had neither been an early marriage of child bride and bride- groom. Mrs. Nash admitted she was twenty five years old when they were joined together . . . When queried on the matter of divorce, Mrs. Nash became almost indignant. "Divorce? I never gave it a thought.

After I had my babies, I said even then 'there'll be no leaving around here,'" Mrs. Nash said with a short but endearing laugh . . .

Certain "choices" like divorce or adultery, which seemed so easily available in the North, rarely occured to the Atlanta branch of the family. Homer Nash, unlike Frank Horne, for example, was not a reluctant man of medicine. And Marie Nash, unlike Cora Horne, was not an unhappy or neglected wife. Possibly because the world outside the family unit was so potentially dangerous, Southern blacks who were lucky enough to have happy family lives and rewarding work cherished them all the more.

Another 1979 newspaper article celebrated Dr. Nash's long practice:

"There was a time when I wasn't the only doctor on Auburn Avenue, there used to be at least 20 doctors practicing on this street. But as opportunities opened up for Blacks all over the city," he said, "they left Auburn Avenue."

In July 1979 Dr. Nash's granddaughter, Cousin Catherine's daughter, Karen Marie Harris, married Stanley Reynolds in Milwaukee's Central United Methodist Church. Karen had graduated from Tufts University in Massachusetts in 1974 and received a certificate from the state of Georgia to teach early elementary grades K–3. Sherry Nash, daughter of Homer Jr., was a bridesmaid, and Hallie Hobson, daughter of Cheryl Chisholm, was flower girl. The bride was employed by the Internal Revenue Service in Atlanta. The bridegroom, a housing code inspector for the city of Atlanta, attended Indiana State University and the Art Institute of Chicago.

In 1980 there was a proclamation from the city of Atlanta by Maynard Jackson, elected in 1973 as the first black mayor of a major Southern city. (In 1959 his mother had been the first Negro to receive a card from the Atlanta Public Library.) He now honored Homer Nash:

WHEREAS Dr. Homer E. Nash has practiced medicine actively in Atlanta for 69 years; and

WHEREAS Dr. Nash has served as president of the Georgia State Medical Association and the Atlanta Medical Association; and

WHEREAS Dr. Nash has also been named Physician of the Year by the Georgia State Medical Association and the Atlanta Medical Association; and

WHEREAS the Atlanta Medical Association has honored Dr. Nash for his outstanding achievements by creating the Nash-Carter Award:

NOW, THEREFORE, I, Maynard Jackson, Mayor of the City of Atlanta, hereby do proclaim Saturday, January 19, 1980 as

HOMER NASH DAY

In Atlanta, and urge our citizens to recognize this day . . .

Homer E. Nash's March 1981 funeral was, of course, at First Congregational Church. The white *Atlanta Constitution* recognized him under the headline "Dr. Homer Nash's Death Ends an Era for Atlanta":

He and his wife, Marie Graves, who were married for 63 years, had five children, two of whom—Homer Jr. and Helen Nash Abernathy—are pediatricians practicing in St. Louis. And in June, Homer Jr.'s daughter Alison is due to become a third-generation physician when she graduates from the Baylor University School of Medicine.

Alison attended Howard University before medical school and completed her pediatric residency at the Oakland Naval Hospital. She married Clarence Dula in 1979 and had two daughters. She joined the U.S. Navy in 1981, reaching the rank of lieutenant commander as a navy doctor. She later went into practice with her father.

When her husband, John Harris, died in 1984, Cousin Catherine moved back to Atlanta from Milwaukee. Wonder of wonders, in 1991 she married her childhood sweetheart, Joseph Page Frye, the "Joe" of her cousin Kathryn's doggerel, a widower who retired as a supervisor with the U.S. Postal Service. Catherine now joined her husband's church, St. Paul's Episcopal. Joe was a member of the St. Paul's Men's Club as well as the Tuesday Bridge Club. And Catherine volunteered at the Atlanta Public Library. Once again, Catherine's activities and concerns were typical of middle-class black Atlanta life—community, church, bridge, and, especially, family. Karen Harris Reynolds wrote about her mother's remarriage:

My dad's illness was long and emotionally draining, but I don't think she would have remarried if she hadn't been here and having social contact with Joe Frye. He went out of his way to convince her it was a good idea. He treated us like we were his children, and we grew to love him too. So I don't think there was a big young love story between them like Harriet who gave up Spelman for her Chiz but they were a great end of life love story and although I miss her horribly I am always glad she was, for her last four years, extremely happy and in love. When she died Joe was devastated and carried on with us as if he had actually fathered me. He was a very nice man . . .

In June 1993 the Calhoun family reunion was held in Atlanta. Cousin Catherine was editor/author of the memorial book *The Calhoun Connection.* As Catherine wrote in the reunion book:

To our ancestors we would like to give praise and thanks for who and what they were. We have become who and what we are because of the strengths, determination, sense of self and pride that you bequeathed to us. We are determined to do the same for the generations following us. This family will continue to grow, working hard to become loving and compassionate people and to develop whatever talents have been given to us.

In its appreciation of Dr. Nash, the *Atlanta Constitution* mentioned the "end of an era." Sad to say, despite great black individual achievements, in the decades following Dr. Nash's death the vicious circle of racism, whose effects move a society in a backward direction, was dragging the South back to, say, sometime before the passage of the Fourteenth Amendment. By the 1990s lynching had returned to the South. And black Southerners suddenly faced a very old enemy: twenty-first-century Republicans were secretly nineteenth-century Democrats. Ostensibly in order to thwart citizenship for the children of illegal immigrants, the Republican Party of 2010 seriously debated the idea of amending or repealing the Fourteenth Amendment. In 2011 Texas Republicans talked about seceding from the Union. In 2012 the National Republican Party was busy finding ways of getting around the Fifteenth Amendment in order to, yet again, deny blacks voting rights. It used to be said of Frederick Douglass, "If only he were white, he could be president." With Barack Obama, the first black president, it might be said, "If he were only white, they would let him *be president.*" From the moment he was elected, Republicans began trying to bring him down, to the costly neglect of every other issue affecting the American people. And just as their nineteenth-century Democratic counterparts began to destroy the black vote the minute the first ballots were counted, twenty-first century Republicans tried to topple the first black president by slyly invoking the *sacred cause* of white supremacy, which seemed to be stronger than God or patriotism—but as proved through the ages, never stronger than love and courage. In freedom as in slavery, white supremacy by definition crushed the hopes and dreams of all but the most fearless and tenacious of black achievers. The black Calhouns were both fearless and tenacious. Thank goodness they were also bighearted and generous with their family gifts, serving not only their communities but also their country.

ACKNOWLEDGMENTS

I have many people to thank—especially my earliest reader, Kevin Buckley, for his encouragement; Lynn Nesbit, my wonderful and supportive agent and friend; and my brilliant editor and friend Joan Bingham, at Grove Atlantic, who made everything better. I also want to thank Joan's Grove Atlantic colleagues—especially Amy Vreeland for her guiding hand, Charles Woods for his art direction, and Morgan Entrekin, Judy Hottensen, and Deb Seager for their enthusiasm and publishing expertise. And special thanks to Nancy Tan for her copyediting.

I want to thank Henry Foner, John Merony, and Ramona Brewer Moloski for enlightening me on the Blacklist days. My thanks also go to Ken Gregory in Atlanta for his knowledge of the Ezzard family. And special thanks to Patrick Callihan for his research assistance.

And of course this book could not have been written without the help and support of my Calhoun cousins: Catherine Nash Harris, Karen Harris Reynolds, Harriet Nash Chisholm, Cheryl Chisholm, Hallie Hobson, and Christopher Lee.

With gratitude to all.

Sources Cited

Atlanta Historical Bulletin: A Salute to Atlanta's Black Heritage. Volume XXI. Atlanta, GA: Historical Society, Spring 1977.

Bacote, Clarence A. *The Story of Atlanta University: A Century of Service, 1865–1965.* Atlanta, GA: Atlanta University, 1969.

Baker, Ray Stannard. *Following the Color Line: An Account of Negro Citizenship in the American Democracy.* Williamstown, MA: Corner House Publishers, 1973 (originally published New York: Doubleday, Page & Company, 1908).

Beiswinger, George I. *One to One: The Story of the Big Brothers/Big Sisters Movement in America.* Philadelphia: Big Brothers/Big Sisters of America, 1985.

Blackmon, Douglas A. *Slavery by Another Name: The Re-Enslavement of Black Americans from the Civil War to World War II.* New York: Anchor Books, 2009.

Blair, Betsy. *The Memory of All That: Love and Politics in New York, Hollywood, and Paris.* New York: Alfred A. Knopf, 2003.

Bond, Julian, and the National Association for the Advancement of Colored People. *NAACP: Celebrating a Century: 100 Years in Pictures.* Layton, UT: Gibbs Smith, 2009.

Chace, James. *1912.* New York: Simon & Schuster, 2004.

Chadakoff, Rochelle, ed. *Eleanor Roosevelt's My Day: Her Acclaimed Columns 1936–1945.* New York: Pharos Books, 1989.

Collier-Thomas, Bettye. *Jesus, Jobs, and Justice: African American Women and Religion.* New York: Alfred A. Knopf, 2010.

Coward, Noël. *The Noël Coward Diaries.* Edited by Graham Payne and Sheridan Morley. Boston: Little, Brown, 1982.

Coweta County Deed Book. Coweta County, Georgia, 1838–1841.

Curry, Constance, et al. *Deep in Our Hearts: Nine White Women in the Freedom Movement.* Athens: University of Georgia Press, 2000.

Dalfiume, Richard M. *The Desegregation of the U.S. Armed Forces 1945–1964.* Columbus: University of Missouri Press, 1969.

Daniels, Maurice C. *Saving the Soul of Georgia: Donald L. Hollowell and the Struggle for Civil Rights.* Athens: University of Georgia Press, 2013.

Deery, Phillip. *Red Apple: Communism and McCarthyism in Cold War New York.* New York: Fordham University Press, 2014.

Douglass, Frederick. *The Life and Times of Frederick Douglass.* New York: Collier Books, 1962.

Du Bois, W. E. B. *The Autobiography of W. E. B. Du Bois.* New York: International Publishers Co., 1968.

Du Bois, W. E. B. *Black Reconstruction in America 1860–1880.* New York: Athenaeum, 1979.

Duberman, Martin Bauml. *Paul Robeson.* New York: Alfred A. Knopf, 1988.

Free at Last: A History of the Civil Rights Movement and Those Who Died in the Struggle. Montgomery, AL: Civil Rights Education Project, Southern Poverty Law Center, 1989.

Friedrich, Otto. *City of Nets: A Portrait of Hollywood in the 1940s.* New York: Harper & Row, 1986.

Hadju, David. *Lush Life: A Biography of Billy Strayhorn.* New York: Farrar, Straus, Giroux, 1996.

Hammond, John, with Irving Townsend. *John Hammond on Record: An Autobiography.* New York: Ridge Press, 1977.

Harwell, Richard Barksdale, ed. *Kate: The Journal of a Confederate Nurse.* Baton Rouge: Louisiana State University Press, 1969 (originally published Louisville: J. P. Morton, and New Orleans: W. Evelyn, 1866).

Haskins, Jim. *The Cotton Club: A Pictorial and Social History of the Most Famous Symbol of the Jazz Era.* New York: Random House, 1977.

Higham, Charles. *Merchant of Dreams: Louis B. Mayer, M.G.M., and the Secret Hollywood.* New York: Donald I. Fine, 1993.

Hine, Darlene Clark, ed. *Black Women in America*. New York: Facts on File, 1997.

Hughes, Langston, and Milton Meltzer. *Black Magic: A Pictorial History of the African-American in the Performing Arts*. New York: Da Capo Press, 1990 (originally published Englewood Cliffs, NJ: Prentice-Hall, 1967).

Irvin, Sam. *Kay Thompson: From Funny Face to Eloise*. New York: Simon & Schuster, 2010.

Israel, Lee. *Kilgallen*. New York: Delacorte Press, 1979.

Jervis, Paul W., ed. *Quintessential Priest: The Life of Father Bernard J. Quinn*. Strasbourg, France: Éditions Du Signe, 2005.

Johnson, Howard Eugene, with Wendy Johnson. *A Dancer in the Revolution: Stretch Johnson, Harlem Communist at the Cotton Club*. New York: Fordham University Press, 2014.

Johnson, James Weldon. *Black Manhattan*. New York: Alfred A. Knopf, 1940.

Kimball, Robert, and William Bolcom. *Reminiscing with Sissle and Blake*. New York: Viking Press, 1973.

Kuntz, Tom, and Phil Kuntz, eds. *The Sinatra Files: The Life of an American Icon Under Government Surveillance*. New York: Three Rivers Press, 2000.

Laurents, Arthur. *Original Story*. New York: Alfred A. Knopf, 2000.

Lesley, Cole. *Remembered Laughter: The Life of Noel Coward*. New York: Alfred A. Knopf, 1976.

Lewis, David Levering. *When Harlem Was in Vogue*. New York: Alfred A. Knopf, 1981.

Meltzer, Milton. *Mark Twain Himself: A Pictorial Biography*. Columbia: University of Missouri Press, 1960.

Meyerson, Harold, and Ernie Harburg. *Who Put the Rainbow in The Wizard of Oz?: Yip Harburg, Lyricist*. Ann Arbor: University of Michigan Press, 1993.

Minnelli, Vincente, with Hector Arce. *I Remember It Well*. Garden City, NY: Doubleday & Company, 1974.

Peery, Nelson. *Black Fire: The Making of an American Revolutionary*. New York: New Press, 1994.

Schoener, Allon, ed. *Harlem on My Mind: Cultural Capital of Black America, 1900–1968*. New York: Random House, 1968.

Sidney, Robert. *With Malice Towards Some: Tales from a Life Dancing with Stars.* 1st Books Library, 2003.

Starr, Kevin. *Embattled Dreams: California in War and Peace, 1940–1950.* New York: Oxford University Press, 2002.

Thomas, Lately. *Sam Ward: "King of the Lobby."* Boston: Houghton Mifflin Company, 1965.

Thomson, David. *Rosebud: The Story of Orson Welles.* New York: Alfred A. Knopf, 1996.

Weinberg, Meyer, ed. *W. E. B. DuBois: A Reader.* New York: Harper & Row, 1970.

White, Walter Francis. *A Man Called White: The Autobiography of Walter White.* New York: Viking Press, 1948.

Woodward, C. Vann. *The Strange Career of Jim Crow.* New York: Oxford University Press, 1955.

INDEX

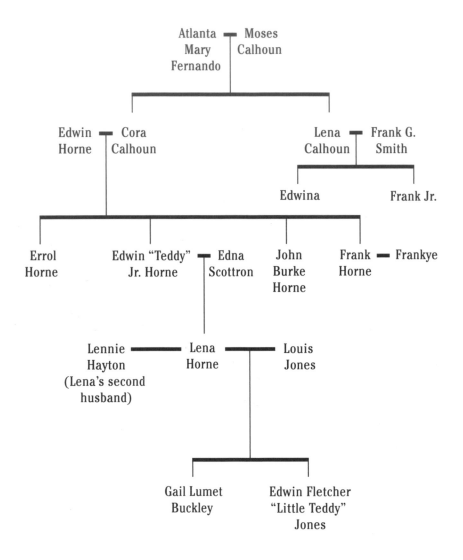